'Informative and articulate in its reflections on the body-mind-spirit connection, this book illustrates how Authentic Movement can nurture personal growth and well-being, explore interoception, alleviate anxiety, and cultivate an ecological self in harmony with nature.'

Tina Stromsted, *PhD, LMFT, BC-DMT, RSME/T, Jungian Analyst,*
Co-Founder Authentic Movement Institute

'This book is simultaneously a retrospective showcasing academic writings from an incredibly full and varied career working in and with Authentic Movement, a practical handbook and guide for those training and using Authentic Movement to support their own and others' processes, and a glimpse of the ways in which Authentic Movement has, can and should be applied to work with different groups and in different contexts.'

Professor Jennifer Leigh, *Reader in Creative Practices for Social Justice,*
School of Social Sciences, University of Kent; Honorary Professor,
Department of Chemistry, University of Liverpool

'Helen Payne's new book on The Discipline of Authentic Movement takes us on a long journey from the days when she first studied the basic form with Janet Adler, the founder of the work, and on through her own multi-faceted process over twenty-five years. After her thorough description of the form of Authentic Movement, including individual, group, transpersonal and universal elements, Payne takes new directions with the form, adapting it creatively to ever more varied territory.

Payne's chapter on the use of Authentic Movement in the natural environment is a gift, as she highlights in depth how by moving and witnessing in the outdoors a unique relationship may be fostered between the human self and the more-than-human-world, stimulating and sensitizing our ecological selves.

I want to mention the attitude of serious scholarship in Payne's work. Her scope is impressive, as we know for example from her research studies which adapt Authentic Movement in tackling issues in the field of mental health, as well as on the edge of the medical field, where symptoms find no diagnosis. With all her rich experience, she goes on to build a variety of training programs for students. The book is dense with ideas, explorations, and a thorough bibliography. Dance therapists and professionals from many additional fields of study have much to discover in the pages of Payne's new book.'

Eileen Shulman, *teacher of Authentic Movement for 15 years*
in the Graduate Dance-Movement Therapy Program,
David Yellin Academic College, Jerusalem, Israel

'In this comprehensive volume, Professor Payne presents a compendium of all the books currently in print on Authentic Movement, with dedicated explanations of the varied components that *Authentic Movement* practice offers to its practitioners. Vignettes of actual *Authentic Movement* sessions render the writing alive and incisively describe how psychotherapeutic adaptations of this practice are shown to ameliorate various psychological disorders, repressed emotional states, chronic illnesses, provide insights for understanding medically unexplained symptomatology, or foster inner growth and self-reflection.

Professor Payne ties together *Authentic Movement* with dance and movement practices from the UK and US, different methods of movement analysis, traditional and contemporary psychoanalytic concepts, Jungian approaches, systems theory, neurobiological connections, phenomenology and philosophy, humanistic psychology, ecopsychology, eco-psychotherapy, relational integrative psychotherapy, ritual and transpersonal experiences. New to the study of *Authentic Movement* is the relevance of research to which Professor Payne has contributed on a wide range of topics with her *Movement Psychology Research Group.*

The value of this work also lies in Professor Payne's weaving historical under-pinnings of the different swathes of body and movement theory with current under-standing of the role the body plays in emotional regulation and mental functioning. A wealth of knowledge awaits both novices and seasoned practitioners in *Authentic Movement.*'

> **Patrizia Pallaro**, *Editor,* Authentic Movement: Essays by Mary Starks Whitehouse, Janet Adler and Joan Chodorow, *Licensed Psychotherapist, Moving the Self Psychotherapy Center, Annapolis, Maryland*

'This book offers a remarkably profound understanding of Authentic Movement in its fundamental and significant essence and traits. The underlying passion conveyed by the most knowledgeable and fervid author throughout the text creates a unique foundation that the reader can sense. A profound and discerning comprehension of embodied consciousness will emerge for the reader, distinctive of Authentic Movement practice and principles.

The author effectively clarifies how various professionals and experts refer to Authentic Movement, from distinct viewpoints, encompassing diverse approaches that help grasp the intricacies and diversity surrounding this unique work's conception and its multiple applications in various contexts.

The reader will be guided through various aspects of Authentic Movement, from its history to the explanations of the practice, including training, its role in supervision, psychotherapy, and the very special additions of the author's research. For example, its adaptation in supporting medically undiagnosed symptoms, and in supporting the concept and experience of the ecological self.

The book is for students in dance movement therapy training and psychotherapy programs and in general for psychotherapists, creative arts therapists, body-somatic therapists. Also, it will be useful for verbally based psychotherapists and psychologists who are interested in embodiment. It will broaden professional learning, inviting personal development, prompting questions and inquiries. It has led my own practice and research towards new boundaries and edges.'

> **Rosa Maria Govoni**, *BSc., MA., BC-DMT., Vice-President, Director Continuing Advance Education, Co-Director Institute Expressive Psychotherapy, Art Therapy Italiana*

Authentic Movement
for Practitioners

This book acts as a guide to understanding authentic movement (AM) in various forms and in differing contexts, covering over three decades of practice across different theoretical and practical topics.

Featuring a selected collection of the author's major works, this book illustrates her theoretical, practical and research contributions to the field. It illustrates a developmental journey of the author's thinking and practice. A multitude of applications of authentic movement are explored in relation to topics such as clinical supervision, body memory, relational integrative psychotherapy, reducing anxiety and many more. The book describes authentic movement in each of these contexts through making connections to theory, research and practice in every chapter. While initial works identify the ways in which the author explores the discipline in relation to clinical supervision and the development of the bodymind spirit, more recent work involves psycho-neurology, body memory and applications to psychotherapy practice.

Both research-informed and practical, this book will be an informative read for any dance movement or body psychotherapists employing the discipline of AM into their practice together with others interested in embodied self-exploration, eco-psychotherapy and spiritual practices.

Professor Helen Payne, PhD., Hon. Fellow & Reg. DMP (ADMP, UK); Reg. UKCP; holds a Chair in Psychotherapy, leads the Movement Psychology Research Group, and teaches and supervises international doctoral students in Education and Psychology at the University of Hertfordshire. She has practised, and trained others in, authentic movement since 2001 and has a clinical supervision and psychotherapy practice.

Authentic Movement for Practitioners

A Culmination of Theory, Research, and Practice

Helen Payne

Routledge
Taylor & Francis Group
LONDON AND NEW YORK

Designed cover image: Photography by Lucie Payne.

First published 2026
by Routledge
4 Park Square, Milton Park, Abingdon, Oxon OX14 4RN

and by Routledge
605 Third Avenue, New York, NY 10158

Routledge is an imprint of the Taylor & Francis Group, an informa business

For Product Safety Concerns and Information please contact our
EU representative GPSR@taylorandfrancis.com. Taylor & Francis
Verlag GmbH, Kaufingerstraße 24, 80331 München, Germany.

British Library Cataloguing-in-Publication Data
A catalogue record for this book is available from the British
Library

ISBN: 978-1-032-76649-2 (hbk)
ISBN: 978-1-032-76643-0 (pbk)
ISBN: 978-1-003-47941-3 (ebk)

DOI: 10.4324/9781003479413

Typeset in Times New Roman
by Apex CoVantage, LLC

I dedicate this book to my two daughters.

Diving into the Wreck
I go down
Rung after rung
the oxygen immerses me
the blue light
the clear atoms
of our human air
I go down
My flippers cripple me
I crawl like an insect down the ladder
and there is no one
to tell me when the ocean
will begin

Extract from Rich, A. (1994).
Diving into the Wreck
(pp. 22). W. W. Norton

Contents

Illustrations

Figures

Line Drawn Pictures

Photographs

Foreword

It is a pleasure to introduce this comprehensive handbook on authentic movement by my colleague, Professor Helen Payne. Helen's longstanding dedication to dance/movement therapy, somatically informed practice and integrative psychotherapy is evident throughout these pages. This volume represents the culmination of her journey with authentic movement, which began during Dr. Janet Adler's intensive summer training for international dance movement therapists, initially in the UK in 1992 until the late 1990s in Tuscany, Italy, and later in Greece.

As a student of the late Dr. Janet Adler, a pioneer in the field, Helen's curiosity and commitment were evident from the start. I first met Helen in the mid-1990s in these formative programmes when I assisted Dr. Adler, with whom I had studied and collaborated since 1985. At that time, I also taught in graduate psychology, somatic/dance psychotherapy and expressive arts therapy programmes, and engaged in and later co-led training sessions for the Marion Woodman Foundation in the US and abroad. In the mid-1990s in response to the growing interest in authentic movement in the international community, I created two additional trainings in Tuscany for experienced movers and clinicians. These international authentic movement intensives continued for over three decades, during which I also offered courses in a variety of countries.

Authentic movement arose from the creative soil of Jungian analysis and Mary Starks Whitehouse's "Movement in Depth" (active imagination in movement) in California. Its lineage is a vibrant tapestry from C.G. Jung's early explorations and Dr. Tina Keller-Jenny's engagement with movement in her analysis with Toni Wolff in Switzerland in the 1920s to Whitehouse's studies with German expressionist dancer Mary Wigman and myth-inspired modern dancer Martha Graham in New York. The practice was then further developed by Whitehouse's students, dance therapists Dr. Joan Chodorow and Dr. Janet Adler, who began teaching in the US and abroad. These influences shaped the rich, intercultural and multigenerational modality featured in this book.

In 1992, I co-founded the Authentic Movement Institute in Berkeley, California, with dance therapist Neala Haze. We invited Drs. Chodorow and Adler to join us as honoured senior faculty. Soon, we were joined by Jungian analyst Dr. Louis Stewart, adjunct faculty and guest teachers – clinicians and educators who continued to enrich the practice in their areas of specialization across diverse populations. Graduates of our programme then began teaching internationally, furthering the evolution of authentic movement in their respective countries of origin, cultures and beyond.

In 2023, at the initiative of Inspirees co-founder Tony Zhou and Italian dance therapists Rosa-Maria Govoni and Marcia Plevin, an International Authentic Movement Teachers' Inquiry group formed with generations of colleagues (including Professor Payne) from many parts of the world. We continue to share and learn from one another about intercultural developments and applications of authentic movement practice.

Professor Payne, among the leading figures in this next generation, has been practising, researching and teaching authentic movement for decades. This much-needed handbook chronicles the practice's development and offers practical tools for its growth. While several valuable collections exist, few resources combine research with clear, step-by-step guidance; Helen's book fills this gap.

Her writings, presented chronologically, trace authentic movement's roots in analytical psychology and dance/movement therapy and its integration into education, clinical work, creative practice and eco-psychology. Her text honours both tradition and innovation, illustrating how theory and lived experience mutually inform each other.

Professor Payne brings professional and academic expertise to this work. At the University of Hertfordshire, where she was conferred a Chair in Psychotherapy, she leads the Movement Psychology Research Group, conducts research and supervises doctoral students while maintaining teaching, clinical and supervisory practices. She has taught authentic movement in numerous countries both online and in person. Her extensive authorship and edited publications have invited a diversity of voices, areas of expertise and international perspectives to our field.

Helen's writing is articulate and down-to-earth, providing a clear and engaging exposition of the principles, structures and rituals of authentic movement. Her handbook is practical and recommended reading for dance movement psychotherapists, body and integrative therapists, creative arts, and health and social care professionals. It is an especially welcome resource for those in training or exploring this path for the first time. With case examples, reflective vignettes and research-based insights, she shows how authentic movement can nurture personal growth, deepen interoceptive awareness, support the management of anxiety and chronic bodily distress and foster an "ecological self" in relationship with nature. Her early life on a farm in the English countryside instilled a reverence for the natural world that is profoundly needed during our current ecological crisis.

Chapters cover a wide range of applications, including clinical supervision, trauma-informed practice, medically unexplained symptoms, and creative and nature-based settings while sensitively addressing questions around inclusivity, ethics, accessibility and our evolving social and ecological context.

Professor Payne's expertise and commitment ensure this book will be a valued resource for years to come. Whether you are a practitioner, student, artist or newcomer seeking a deeper connection to self, others or nature, you will find guidance here. The reflections and open invitations in these pages encourage us to step into the unknown and discover new possibilities.

Her book honours authentic movement's origins and supports its continued growth. As founder Mary Starks Whitehouse said, "There is that in us which has moved from the very beginning; it is that which can liberate us" (Whitehouse, 1999, p. 53).

In today's challenging world, embodied wisdom, authenticity and community engagement are needed more than ever. I hope you'll dive into this text and let it move you!

Tina Stromsted, Ph.D., LMFT, BC-DMT,
RSME/T, SEP, Jungian Psychoanalyst
Co-Founder, Authentic Movement Institute
Director, Soul's Body® Center, San Francisco, California

Reference

Whitehouse, M. (1999). Physical movement and personality. In P. Pallaro (Ed.), *Authentic movement: Essays by Mary Starks Whitehouse, Janet Adler and Joan Chodorow* (pp. 51–57). Jessica Kingsley Publishers.

Preface

This book is essential reading for dance movement psychotherapists, counsellors, psychotherapists (whether verbal or employing embodied methods), arts therapists, mental health professionals, university teaching and mental wellbeing staff, mental health nurses, clinical psychologists, other relevant health professionals, policymakers and those who commission health services. Academics from health psychology and others with an interest in chronic bodily symptoms for which tests and scans come back normal, self-management strategies or anxiety might also find it of use. People experiencing anxiety or bodily symptoms with no medical explanation may find it helpful. Anyone pursuing personal development through embodied consciousness, spiritual/mystical practice or the creative arts will find some gems here too. Finally, trainees on authentic movement training programmes will find it helpful to refer to the book as part of their training.

The market for this book is likely to grow as separation of body and mind is abandoned in favour of bottom-up embodied approaches. It is also possible that shifts in our understanding of neurobiology and neuroscience will increase support for the use of authentic movement. The need for embodied consciousness has never been greater.

Undertaking this book has been a passage of reflection, connection, new thinking and enrichment. It has brought up echoes on past thoughts and feelings about my training in the Discipline of Authentic Movement (AM) with the founder, Janet Adler, and my previous preparatory trainings. I have been excited to document the adapted ground-form of authentic movement for working with people experiencing bodily symptoms for which there is no known pathology or treatment. Some of the writing has been personal, acknowledging my vulnerability in reporting on my peer dyadic practice, training workshops, as well as illustrating how I employ authentic movement in my private practice with individual clients.

My trajectory into authentic movement began in 1978 in a workshop with Mary Starks Whitehouse. The seed was sown! However, it was not until over a decade later that an opportunity arose to invite Janet Adler to England to begin an intensive training in the 1990s for many colleagues from across Europe. Compiling this book has been a wonderful chance to reflect upon, and to share with you, dear reader, the decades of theory, research and practice in the Discipline of Authentic Movement.

Many of the contents have been published before in newsletters and peer reviewed journals and book chapters. However, I have updated much of the content to mirror my thinking nowadays. Of course, that will probably also change over time as I further develop the work.

This book is a culmination of theory, research and practice all in one place as my contribution to you, whether that be to your studies, research or practice. I hope it inspires you to delve deeper into this wonderfully creative and powerful model for transformation, a method employed in dance movement psychotherapy, but which can also be adapted organically to be delivered in a variety of settings and populations within a range of contexts as you will see illustrated in these chapters themselves.

The Discipline of Authentic Movement was taught to me by the founder, Janet Adler, whilst I was training intensively with her as her personal student in the 1990s. Although, not taught as a solely mystical practice during those years, Janet's teaching later evolved to focus mainly on that element which can arise at any point through the practice of the discipline. Since the early 2000s, authentic movement has evolved within me to become a long-standing in-depth methodology in my life. It is teaching me still to this day, how powerful it can be when, within a safe, benign relationship, as a mover and a witness I learn more and more about myself and my interactions with the world (including the spiritual element). Being seen and seeing others without interpretation, projection or judgement has served to enhance my embodied and verbal psychotherapy practices, training programmes and research.

Authentic movement as explored in this book responds to the following questions:

How can working with authentic movement help to support people into embodied consciousness and personal transformation to become more of themselves?

How can working with the interrelationship of body, mind and spirit develop a greater sense of wellbeing?

Can authentic movement nurture our ecological self?

What is the relationship between interoception and authentic movement?

How can an adaption of authentic movement with its focus in interoception support people with undiagnosed chronic bodily symptoms and excessive distress and people experiencing anxiety?

This book holds some of the answers.

The aim is to showcase entirely new material developed specifically for this book as well as previously published, yet updated, articles on authentic movement.

The book shares insights into the theory, research and practice of authentic movement tracking writing from over three decades. An Introduction presents an overview of authentic movement, its roles, rituals and protocols, followed by a chapter illustrating the roles of witness and mover with examples from practice. The scope of the book explores the application of authentic movement in relation to clinical supervision, groupwork, body, mind, spirit and wellbeing, body memory, interaction with psycho-neurology, a method to connect with nature, relational integrative psychotherapy, interoception for supporting people with chronic undiagnosed bodily symptoms, reducing anxiety and training. The book describes authentic movement in each of these contexts through making connections to theory, research and practice in every chapter. Finally, in Chapter 12 there is an Epilogue which looks back at the contents of this book and forward to the future.

Professor Helen Payne, PhD., MPhil., PGDip., BEd., Laban Cert., is a Fellow of the Higher Education Authority and a registered integrative psychotherapist with the United Kingdom Council for Psychotherapy. She is an Fellow of the Association for Dance Movement Psychotherapy, UK. She works part time at the University of Hertfordshire where she holds a Chair in Psychotherapy, leads the Movement Psychology Research Group, and teaches and supervises doctoral students in both the Departments of Education and Psychology. She has a small clinical supervision and psychotherapy practice and is a founding member of the International Teachers of Authentic Movement Inquiry Group. She has been practising and training others in authentic movement since 2001 both nationally and internationally.

Please note the terms "her/herself" and "they" are used whilst recognizing that participants are of various genders.

Acknowledgments

To all the movers throughout the world I have had the honour of witnessing. To all those who have witnessed me as a mover. To all who intend to make the invisible visible. To the professionals and colleagues who have engaged with me in discourse about authentic movement, supported my aspirations and given feedback on this book, including the publisher, Routledge. I am indebted to all the trainees and participants in our open circles who have truthfully engaged with me during their personal development and transformation through authentic movement. Appreciations to those clients for their vulnerability with me in The Empty Studio, and to Chris, my dyadic authentic movement partner whose reliable presence as my witness these many years now has enabled my moving self to be fully present. I am grateful to Dr. Chrsitina Bracegirdle for her support in reading a draft of this book and for all her wonderful poetry illustrated throughout the book. Appreciations also to Elyne Selu, Jonathon Gibson, Andrea Zaccaro, my friend and colleague Eila Goldhahn, long-standing colleague Susan Brooks and co-trainer Silvana Reynolds for their various contributions and comments on drafts of chapters 9 and/or 10. Many thanks to Jane Batchelor, my student research assistant at the University of Hertfordshire, for her efforts assisting me on producing this book. Finally, I would like to send gratitude to my family for their patience and support in this endeavour with a very special thanks to my daughter Lucie for the beautiful photographs.

Disclaimer

The interventions and materials in this book may be beyond the authorized practice of mental health professionals. As a licensed professional you are responsible for reviewing the scope of practice including activities defined in law as beyond the boundaries of practice in accordance and compliance with your profession's standards. It is recommended a full training in authentic movement is undertaken before delivering the practice to clients/patients in the context of mental health.

Introduction

Abstract

This Introduction leads the reader towards the topic of authentic movement, the book's aims and who might be its audience. It provides an overview of the chapters, indicating the main theme to be covered and contextualizing the works in terms of chronology and publication details. My positionality is offered to illustrate from where the contribution emanates. Finally, an extensive overview of authentic movement is introduced highlighting the significance of the roles, rituals and requirements for safe practice and other important elements.

Introduction

The idea for this book arose out of practitioners requesting an in-depth understanding in the discipline of Authentic Movement (Adler, 2002) and the frequent need for more information on my research and practice. It was inspired by a dream to showcase in one place my writing on authentic movement over the past two and a half decades. Therefore, the book is a culmination of a lifetime's writing on the theory and practice of the discipline of Authentic Movement since the 1990s when I became immersed in an intensive training as a personal student with the founder, the late Dr. Janet Adler (and later with Dr. Tina Stromsted who assisted Janet at those trainings).

My first taste of authentic movement was years before, though, in 1978 when I was a delegate at an American Dance Therapy Conference in Seattle. I was moved to attend a workshop with the late Mary Starks Whitehouse who termed the method "movement-in-depth". It was something quite different to the way I had used creative dance and movement with which I was familiar. I had been developing my practice within my employment as a movement therapist in a special school for children and adolescents with moderate learning difficulties, emotional disturbance and autism employing elements from creative dance and movement (Payne, 2020) to support them with their emotional struggles. I attended the conference as I was keen to learn more about dance movement therapy (DMT) which appeared to be more recognized in the USA than England. I also participated in another offering from Zoe Avstreih on authentic movement. In those conference workshops the kernel for this new way of moving had been planted.

DOI: 10.4324/9781003479413-1

This book is timely since many more professionally trained dance movement psychotherapists are practising authentic movement all over the globe. There is also more interest in embodied approaches in general amongst arts therapists, counsellors/psychotherapists and clinical/counselling psychologists. In the 2023 World Arts and Embodiment Forum (WAEF23), the authentic movement stream I organized was the most popular with 273 delegates and 23 presenters demonstrating the strength of interest (Registration Link: https://inspirees.glueup.com/event/authentic-movement-summit-68830/) Furthermore, for artists, poets, dancers and choreographers it can be stimulating for their creativity and choreography respectively.

A word on terminology. Since my training was over many years with Janet Adler, I employ the term discipline of authentic movement as in the title of her primer in 2002, published subsequently to that training. With reference to Janet's key focus on mysticism and transpersonal elements, in my experience these emerge naturally for participants, often without any intention. Although the term discipline of authentic movement has been adopted, throughout this book it has been shortened to authentic movement (AM) for ease of reference.

It may be helpful to define the term "authentic" in the title of authentic movement. Although the title authentic movement only refers to movement being authentic, it does embrace the authenticity of the witness role too. Within this context "authentic" refers to something that is genuine, real or true to its nature, origins or intentions, implying a lack of falseness, imitation or deception. An authentic action/movement or experience in the presence of the movement, whether that of a mover or witness respectively. The movement is intended to be original rather than performative, insincere or fake; it is what must be done. Being authentic means behaving in a way that is true to one's own personality, values and beliefs, rather than conforming to external pressures or expectations. There is no intention to create an effect or impression on an audience; rather the movement arises naturally or spontaneously. The action/movement is not done for show, to fulfil a social role or to convey a particular image; rather it reflects genuineness (for example, in feelings or intentions).

Mary Starks Whitehouse defines "authentic" as:

> When the movement was simple, and inevitable, not to be changed no matter how limited or partial, it became what I called "authentic" – it could be recognised as genuine, belonging to that person. Authentic was the only word I could think of that meant truth – truth of a kind unlearned but there to be seen at moments.
>
> (Whitehouse, 1999, p. 81)

For the witness, authenticity is about being true to the experience of the impact of the movement on their being. Being faithful to their experience in the presence of the movement when sharing with their mover any images, kinaesthetic impulses, feelings, sensations or thoughts even though they may not directly mirror those of the mover's experience. Furthermore, being loyal to the mover's actual physicality as reported by the mover seen by the witness in that only those movements the mover has recalled are spoken of in the authentic witness's offering.

Who Is the Book For?

The aim of this book is to bring forward the culmination of my writings over 25 years as well as offering new content to a range of people, both the professional and the layperson. The chapters are presented in chronological order of publication from 2001 to the present day to show the trajectory of my thinking and my employment of authentic movement in different contexts. This book has been birthed at a time when there is a growing interest in the literature on authentic movement, increasing numbers of facilitators/teachers/therapists practising worldwide and tentative beginnings of research. Currently, the number of texts is insufficient, and significant research has barely been embarked upon. This book provides for some first steps on several new pathways upon which authentic movement can travel.

This book is mainly for psychotherapists including dance movement, arts, body, gestalt, Jungian, integrative and verbally based counsellors/psychotherapists and counselling psychologists. Anyone with an interest in embodiment and/or its integration into the arts, such as visual/dramatic artists, dancers, poets, somatic practitioners and followers of nature may also find this book of interest. For health and social care professionals, it will offer an insight into another, different intervention which may be recommended for clients and service users. It can act as a balance to the talking therapies which are limited to verbal communication. People can over-use language as a defence or over-intellectualize, while others have experienced pre-verbal developmental trauma which cannot be accessed through language. A focus on the body and expressive, spontaneous movement arising directly from the unconscious within a safe relationship may be more accessible.

The book will be a basic textbook for students and staff on programmes for training in authentic movement, dance movement psychotherapists, body psychotherapists and arts therapists. It can be recommended as further reading for psychotherapists and for those in the arts, health and social care professions. It can also be of interest to the layperson and those engaging in personal growth or spiritual longings.

Whatever your background it is anticipated you will gain insights and resonances in this volume. You will glean greater insight in the practice of this discipline and hopefully enhance your own practice, extending your professional learning, raising questions and taking you to new edges.

How Is the Book Structured?

The book is structured chronologically from my first writings in 2001 to the present day which, at the time of writing, is 2025. All subsequent chapters provide for an abstract and a list of relevant references. The previously published material has been updated.

Following this Introduction is Chapter 1 which builds on the descriptive elements in the ground form and group formats found in the Introduction by offering illustrative examples from each.

Next is Chapter 2 which delves into the notion of authentic movement and how it can support clinical supervision. It was first published in the Association for Dance Movement Therapy UK newsletter in 2001.

Chapter 3 is also from an article first published in an association newsletter, this time in Australia (The Dance Therapy Association of Australia). This updated version has a focus on authentic movement, group process and the transpersonal.

Chapter 4 describes the integration of the body as container and expresser in the framework of authentic movement and the development of wellbeing in our bodymindspirit. This was a chapter published in the book of proceedings of the United Kingdom Council of Psychotherapy conference, in Cambridge, UK titled Working with the Embodied Mind in Psychotherapy. I was one of the three editors of the book titled *About a Body: Working with the Embodied Mind in Psychotherapy*, published by Routledge in 2006.

Chapter 5 is based on a chapter co-authored with one of my authentic movement trainees, Ilka Konopatsch, called Bodies Becoming Conscious. The book in which it can be found, published by John Benjamins in 2012, is titled *Body Memory, Metaphor and Movement*, edited by Sabine C. Koch, Thomas Fuchs, Michela Summa and Cornelia Müller.

Chapter 6 encompasses the neuroscience of embodiment based on an article first published in the *American Journal of Dance Therapy* in 2017 called The Psycho-neurology of Embodiment with Examples from Authentic Movement and Laban Movement Analysis.

Chapter 7 shows how authentic movement can lean into the climate catastrophe to be employed to develop an ecological self. For many years I had been experimenting with facilitating authentic movement circles outdoors. My more recent teaching on a Masters' programme in outdoor environmental education stimulated me to consider further with how authentic movement might enhance our connection with nature. Subsequently, as my thinking about this topic deepened, I wrote an article for the international peer reviewed journal *Body, Movement and Dance in Psychotherapy* called Nature Connectedness and the Discipline of Authentic Movement which was published in 2023.

Chapter 8 presents a discursive piece based on a newer article published in 2024 in the *American Journal of Dance Therapy* called Relational Integrative Psychotherapy and the Discipline of Authentic Movement. It brings into focus how psychotherapy, formulated as relational and integrative, can be enhanced by employing authentic movement as an embodied psychotherapy method.

Chapter 9 brings into play the research and practice over many years since 2004 when I first embarked on a pilot study to explore an embodied approach to supporting people experiencing undiagnosed or medically unexplained symptoms (MUS), now under the umbrella diagnostic category of body distress disorder. The practices were trialled in the National Health Service, primary care with this hard-to-reach patient population and include many using an adapted form of authentic movement (aAM) where there is an intention to bear the symptom in mind when entering into movement. This is a new piece of writing but based on two decades of research and practice with this patient group in the NHS and from the training of facilitators in The BodyMind Approach (TBMA). Three vignettes illustrate the powerful outcomes for participants with these undiagnosed symptoms when engaging in aAM.

Chapter 10 examines an innovative research interest I am developing which marries my studies in student mental health, The BodyMind Approach and authentic movement. It investigates how interoception, cultivated in AM, whether in stillness or during movement, can moderate anxiety, particularly for students in higher education institutions, many of whom have anxiety. The numbers have risen exponentially in the last five years. This theoretical argument is based on the outcomes from the studies of TBMA (which includes key practices from authentic movement) demonstrating anxiety was reduced post-group and at three and six months' follow-up for this patient population with chronic somatic conditions. A pilot study with students experiencing chronic anxiety in two universities in England conducted in 2023 showed encouraging outcomes.

Chapter 11 presents as a context, my professional background which prepared me to design a training model in authentic movement. The model is designed for those who wish to train to facilitate authentic movement in groups or individually in their various settings, as psychotherapists, arts therapists or as a method from which to create art. It also contains references to other training programmes and workshops conducted by trained and seasoned teachers/trainers/facilitators.

Chapter 12 is the Epilogue which concludes the book with some final thoughts and recommendations for research and practice in authentic movement.

There is then a resources section for further information including relevant professional associations and training programmes and links to films, and finally there is a useful subject and author index at the end for reference.

Authentic Movement

This is an overview of authentic movement, the roles, formats, rituals and requirements for safe practice together with other important elements for practice. Authentic movement is a somatically expressive practice integrating movement, mindfulness and self-exploration. It can be a form of embodied psychotherapy, a mystical practice or a creative process in which individuals enter the unknown in movement, with eyes closed, spontaneously and authentically in response to inner impulses, feelings and/or sensations. The intention to be present in the moment is important, allowing the body to guide the movement without judgement or preconceived ideas. A benign, present inner witness (or observing self) is cultivated in both mover and witness. Authentic movement is often described as a "meditation in motion" (Marcow-Speiser & Franklin, 2007) because it combines the inward focus of attention qualities of meditation with the expressive power of movement. It is a deeply personal and transformative practice that honours the wisdom of the body and the uniqueness of each individual experience in making the invisible visible.

Roles

There are several roles which can be taken by those participating in this practice. There are those of the mover, witness, silent witness, collective and moving witness.

The mover: This is the one who closes their eyes and engages in spontaneous movement from an inner impulse and engages their inner witness to track their action and/or sound, sensations, images, thoughts, memories, any contacts, feelings, compulsions and attending to, and being present to, their internal experience rather than any external performance. They practise developing their inner witness. Sensation, images, feelings, stories, memories, personal content and mythical journeys can all arise from the movement, sounds, touch or smell. It is the mover's responsibility to ask for witnessing if they wish.

A note on closed eyes: Memories may be stimulated during the practice, particularly as a mover with eyes closed. Vredeveldt et al. (2011) found visual and auditory distraction selectively impaired memory for information presented in the same modality, supporting the role of visualization (image-making) in the eye closure effect. This is why images and memories are commonly experienced by the mover in the practice of AM. The closing of the eyes also detaches the mover from the ordinary world enabling attention to the self and other beyond the everyday. Regression to earlier states and repressed emotions have been found to emerge for some individuals when moving or witnessing in AM (Lucchi, 2018; Stromsted & Haze, 2007) as they surrender to themself. Memories which have been held in the body, for example, of early childhood adversity, or other traumatic events as well as positive memories. Closing eyes during the movement removes visual distractions, and this may lower the cognitive load which may otherwise be monitoring the environment, for example the social setting, according to Vredeveldt et al. (2011). It also helps to remove body shame, a barrier for some movers.

The witness: This is the one who, with eyes open, is present to, and intending to clearly see, the mover with compassion and with supportive, mindful, non-judgemental attention. They are both a receptive mirror for the mover during the movement and, if they choose, an active mirror in the gestural and/or postural "offering" they share with the mover. The witness makes an offering, when invited by the mover (following the mover's recall of their actions etc.), which is respectful, non-interpretive, non-directive and non-judgemental and uses percept and self-referential language (for example, using "I" statements). The witness can be a partner in a dyad, members in a group format or the facilitator. The witness holds the psychic space for the mover, does not move from their place but remains a predictable, reliable presence, ready to make eye contact with the mover (if required) at the ending of their moving time. They are practising developing a clear, receptive, seeing inner mover as their mirror neurones fire up with each action they see. In the ground form, the witness is usually the timekeeper. After the mover has spoken, the witness is ready to share the impact of the mover's physical action on them, their feelings, sensations, thoughts, memories, imagination or physically wanting to join the mover (or as in an imaginary gesture or posture etc., wanting to be enacted, but never acted upon whilst the mover is moving, it can be part of the offering later though). The offering does not interpret the mover's intentions, feelings, thoughts, sensations etc. Any evaluations of what is seen as happening in the action arise out of the effect and impact it has on the witness herself. All interpretations, projections and judgements, if offered, are owned as belonging to the witness. The witness only shares their offering if invited by the mover for an offering and only mention their experience as it relates to the movement recalled by the mover so there may be some need to contain some of their expression. A dialogue between mover and witness can then ensue which may help the mover process their experience. To follow, track and mirror the mover the witness must identify and suspend their biases and interpretation of another's movement, and rather intend to internalize their mover, be receptive, neutral and present to the content stimulated by the mover's action, sound, touch etc. The inner mover in the speaking outer witness is cultivated the more they learn to clearly see a mover. In receiving the mover's action, sound etc. the mirror neurones fire and embodied simulation (Payne, 2017) is stimulated. The witnesses' direct experience is then perceived, i.e., the sensations and the feelings felt, the images imagined, the story unfolded, the sounds heard, and the event is interpreted from the witnesses' perspective.

Silent witness: This is the one who witnesses but does not become a speaking witness and instead contains all they see and hear. Art making and/or journalling can be used to process the experience during transition. It is nominated by the one wanting to be this role at the outset of a session of any group format session. To become a silent witness is one of the most lucrative learning experiences.

Collective witnessing: This is where a witness sees a larger story or event in the way a group of movers interact with each other through the movement expression as a collective body. It can integrate the group dynamics to reveal a rich tapestry of shared experiences and can create a sense of unity and mutual understanding promoting connection. Collective group energy can enhance the depth and intensity of the movement experience and further a sense of belonging and shared humanity. Ancestral, primordial or collective memories can be named in this way.

Moving witness: This is the one who is a mover and who resonates with a speaking mover's experience because they have been involved with the event or heard it. As movers they can speak as moving witnesses to that event.

Free-floating witness: In a group format such as the breathing or long circle, the witnesses may follow any mover they are drawn to for as long as they feel connected to them.

Designated witness: In any group format a mover can ask a witness to be their witness solely for the whole duration.

Formats

The various formats are as follows:

Group Move

There is one witness (the facilitator) in the group move. This is normally the format employed at the beginning of a group starting to practise. The witness-facilitator uses this format to model the languaging in their offerings to movers. Movers make eye contact with each other and their witness and are invited to notice an impulse to move in the space with closed eyes for the allotted time. At the end they enter the transition phase followed by speaking about their movements and any associated images, feelings etc., and asking for witnessing. The time duration is normally short, working towards up to 15 minutes. Specifically, this format leans towards introducing the aspect of the inner witness in the mover, the movers' languaging in the present tense and their recalling of actions (or a pool of action) as well as any surrounding content, if any. As their practice develops there may be one or more silent witnesses added to the outer circle cultivating, for them, containment of experience as there is no requirement to offer witnessing. They may write reflections or make marks on paper as a way to process what is seen.

Dyad

This is the ground-form, and each pair take it in turns to move and witness each other. The time duration is agreed at the outset. There is eye contact (see more later) between them before the mover waits for the impulse to move. Following transition there is a sharing of experiences, the mover requesting witnessing if they desire it. They then change roles.

Triad

There are two formats in a triad. The first is where there are three individuals: one a mover, the other two speaking witnesses, or a speaking and a silent witness. Roles are changed each round. This structure facilitates a mover experiencing two pairs of eyes witnessing them, and the witnesses can see differing aspects of the movement depending on where each one sits in relation to the mover. This can provide for different perspectives on the action seen which may be helpful to the mover. All change roles each round.

Another triad format is where there are two movers and one witness. This provides for the movers to have an opportunity to be in relationship, maybe in physical contact scaffolding them into the group formats. It also provides the witness the experience of free-floating their attention between two movers rather than on a specific one, preparing them for the group formats.

Fours

In this format there can be two witnesses and two movers, three witnesses and one mover, or one witness and three movers. Alternatively, one can be in the role of a silent witness. All are introduced at different stages as preparatory steps for the group circles presented next.

Breathing Circle

This is one of the group formats where a group of individuals participate in the roles of both movers and witnesses, creating a shared space for movement, witnessing and dialogic reflection. It expands the traditional dyadic structure of authentic movement (one mover and one witness) to a group setting, encouraging a sense of community, interconnectedness and collective awareness. Seated in a circle the time duration is agreed upon. Half the group volunteer to move whilst the other half become witnesses seated equidistant from each other. After contemplating the empty space inside the circle, the first group enter the space, make eye contact with each other and their witnesses, and then the sound of the bowl begins the time. They close their eyes and wait for an impulse to follow. They may move outside the containing witness circle if they wish. They move for the allotted duration and then opening their eyes make eye contact again with each other and return to their place in the outer circle of witnesses. They may make eye contact with the witnesses who sprout (see later) their arms to welcome them back. After contemplating the empty space again, the second half of the group become movers. The cycle is repeated followed by transition and then movers from the first group speak of their movement if they wish. They can ask for witnessing from all or only one or two witnesses. The mover knows when they have had sufficient offerings. Any witness who has resonated with the mover's recollections may make an offering. There follows a dialogue for each mover.

Long Circle

This is designed to take a long time, perhaps an hour or more. There are free-floating witnesses and movers. Witnesses are all free-floating, that is, they witness different movers or pairs or groups of movers as they are drawn to them. A mover can request a designated witness to be solely for them for the whole duration of the circle, while another may elect to be a silent witness throughout. All sit in a circle and contemplate the empty space; when it is time to begin any mover can go into the space at any time, as many or as few times as they are moved to. There needs to be a minimum number of witnesses in the circle at any one time, however how many depends on the number of members of the group. For example, a long circle of eight members might need three minimum to be present as witnesses. Movers may return to become witnesses at any time. They are welcomed back to their place with witnesses sprouting their arms (see later) and making eye contact with each mover (if it is thought to be wanted) and with each other. When it comes to movers speaking, after the transition which may be quite long, movers speak in chronological order. They may invite witnessing for each time they went into the space as movers.

Benefits of Authentic Movement Can Include

- Enhancing self-awareness, empathy, compassion and emotional expression.
- Promoting regression, healing and integration of body, mind and spirit.
- Encouraging authenticity and spontaneity.
- Fostering a deeper connection to inner worlds and intuition and the transpersonal/spiritual realms beyond the little "I".
- Creating personal embodied consciousness.
- Contributing to collective embodied consciousness.

Rituals and Protocols for Practice

Rituals are sets of fixed actions, gestures or ceremonies performed in a specific order, often with symbolic meaning, and usually rooted in tradition, religion, culture or personal practice. Rituals are typically repeated regularly and serve various purposes.

There are many rituals performed in the discipline of authentic movement. Many carry deeper meaning beyond their surface appearance. Some were developed during the training with Janet Adler, and others have emerged since practising the form over time from issues raised in groups or from individuals pertaining to, for example, safety. These rituals provide a sense of order, continuity and purpose, often helping individuals and groups navigate the transitions or uncertainties. The discipline of authentic movement incorporates firm rituals despite its nature of freedom to move from within. Analogously, the requirements for practice also have meaning rooted in comments from participants addressing a concern or creating methods to enhance the practice.

Preparing the Space Before Practice

There is a ritualistic set of actions the facilitator will perform prior to the individual or group members arriving to protect the space. In this way they prepare themselves for the session through preparing the space. The facilitator's role is to secure the space as private, confidential and clear of any interruptions as well as papering over any windows through which public could view the space. They should also clear the space of as many objects as possible to reduce the possibility of injury for the ones with eyes closed. The floor should be inviting and clean and bolsters, cushions, mats or chairs provided for participants. Participants are invited to remove shoes before entering the space. If even one person cannot agree to this then shoes are kept. Chairs, cushions or bolsters are arranged in a circle so participants can sit in a circle. All participants' belongings, for example, bags, are left outside the space. Facilitators/teachers or group psychotherapists would likely offer a bodily warm-up prior to beginning the practice. For example, getting to know the room through moving in the space, exploring the walls, ceiling, corners, windows, curtains etc., visually then through touch. Acknowledging others in the space through eye contact, a gesture or mirroring movements. Following this an individual preparatory practice of, for example, standing to lying and then to standing, again taking time with half closed eyes to attend to the body and breath as the movement takes place. To encourage reflection on closed eyes, foster the inner witness and begin to develop relationship, participants might be invited to pair up, one with eyes open the other with eyes closed. For two minutes they experience what happens inside of them (feelings, kinaesthetic impulses, sensations, thoughts, images or memories) in the presence of the one with eyes closed or the one with eyes open. They change roles. Afterwards, they each in turn reflect on their experience, perhaps requesting they speak in the present tense as a preparation for later in the practice. It is important to prepare participants for the various roles, responsibilities, protocols and rituals etc., found in authentic movement.

Ground Rules for Safe Practice

All groupwork requires ground rules for safe practice. People will have their own, and groups often have input into the ground rules at the start of the group. Here are some suggestions:

1. Any additional needs adjustments will need to be discussed before the group starts. An application form for all participants to complete prior to attending the group could include the request to disclose any special needs adjustments with reference to disability, health, medication and so on.
2. The group content will remain confidential. Any discussion of participants' own experiences outside the group is fine, but any content or identifying details of other participants need to be kept confidential. This is to ensure a trusting, safe ethos to the group.
3. No drinks or food is to be brought into the group, as there will be regular breaks to consume these.
4. Timekeeping when returning from breaks is very important; we can help each other to return promptly.
5. When moving, if strongly and quickly, half open eyes to ensure you do not hurt yourself or anyone else.
6. The ethos of this group is non-judgemental and respectful of others' contributions.
7. Please report any concerns to the group at the check-in.
8. Please refrain from speaking about your experience of the group with the facilitator or other participants during breaks. If you do, please bring the content

back to the group at the next opportunity. This prevents leaking of the collective content and keeps it held by the group and facilitator.

9. It is important to own all projections, interpretations and judgements. The use of self-referential and percept languaging can help with this.

10. Touch between movers is always non-aggressive/invasive and non-sexual. You have the choice as to whether to accept and "go with" any contact from another mover or withdraw.

11. Ensure you have safe space in which to continue to process issues which may arise as this group has a finite ending.

Timekeeping

The facilitator would normally hold the time or share this task amongst group members or if a dyad each witness would take it in turns. A singing bowl has been the usual way of noting the beginning and ending of a movement piece and the transition time boundaries. One sounding to begin and three to end. The bowl sounding once after the eye contact indicates to the mover it is time to prepare to dive down into moving and for the witness to enter the role of witness. Normally it is the witness who chimes the singing bowl and times the pre-agreed movement duration. The three chimes to end gives sufficient warning for when movers are coming out of an altered state to re-orient themselves and for witnesses to be present to their mover/s for eye contact if wanted. This is another ritual which supports safety in that the there is a discipline to keeping to time boundaries, staying in the role of a mover/witness until the time is up.

Order of Practice

In all the formats, the dyadic ground form, small groups and the larger circles once the mover/s has moved and returned to their witness/es the mover always speaks first. They can request the witness's offering afterwards, provided there has been physical movement recalled by the mover. In the group move circle, movers speak as they are moved to or not. In the breathing circle after the final breath (group of movers) have finished, and following the ensuing transition period, the initial group of movers (the opening breath) speak first in any order. In the long circle, movers are invited to speak in the chronological order they went into the space to move. If they moved more than once, they would wait to speak in the order they moved. If they went in at the opening of the long circle and moved the whole of the time they would speak of that move as the first to speak or, if they went in a little later after another mover, from when it is their turn to speak.

Eye Contact

This important ritual takes place in several important junctures of the practice. At the outset of a moving piece and between the mover and witness if in a dyad or between movers and witnesses if a group format, a receptive, empathic, accepting gaze should be available from the witness to the mover if the latter wishes. This takes place before a mover enters the space to move. The gaze is direct, benign, mutual, more a regarding than intense intrusive gaze, reflective of the I-Thou relationship of which Buber (2008) speaks. Both are present to each other, with an openness and readiness without judgement, qualification or objectification. The witness carries this quality of gaze with their whole being in their witnessing role as a supporter in the service of the mover, offering unconditional positive regard (Rogers, 1957).

The Empty Movement Space

Prior to entering the movement space there are a few moments to contemplate the empty space. If an individual mover after entering the space, there is a time of waiting for an impulse, be that movement, to remain in stillness or make sound. Next, in a group format a mover enters it, and content is made. At the end of the movement when all movers have returned to their place in the outer circle there is again the ritual of a few moments of contemplating the empty inner space.

Pre-Agreed Time Duration

This is a crucial element on the discipline. The mover usually indicates the amount of time they would like for moving. The witness enables the mover to keep to that time duration by holding the time and singing bowl. Or if there is no bowl just say, "now it is time to begin" and "now it is time to bring that experience to a close". It is important to adhere to the time duration agreed. For the group format it is usually the group who decide the time duration. The transition duration is normally decided by the facilitator, mostly about half of the movement time.

Moving Quickly and Strongly

For safety if a mover is moving quickly and strongly it is strongly recommended that they half open their eyes to avoid injury to themselves or another participant. Attending inwardly is still important to retain even with half open eyes.

Inner Witness

The mover attends to their bodily sensations, emotions, kinaesthetic impulses, memories, images and thoughts as they arise, allowing the movement to emerge organically from this inner witness awareness. This awareness is continuously developing. Being seen over and over as a mover can support and strengthen still further the inner witness which also needs to be active in the witness. The two roles of witness and mover support each other in the developing inner witness, also called the observing self.

Inner Mover

The inner mover in the outer speaking witness attends to the actions of the mover and notices their bodily felt response. This can be a kinaesthetic urge to move which is not acted upon unless in a long circle. It could be a bodily sensation experienced by the witness in the presence of their mover's actions or a group of movers. The inner mover is cultivated by the tracking of their movement by their inner witness when in the role of mover. Interoception is stirred and inner responses follow, for example images, thoughts, sensation, feelings and so on, arising out of the witnesses seeing (or hearing) their mover.

Speaking Witness

When a witness begins to speak, they may recall certain movements the mover has remembered. It is suggested they begin their offering by saying "I am the One who sees [add here the action/sound/contact spoken by the mover] and in the presence of this I . . ." repeating the movement words shared by the mover first and then adding their own experience in the presence of that movement event.

Integral Witnessing

There may be an element in a witness's previous mover or witness role which they feel resonates with a mover's experience. This can be shared with the group, as long as confidentiality has been agreed. Offerings amongst participants are not solely based on experiences in the moving witnessing circle. Adler (Morrissey & Sager, 2022, p. 218) defines integral witnessing as:

> the experience of the speaking witness expands, matures into an integral witness . . . witnesses, listens and responds by speaking consciously from multiple perspectives. She responds to whoever speaks from whatever original role in the preceding round of moving and witnessing practice. Feeling seen, seeing herself and seeing each other one simultaneously –

All fully participating in the intimacy of direct experience, the bell for timing, eye contact and former roles of witness and mover melt away. Movers move into the emptiness, witnesses do not, all voices speak what matters, all listen and there emerges a unitive consciousness, an energetic field of shared awareness. Intuitive knowing in the ritual of what is possible, all voices blend into what Adler names as vibratory resonance, a collective consciousness ceremony (Morrissey & Sager, 2022, p. 187/221). This connects to the notion of the universal "throb", the initial movement that begins and supports all creation into its many forms and endless cycles of expansion and contraction (Singh, 1980, cited in Marcow-Speiser & Franklin, 2007).

Non-Judgemental Attitude of Mind

Self-criticism is left at the door in this practice. There is no need to perform. There is a strong fostering of honest, unfiltered expression.

Sprouting

This ritualistic practice is to help witnesses who may be overwhelmed or tiring in a breathing or long circle which could go on for an hour or more. The arms of all those witnesses in the outer circle rise and open out in a sprouting gesture, eye contact is made with each other and thereafter arms go down. Any witness can begin the process of sprouting if they feel their presence is dropping off. Similarly, after the breathing circle or a long circle as the movers return to their places all the witnesses sprout their arms to acknowledge their return.

Subsequently, at the end of the movement but before the next round or transition the witness needs to have their accepting gaze available again to meet the eyes of the mover if the mover wishes. It is the mover's choice. Some movers may need longer to come back to consensus reality and not wish to meet the eyes of their witness at that point. Others need to see they have been seen by their witness and the gaze can augment this feeling (as in "I see you seeing me seeing you").

Furthermore, this eye contact is made with each witness in the breathing and long circles before movers begin their time as movers and after it has ended either whilst still in the inner circle space or once back at their place. In the long circle when each mover returns to their place and the witnesses sprout, they also offer eye contact to that mover welcoming them back as a witness. Movers can choose to engage or not in this ritual.

Transition

This is a major phase to the practice of this discipline. It is the middle part of the three-phase ritual: a) movement, b) transition for both mover and witness, and c) mover and witness speaking together. Transition could be viewed as a crossing over or bridge between the nonverbal and verbal phases, a turning point towards connection between two worlds or realms. In fairy tales bridges and crossings can symbolize a transition between worlds, realms or states of being. There are many ways to undertake transition. Art materials, for mark-making on paper, collage and clay for sculpting are often made available. Many write in their personal journals in transition (for further details please see Bracegirdle, 2023). This nonverbal bridging by using the arts between moving/witnessing and speaking fosters self-reflection and meaning-making. The expressions are directly related to the embodied experience and may be shared when speaking as a mover or, if resonance is felt with their mover's experience, by the witness too, however, until such a time the material is kept back. Sometimes participants prefer to simply contemplate/reflect quietly. There is the option of offering collective witnessing of artifacts and writing created in the transition.

Dialoguing

This refers to the phase whereby the mover, in the presence of a compassionate, benign, supportive witness, speaks in the present tense of their movements and any accompanying feelings, thoughts, sensation, kinaesthetic impulses and images. They may request a witness offering if they wish. If asked, the witness speaks in the present tense in percept language of the same movements adding their own content whether or not it resonates with the mover's content. Both use self-referential languaging. If they are very similar experiences that is called a unitive experience, and if different then that is called a differentiated experience. We are both connected and separate at times, we are both seen and unseen by the other, and both seeing and not seeing the other.

Pools of Movement

In group formats as well as the ground form it becomes more and more clear that significant moments or pools (as in pools of water in the foreground with the earth as the backdrop) are what really matter to the mover. Movers reporting only those substantial moments may be helpful in group formats whereby every mover telling their whole movement story may take far too long. Asking what the most important one or two pools might be may hone the mover's experience, refining the recall by helping to identify the resonance in both mover and witness. So, movers are invited to select a significant section of their moving/non-moving journey and which they would like to speak of, and on which, perhaps, they would like to request witnessing.

Hands on Floor (or Thighs if Sitting in a Chair) after Speaking

To support respect for each contribution in the speaking circle or dyad the ritualistic practice of making a gesture with hands towards the floor is given once the speaker has finished speaking. Everyone knows there is now space for another to speak.

Speaking in the Present Tense

One substantial requirement for effective practice is that both movers and witnesses are invited to speak in the present tense during the dialogue following the movement. This helps to keep alive the previous movement experience for the mover and the previous witnessing experience for the witness.

Self-Referential Languaging

This requirement is where the languaging highlights the speaker's experiences, to help them to focus on their own experience, owning it. Using "I", "me", "my" and "mine" etc., for example "I am the One who sees (followed by speaking the action etc. the mover has shared, subsequently describing the present-moment experience in the presence of that action, interaction, sound etc.) . . ." when reporting mover and witness's experiences can cultivate staying with the direct experience of the self. It challenges assumptions about communication by highlighting the ways in which language can influence thought, perception and reality.

Languaging in the Present Tense

With reference to the use of the present tense, percept and self-referential languaging it is of interest to note Gallese (2025) reviewed evidence showing that different sensory modalities and motor systems collaborate to form a coherent linguistic experience. Apparently, understanding language involves the activation of neural circuits associated with motor actions, perception and social interaction. The integration of the body's multimodal experiences into language processing provides a more comprehensive framework for understanding language as an embodied and interactive phenomenon. This is relevant to the discipline of authentic movement in that the direct experience of the self for both mover and witness will be even more deeply rooted in embodied consciousness due to the languaging protocols which guide the speaking.

Projection and Interpretation

The practice of owning any projections, for example from a witness onto the mover, aids in cultivating clearer seeing. Witnesses do not interpret what they think might be happening in the mover, helped by the languaging protocols. Witnesses need to be mindful of these. Be mindful of these and acknowledge and own them openly if they happen. Similarly, any interpretations need to be owned and communicated.

Percept Languaging

The term "percept language" was coined by John and Joyce Weir (Weir, 1975). It refers to their process of restructuring verbal expression to encourage ownership of what may be projected onto others. Percept language is a tool for self-discovery and personal growth, encouraging individuals to investigate their perceptions and take responsibility for their experiences. It is a way to become more conscious of how reality is constructed through language and perception. It reduces praise or blame, thus decreasing judgements. It clarifies to others that I am describing internal experiences or personal interpretations of our world (the one in each of us). It captures subjectivity minimizing defensiveness, increasing the capacity to listen to others, offer compassion and improve connection. Observing and owning projected parts of the self develops a new self-awareness, creating self-differentiation. Speaking in this way focusses the person on the transferences underlying most perceptions and interactions. The intention is to enable each person to follow the path towards their own personal distinction, becoming more differentiated into their unique individuality, which in turn can lead to self-differentiation. There are no impersonal pronouns used such as "it", "one", "you", "that", etc., instead "I", "me" and "mine" are substituted. Speaking in the present tense and in percept language allows a re-centring of the self, bringing the present moment to the forefront, since it is this which can be most easily influenced. It is a practice and requires discipline.

In contrast to a description of the action, those bodily movements and/or sounds witnessed, percept languaging uses subjective and descriptive words to evoke sensory experiences or emotions. It is concerned with translating sensory experiences or observations into a form that can be understood or communicated, often emphasizing the subjective or experiential aspects of perception. It is closely tied to how humans or systems interpret and make sense of the world through their senses.

Percept languaging conveys information based on percepts i.e., the mental impressions or interpretations of sensory input (what we see, hear, touch, taste or smell). It is a way of describing or encoding experiences, observations or phenomena in a form that reflects how they are perceived, rather than relying on abstract or symbolic representations. It does not judge (the mover/movements), interpret (what is thought to be going on inside the mover) or project (the witness's own content onto the mover as though it were theirs) without recognizing and owning each of these if they do occur.

Percept language might focus on, for example, seeing the "sinewy" movement, feeling the great "effort" needed to move, or imagining the "warmth" of the sunlight on a mover's back, and the feeling of tranquillity it evokes in the witness, rather than stating as if facts about the sun's position or atmospheric conditions.

Witnesses Only Speak of those Movements the Mover has Reported

Just as in person-centred psychotherapy or dream work in Jungian analysis only those elements of physical movement the mover recalls can be referred to by the witness in their offering. If not remembered, they were not so significant to the mover. Although perhaps they were to the witness nevertheless, they do not share the impact of them on the witness. The agenda for the dialoguing between mover and witness is necessarily based on the mover's agenda, rather than that of the witness. Despite this, movers do like to hear of movements they forgot to recall which is alluring to the witness so they might give them everything they see.

The Witness Remains in One Place

Whilst the mover or movers move the witness remains seated without moving, for example, to support a mover or speaking. They do not attempt to see a mover who is behind another mover, or a pillar or curtain, for example. They have one perspective from the place they inhabit. If in a group format other movers will have different perspectives on the mover/s since they are seated in different spaces around the circle of witnesses. The witness holds a clear presence engaging their inner mover as they regard their mover/s.

Movement/s the Mover has Shared with the Witness

There is an obligation on the witness to make sure the mover does not see a movement they have experienced in their own body. Hence, it is recommended the witness does not repeat on their body any of the movements the mover has shared with them. A movement may feel different if seen on another's body. The direct experience of it may be changed for the mover. There is a ritual, therefore, especially for the first few months of practice, that witnesses sit on their hands to avoid falling into the unconscious trap of repeating movements the mover has shared, or the witness has seen.

Witnesses Echoing Words or Phrases Heard from the Mover

At times the witness may hear a significant phrase or word from the mover which it is thought could do with emphasizing. Echoing these can be helpful for the mover to hear.

Mover has Closed Eyes

Normally when authentic movement is practised between humans it is a prerequisite for the mover to have closed or half-closed eyes. It is important to make it clear they can open them at any time; however, an inward focus needs to be maintained. The idea here is that with closed eyes there can be more opportunities to delve down into the unconscious, to allow what needs to be surfaced to arrive. The visual pull is so strong it can be difficult especially for novices to retain inward attention.

Mover Reports Movement/Sound

In the same way that we only remember significant elements of our dreams there will be movements which cannot be recalled. It is accepted that movers will not recall every physical movement. Neither will they recall all the content around that movement. What is recalled is what is remembered, what is becoming conscious. The mover recalls their action and whatever accompanies it and, if they wish, can request a witness offering. It is important to note the mover and witness can only meet in the physicality of the movement as enacted or as seen and/or sound heard respectively.

In the same vein witnesses may not recall all the mover's actions. Often what is not remembered by the mover is also not remembered by the witness. It cannot have been meaningful. What is significant is usually always remembered though.

Summary

This chapter has introduced the topic of authentic movement, the book's aims and its audience. An overview of the chapters is provided, with their main themes identified, and a context to the works with reference to chronology of publication and new writings, together with my positionality is offered to illustrate from where my contribution emanates. Finally, a brief overview of the form itself is introduced highlighting the significance of the rituals and requirements for safe practice of this discipline.

References

Adler, J. (2002). *Offering from the conscious body: The discipline of authentic movement.* Inner Traditions.

Bracegirdle, C. (2023). A mover's practice of transition in authentic movement: An embodied non-dual lived experience. *Body, Movement and Dance in Psychotherapy, 19*(4), 381–396. https://doi.org/10.1080/17432979.2023.2254834

Buber, M. (2008). *The I and Thou.* Simon & Schuster.

Gallese, V. (2025). Language and bodily multimodality. The role of embodied simulation. *Sistemi Intelligenti, 2,* 165–182. https://doi.org/10.1422/117529

Lucchi, B. (2018). Authentic movement as a training modality for private practice clinicians. *American Journal of Dance Therapy, 40,* 300–317, 305.

Marcow-Speiser, V., & Franklin, M. (2007). Authentic movement as meditative practice. *Pedagogy, Pluralism & Practice, 3*(4), 68–74.

Morrissey, B., & Sager, P. (Eds). (2022). *Intimacy in emptiness: Collected writings of Janet Adler.* Inner Traditions Press.

Payne, H. (2017). The psycho-neurology of embodiment with examples from authentic movement and Laban movement analysis. *American Journal of Dance Therapy, 39*(2), 163–178. https://doi.org/10.1007/s10465-017-9256-2

Payne, H. (2020). *Creative dance and movement in groupwork.* Routledge.

Rogers, C. R. (1957). The necessary and sufficient conditions of therapeutic personality change. *Journal of Consulting Psychology, 21*(2), 95–103.

Stromsted, T., & Haze, N. (2007). The road in: Elements of the study and practice of authentic movement. In P. Pallaro (Ed.), *Authentic movement: Moving the body, moving the self, being moved; A collection of essays.* Volume Two. (pp. 56–69). Jessica Kingsley Publishers.

Vredeveldt, A., Hitch, G. J., & Baddeley, A. D. (2011). Eyeclosure helps memory by reducing cognitive load and enhancing visualisation. *Memory & Cognition, 39,* 1253–1263. https://doi.org/10.3758/s13421-011-0098-8

Weir, J. (1975). The personal growth laboratory. In K. Benne, L. P. Bradford, J. R. Gibb, & R. D. Lippitt (Eds.), *The laboratory method of changing and learning: Theory and application* (Chapter 13). Science and Behavior Books.

Whitehouse, M. S. (1999). C. G. Jung and dance therapy, two major principles. In P. Pallaro (Ed.), *Authentic movement: Essays by Mary Starks Whitehouse, Janet Adler and Joan Chodorow* (pp. 73–105). Jessica Kingsley Publishers.

Photograph 1.1 Four movers

Credit: Photography by Lucie Payne

Chapter 1

Illustrative Examples of the Ground Form and Group Formats

Abstract

This chapter recognizes the abstract wording of the discipline of authentic movement might be rather vague and confusing for the reader, so some clarification is offered. The illustrations provide examples of how the various protocols are interwoven into the mover's story and the witness's offering. The first section refers to the ground form, the dyad, where there is a mover and a speaking witness. The second section highlights the group formats, the long circle and the breathing circles.

Introduction

Authentic movement is a term fraught with misunderstandings, assumptions and interpretations. There is confusion of the use of the term "discipline" as in the discipline of authentic movement, for example. The capitalization of "Discipline" was made by Adler (Morrissey & Sager, 2022, p. 21) to distinguish it from the term "discipline of authentic movement" (Adler, 2002). The latter refers to the deepening and widening of the work to include transpersonal phenomena. In Adler's developmental model it has been suggested she specifies the final phase as "an embrace of the full arc of embodied consciousness" and a "wholeness within the evolution of this contemporary mystical practice", calling it the Discipline of Authentic Movement with a capital D for Discipline (Adler, 2002). The emptiness and fullness referred to in this model of contemporary mysticism is of a non-dual experience, a potential, mysterious unknown into which we can journey.

To clarify, "authentic" in this discipline may be defined as referring to movements that emerge spontaneously and genuinely from within, unfiltered by pretence or external influence (Adler, 2002), although it is now acknowledged the movement or sound response from within can also be responsive to external stimulus such as contact between mover, sound or other elements. In any event, the "direct experience" of mover, witness, collective and unitive consciousness are essential (Morrissey & Sager, 2022, p. 21) which Adler (2002) describes as a developmental arc towards non-duality.

Sometimes AM is referred to as a form of dance/movement improvisation. Some differences might include that the intention in AM is different from improvisation,

DOI: 10.4324/9781003479413-2

listening inwardly and following an intuition of what needs to be expressed and seen in the moment and without an agenda. Another important distinction is that in AM the mover has closed eyes and an outer witness, who is integral to the discipline. Additionally, the very specific protocols and rituals differentiate AM from improvisation. In AM the mover goes into another realm, sometimes described as a dream state whereas in improvisation finding movement is the main purpose for the choreographer/improviser.

This chapter continues by providing examples of the ground form to illustrate the speaking of both mover and witness in the present tense, with percept (Weir, 1975) and self-referential languaging. The owing of projection, interpretations and any judgements and the accurate, clear seeing of the movement which has been recalled by the mover. Projection is a psychological concept occurring when a person unconsciously attributes their own thoughts, feelings or traits to someone else, externalizing their own emotions or characteristics onto others. Despite the unconscious nature of projection, mindful attention can lead to identifying when it is taking place. If a witness feels insecure about their abilities, they might speak of a mover being less confident in moving if they have chosen not to move, for example. Interpretation is the making sense of information, experiences or events based on one's perspective, cultural background, knowledge and understanding, for example. It involves analysing, explaining or giving meaning to something rather than unconsciously attributing one's own feelings onto it/others. Interpretation is constant, and we are aware of it when it happens. How much of interpretation includes projection is often unclear though. The witness intends to refrain from interpreting the mover's feelings, thoughts etc. in their offering. Value judgements too are owned. The intention is to work towards avoiding all three as a speaking witness to cultivate clearer seeing.

The Ground Form

This section illustrates the ground form of the dyad, where there is one witness and one mover. The examples show how sometimes there is a unity of experience, whereby the mover will feel seen and validated by their witness. At other times there is a differentiation of experience, where the mover and witness's experiences of the same movement differ. The movements may have been seen by their witness, which provides for some validation for the mover. However, the elements surrounding those movements will not be the same, or even similar. When dissimilar, the mover can either ignore the witness's offering or consider it as food for thought. Note the use of self-referential languaging, always speaking from the direct experience of the self when both mover and witness.

There are two examples in the following of a mover speaking and a witness's offerings avoiding phrases which do not resonate with the mover's recall of her actions so are placed in the square brackets []. These words are not spoken, although seen, by the witness. These curved () brackets identify when an interpretation is made from the witness's direct experience (rather than putting an interpretation onto the mover as in "you felt sad") and owned, that is, spoken as an interpretation by the witness in their offering.

1. *A mover speaks*: I begin full of stiffness as I have been sitting for so long after a 7-mile walk. I need to stretch and regain flexibility. I find the wall and lean against it, sitting upright. I am wobbling my legs. I am sliding down the wall, stretching my neck until I am flat on my back. Hands push against the wall, it feels good to feel strength. Turning around and I feel, and find, the wall again. I paint an abstract on the wall. I crawl to another place like a crab, sideways, very carefully placing hands, hips and knees down on the floor. I find myself curled up in a child pose. Slowly I become more upright and begin to bounce on my knees halfway up which is soothing, relaxing and satisfying. Sadly, the sound of the bowl awakens me. I do not want to stop, and I say to my witness "I am enjoying that!"

    Witness offering: My mover drops to the ground on all fours [and turns herself around as though seeking direction. I am reminded of a cat or dog circling before lying down]. She finds the wall at a corner and sits, legs in front of her, back upright against the wall, stretching legs and rolling thighs [and pulling up her socks]. After some while she lets herself slide down the wall and stretches her body onto the floor with hands behind her. There are some movements that seem like hip exercises. [Then a switch back to lying on the floor with her feet on the wall, tapping, before another movement where she again moves away from the wall, this time looking like a sea lion or walrus (my interpretation). The same sense of something long and rolling in her body.]

    After a while she moves across the room sideways, somewhat like a crab (my interpretation), until reaching the curtain – and this time moves away to kneel, prayer like (my interpretation), head hanging between her arms – and now strong arms push up her shoulders like a powerful animal. At the end she rolls up into full height and shakes out her body in delight.

2. *Refugees* (sometimes a title emerges from the dialoguing between witness and mover)

    A mover speaks: My mind is full of Ukraine, so it takes me a while to be fully inside my body, and let it lead me. My first impulse is to fling my arms wide, but I think this might just be a head thought, so instead I fold my arms inwards with hands on my heart, feeling it beat, feeling my own aliveness. There is then some reaching out into the room but the image I have is of holding others near me, in my heart, picturing women carrying small children and babies as they flee.

    I sway a little and feel energy coming back. I shake my body into vitality and rage, legs and arms, wrists and shoulders, blowing out the trapped air in my lungs to a better form of physical functioning. I then picture the evacuation and imagine walking with them, but my feet hardly move. One step forward and two back. I get to a nearby wall but it's not satisfying, so I walk in the other direction and find the curtain, feeling the strangeness of its texture – and again thinking of the destinations these women will come to, the comfort of new surroundings but also the strangeness. I return to the centre of the room and take small running steps, moving my arms as children do when mimicking a train. This is what they are doing, getting trains to somewhere, anywhere. I pause hand on heart again, and it is time to stop.

Mover's reflection: Overwhelmed by world events, I feel in my body a connection with women whose lives have been completely upended. We are subject to inner and outer influences, and don't often know how much the plight of others affects us all.

Witness offering: Hands on upper chest fingers overlapping I see an empathic posture in my mover (my interpretation), in the presence of this I feel full of feeling. Constriction follows, shoulders come forward, head goes down, hands disappear. Then the upper body opens welcoming all. I hear the breath in and out as the mover's body opens and closes. This is repeated several times. I see arms together moving in synchrony swinging and shaking, feet move up and down, as if shaking off something. I see arms together in synchrony going behind the torso in a swinging motion. Elbows become prominent, elbowing others out of the way and creating space for herself (my interpretation). Arms in front moving something away so sufficient room (my interpretation). She stops. Walks towards a wall then retreats, walks tentatively forward again and then retreats. She repeats this twice more until finally is brave enough (my interpretation) to meet the wall. She leans her head and hands against the wall. As she is leaning, I see a person at the wailing wall in Jerusalem (my interpretation). She turns and walks with one had outstretched seeking the opposite wall and finds a curtain. Feeling its texture, her hands slide down it as she turns and walks to the centre of the space. Another swinging of the arms before there is stillness.

3. *Gratitude*

A mover speaks: I begin with a heavy feeling in my legs pulling me downwards – not sure if I want to reach the floor, so I crouch for a few moments and then let myself sit legs in front of me, before lying back. The swishing of my feet on the floor takes my imagination and I hear the sound of waves. I deliberately make this sound a few times, starfish-shaped on the floor, thinking I haven't heard the sea for a while. Having had enough I let my body curl to one side and then the other, then lie back down with my hands behind my head. I notice it's not easy to hold this position on a hard floor and seek to burrow, insect-like, into the ground with my back.

I must have had the impulse to rise again because I find myself arms open, swaying. It makes me think of knowledge all around me and wanting to bring that into me. I think of PB and feel sad that he's died but know that he would want me to stand up straight and bring the world in towards me. I think of him and other elders who've left the planet and imagine pulling down their wisdom onto my head. So many have helped me in my life and are still there for me.

Mover's reflection: A moment of gratitude and reflection, led by the body.

Witness offering: Beginning by going down in a squat, one hand on the floor I am reminded of a sumo wrestler or American footballer in the ready position. I see my mover lie down on her back making "angles in the snow" movements arms and legs opening and closing in synch making a swishing sound. [She pulls herself up to bend over her legs and goes back down again in a whole-body movement.

Repeated several times. I feel a pull on my abdominals. She sits on her side look-ing away from me and I see a young girl on the edge, watching.] She stands and purveys her everything all around her, swaying side to side, arms outstretched in an open "look at it all" statement in all directions. At one point the arms push some-thing out from the space and a twisting movement follows. The arms rise up, hands clasp together, and she brings something into the crown of her head which bows in receipt and appreciation three times (my projection). I see a ritual.

4. *After the injury*

A mover speaks: After swaying gently, I lift my arms above my head and think that I haven't dared move from side to side, putting weight on just one foot, for weeks and weeks. It feels such a relief and release to stretch my arms, my left arm particularly, up to the sky: I can feel my body sigh. I move cautiously from one foot to the other, facing towards all four corners, though hardly mov-ing from where I stand, just stretching and breathing. At some point I clasp my hands together and feel one hand supporting the other. I dare to reach down and come up again, still scared of falling, but in the reaching down I become aware that my whole body needs to be touched. I have protected myself from anyone touching me for the last two months, so I explore with pleasure the feeling of my own hands touching every part of my body, putting myself back together again. I cradle my arm for a bit, holding it against my right shoulder and then my left, feeling sorry for it, sorry for me, heart-felt. After a while I feel strong enough to reach out for a wall and am nearly there when the gong goes.

Mover's reflection: This is an example of how the body's needs are often hid-den in everyday life, only becoming apparent when afforded the focus of my less conscious self. It takes only seconds to locate and respond to a deep need for healing in the body.

Witness offering: Leaning back on her heels my mover stretches upwards then moves backwards into the space behind her. I see her stroking her legs, back, torso and shoulders. In the presence of this see a sensory experience (my interpretation).

She takes her wrist into her body near her neck and cradles it with compas-sion, nurturing it (my interpretation), gently stroking the arm and wrist. I see self-care, self-compassion and imagine this has been an injury (my interpreta-tion). I see my mover bend over and place her hands on her feet then her knees, waiting there. Is she looking at something on the ground? I see her stand upright and arch backwards. Coming back to her centre she takes steps with her right arm outstretched as if anticipating finding a wall (my interpretation). I sound the singing bowl to end the piece, and she jumps, startled (my interpretation). I have made an interruption (my interpretation).

5. *Untitled*

A mover speaks: I find myself walking backwards as though retracing my time-line to Canada. I can feel the tug of my family and the different time-zone and wonder about it. As I stop, I feel the wall behind me and have the thought: "She's got my back" as I stand with my back supported. But thoughts and body lead me downwards and I find my knees buckling as I slide towards the floor and then forward on knees and then prostrate. I put my hands in a prayer position in front of me and think "It's important to be like an arrow for them – straight and true and strong". Coming up to my knees I feel stronger and, reaching out, discover the radiator at my side – something on which to lean as I get to my feet again. I use it for a while as a ballet barre, leaning outwards and then in, enjoying the flow of movement from a safe position. I find I want to shake my head – a "No" – and then nod my head – a "Yes". But I have soon had enough, and I turn outwards again with the thought that my family both constrains and "holds" me in the sense of keeping me safe. I begin to walk forward and noting freedom in each step, reach forward into the unknown of older age and death.

Mover's reflection: An example of coming to authentic movement with a powerful thought in my head, which then moves as my body moves.

Witness offering: Retreating backwards away from me, my mover finds a wall with her foot. Arms reach to each side, and she finds the wall behind and to one side. She sinks to the floor, her back sliding down against the wall and crouches there as though waiting, then goes forward onto her knees and sits back on her heels. I see her torso only, no lower legs. My mover has an acceptance of this limitation (my projection). She slowly folds and goes down to the floor hands folded in prayer, a type of supplicant worshipping the other (my interpretation). She stretches onto the floor, fully long, and thin fingers point forwards piercing through something – a barrier (my interpretation). Then rising up onto one knee she finds the radiator and supporting herself to stand she is at the "ballet bar" making her exercises (my interpretation). She's turned sideways to me standing like a soldier with her hands in her "back pockets" (my interpretation). She conducts a head dance shaking side to side, up and down and turning. I see a strong "No!", a "maybe" and a "Yes!" and then another "Yes" (my interpretations). I notice her hair swinging each way as she moves her head. Turning sideways to me she walks forwards arms outstretched in front of her cautiously (my interpretation). It's a new pathway and she seems uncertain (my interpretation).

6. *Enlargement*

A mover speaks: I am aware of my stomach feeling large and touch it, feeling its warmth. I imagine myself grossly fat and old, leaning backwards to hold my weight as though I have become enormous. I then recover my upright posture, feeling the heat radiating from my centre, and wonder if the message of my full stomach is to make myself larger. I experiment with my hands making circular movements around my body as though expanding my presence in the world – larger and larger in circumference, feeling energised and more substantial. This is what I need to do, and I can feel my fingers buzzing and vibrating. Eventually I can grow no bigger with my arms and hands and let them float upwards. I then have an image of K standing in front of me and decide to radiate the heat of my arms into his body. I do this several times as though my energy can rid his body of cancer, changing the movements to pour love into him. This feels good. I am then at an end and can easily stop there, but it is not time yet and I stretch forward towards the light coming through the window. I am not sure how near it is, so I edge forward slowly reaching out with my fingers . . . and I think that old age and dying is like this, tentatively reaching out towards the light.

Mover's reflection: This is an example of trusting where my body leads and trusting that my witness will not judge me. The enlarged body leads to enlarged feelings I would not have contacted otherwise. The buzzing in my fingertips is a message that I am fully alive.

Witness offering: Her hand is on her on abdomen, I feel my own, both her hands meet on the abdomen, and I see breathing as they move with the breath in and out. My mover arches back her whole body and becomes gigantic. I imagine a very overweight person trying to walk (my interpretation). She begins to move her arms in a scattering motion and leans into the movement. I imagine a work task is taking place (my interpretation). Then I see a giant or large deity overseeing the little people, clearing the toxins from them, making sure they are safe (my interpretation). There is a reaching out of the hands to offer or receive something in return, then gathering and turning arms over each other towards the sky and opening out again. Now turning away from me I see quiet slow movement as she travels to the back corner of the studio. Her right hand leads the way, is she pointing? I cannot see clearly. Aiming for something there and keeping focussed on it there, it must not be disturbed so I (she), needs to tread very carefully (my projection). Time is up, but she has not yet reached it or arrived there according to my story.

N.B. Here the witness becomes entangled in her story-making in the presence of her mover's actions. She identifies so strongly with the story and images she sees that she uses "I" rather than "she" as if owning and moving the actions herself. The witness interprets her mover's actions making sense of them as a story in her imagination. It is as though she merges with her witness both being "as if" her and being herself in the experience at the same time.

This section refers to illustration group formats, specifically extracts of movers speaking and witness offerings, including collective witnessing in the long circle and the breathing circle.

The Collective Body

The Long Circle (an extract)

A mover tells her story. Afterwards, a moving witness speaks of experiencing her father's rage. Then there is an example of witnessing the collective body. A witness sees many movers enacting a scenario. As a result, she is then moved out of compassion to become a mover. This mover goes again into the moving circle. She makes pictures during transition, then speaks of her experience and asks for witnessing.

This is the sequence, after transition, when movers speak and ask for witnessing, if they wish.

A Mover's Story

I am a mover. My arms come down as my foot begins to stamp. My hands join in a fist forming a huge sledgehammer beating, beating in time with my feet. It is slow, monotonous, stamping but it destroys whole villages with each strike on the earth. I reach to the sky hoping I do not have to continue but my tears tell me it must go on. Sledgehammer feet alternating with a sledgehammer-hands beating, beating the small defenceless sound in front of me.

I feel hands trying to hold my foot to the floor. I do not want to hurt them, but I must go on beating out destruction with my sound and my sledgehammer limbs. I'm careful not to lift my foot too high in case my destructive foot will smash someone's finger straying to the floor underneath the sole of my foot. I feel hands clawing at my back and waist, but I must go on, others are trying to hold my leg, but it is easy to resist their efforts, as I must pound on.

All at once hands come between mine and breakthrough my fist. My upper body collapses into those hands and I turn, weeping, to walk away, the relentless monotonous rhythm of my feet slamming the floor stops. The sledgehammer is disintegrated. I am a weeping woman shuffling, wandering on my way.

A Moving Witness Tells her Story in the Presence of these Actions

I see my father's rage, his complete ranting rage and I know I can just watch it (a projection). I do not need to stop it. I can wait until it passes then slip in when the timing is right. The timing was never right when I was a girl (a projection), but this time, I was able to comfort, and I did my job successfully (a projection).

A Speaking Witness Tells their Story as a Collective Witness

First there is a Reaper slashing purposely surrounded by the beautiful flying birds and the dead bodies. Death is being accomplished, and it is hard, anguishing work. The bodies are needing to be buried. Then I hear cries, the screams of those suffering at the hands of the scythe, and the pain of the destroyer. There is nowhere left to go (my interpretation).

I feel terrified, the destruction, the relentless cutting down of life, of creation. It must stop, this brutalization and perpetual attacking of the world, but why stop the inevitable death of life? (my interpretation) Surely it is necessary and needs to be undertaken by someone. This mover holds that role now. Death is part of life after all. Nothing seems able to restrain the Reaper as he moves on over the earth, pounding forward like a powerful machine (my interpretation). I try to contain my tears. I cannot.

A mover speaks: Upon witnessing this collective I invite myself, in fear, to enter the moving circle. It must stop, this total destruction before all is raped and annihilated, gone forever. It is a matter of life or death for the earth. Feeling impelled to approach the Reaper (see Picture 1.1) I gently hold their hands wielding the scythe (my interpretation). Gradually as we move together my hands come between his (in my imagination they are masculine) hands, opening them. I am able to extract the tool of death from him. I place it out of reach, and he is released from his painful task. My left hand, which has briefly held the scythe, begins to quake. It trembles through my arm and my body, bit by bit. It is now flowing into my other arm and up, up, towards the heavens.

This enables a kind of energy to connect and to be brought down from the gods above in an angelic host, singing in colourful light. I feel beautiful in this presence.

I withdraw from being a mover to become a witness again.

A mover speaks: Later I go into the movement circle again purposely to dig a grave. I try to pull one body into it but notice she is alive and would not go. I leave those that are in the grave there, although after having had some contact with them I feel they are not so completely dead as I had presumed. However, on listening to the ground I hear the sounds of their disintegration. A digestion. A transformation. The worms come from the earth. I listen to the earth sounding with my ear close to the ground. The bodies disappear into the earth leaving a chasm, a void into which I need to go. It is the abys. I feel scared to descend into it, hovering on the edge at first. I eventually let go with a roll and tip myself over into the lip of the edge. I am falling, rolling, squirming and floating into the blackness. I find two more of me. We, ourselves. I touch myself onto them and they onto me.

I withdraw from the movement circle and become a witness again.

Later I become a mover again.

A mover speaks: In the third time in the moving circle, I am a cell. I begin to feel trapped by one other companion cell. I leave to find myself holding onto a large object. I must bring it from behind me to in front of me, as I lay on my back. It takes ages and ages to do this. I am moving my arms very, very slowly. I find it very difficult, painful; my arms totally seize up. I begin to tremble. Someone touches my hair. I am not alone and feel encouraged to continue. I take another deep breath into a shuddering and then a shaking. Finally, I manage to bring the object forward. It affects my whole body. The object is vibrating strongly and makes a channel up from my heart chakra to the heavens. I do not want to end when the bell sounds. I feel tired and strange as though a new life has been created.

Whilst I speak as a mover, I show my pictures during the speaking time after the long circle and ask for witnessing. In Picture 1.1, made during transition following the long circle, the dead bodies and the Reaper with scythe are illustrated. In Picture 1.2, I portray the abys, as I reflect upon my need to stay with the intention of needing to bury the dead bodies and fall into the abys. Picture 1.3 depicts the object I bring in front of me which I later learn from a witness's offering is a symbol for healing, the Caduceus with two snakes entwined around the staff.

On requesting witnessing a moving witness speaks of their need to stop the relentless destruction to give a breathing space for re-creation to begin. Another witness says to me that she sees someone preparing a burial ground. A third witness tells me that Picture 1.3 resembles a symbol for healing.

The symbol for healing shown in Picture 1.3, "Caduceus", is a staff with two snakes coiled around it – the magic wand carried by Hermes, messenger to the gods. It represents balance and harmony which healing requires, and the wings at the top represent swiftness.

The next section highlights collective witnessing and how mystical experiences can be experienced at any time. The movements for making Picture 1.4, were made known to the mover over the period of three consecutive breathing circles.

Picture 1.1 A line drawing of a circle with bodies inside it and a head and hand holding a scythe, a black bird flies above

First Breathing Circle

A mover speaks: I go to the window and embrace the light. I move along the window to find a hand. We have a hand dance. Then I feel encouraged to go back into the circle with her. I feel her back, her hair and then we separate gently. I point my fingers downwards to make a pendulum with each arm as it circles around, my torso hanging over. This I witness powerfully as a gathering of energy. I make one circle with one arm which crosses over and converges with the other, one after the other on concentric circles. It makes an eye in the middle as in the symbol in Picture 1.4.

Second Breathing Circle

A mover speaks: I find another mover clapping each time we make contact. She leaves and I wait until the magic dust appears in my fingers. I must sprinkle it all around. I do this in a circular motion making the same symbolic shape as yesterday's breathing circle, arms crossing over each other as I hang over myself, making an oval shape in the centre (see Picture 1.4). Then I shoot my arms up, up, to the sky in a shaft. I bring them down and turn them to make an offering to something/ someone and bring my hands to my heart to end.

Picture 1.2 A line drawing of a dark centre inside a circular hole in the earth

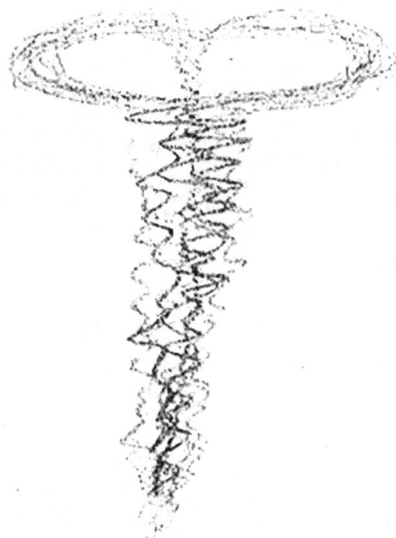

Picture 1.3 A line drawing of the symbol for healing-two snakes curled around the central rod with two wings on either side

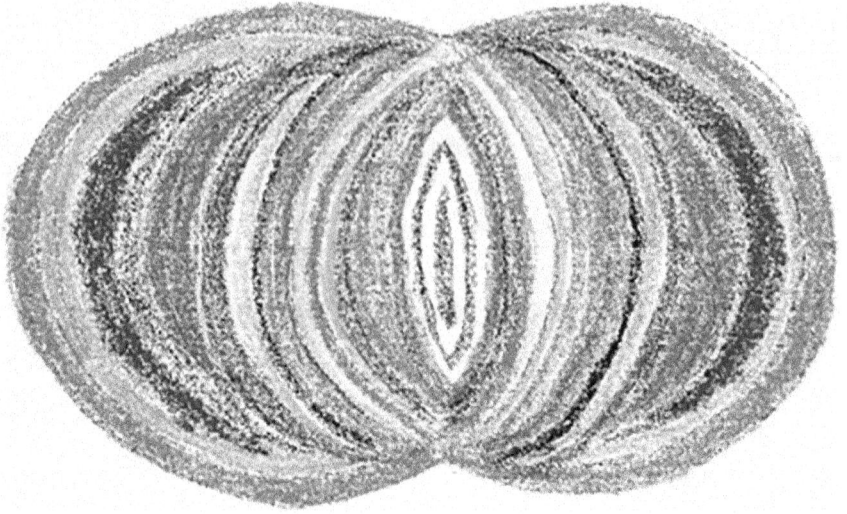

Picture 1.4 A line drawing showing the shape of the madorla, two concentric circles overlapping to make an almond eye shape in the centre

Third Breathing Circle

A mover speaks: I walk into the circle and to my surprise meet another. We embrace
and sway together. I am touched by the care to become as if one together. We
are joined by another who also embraces us. We form a circle of three contacted
through hands, as slowly and delicately we separate. I am reminded of my depar-
ture and I'm sad as it is premature. It disturbs and disrupts the group. I move to
the floor and make shapes on it with my hands and fingers. Out of this that same
shape is happening again (see Picture 1.4). Is it seen? I trace the outline of the shape
and into its centre and point my fingers into it, point at dark space in the middle,
the abys. I dive down through it. I am now moving towards the light. I find a step.
I make my heartbeat with my heels on it, and then my hands drum on it before
sitting up and sounding "Ohm" and then make bird songs in whistles. I am in an
aviary, participating in the birds' songs.

Witness offering: A witness explains the symbol is called a mandorla and is connected to Janet Adler's process where she highlights the mystical pathway.

Mover's reflections: In this breathing circle there is an example of how a symbol
can make itself known through several phases of a group process in the format of
a breathing circle.

Janet's initiation into the mysteries is documented in Adler (1995) and she speaks
to the mystical path in Adler (1999). This path claims to attain, or believes in the
possibility of attaining, insight into mysteries transcending ordinary human knowledge, by direct communication with the divine or immediate intuition in a state of
spiritual ecstasy. It concerns altered states of consciousness. The encyclopaedia

Britannica defines mysticism as the practice of religious ecstasies (experiences during altered states of consciousness), together with whatever ideologies, ethics, rites, myths, legends and magic may be related to them. Mystical experiences may occur during the practice of authentic movement since it too fosters an altered state of consciousness whereby experiences may make connection with an extrasensory dimension of reality (spiritual). Phenomena whose existence cannot be detected through sense perception become apparent during mystical experiences perceived directly, with a depth of feeling (heartfelt), by the soul, mind or imagination. They are said to be mysterious, awesome, urgent, fascinating and numinous.

With reference to a psycho-spiritual journey the mandorla has ancient origins and great power. It is a mystical symbol. It hints at another shape, the yoni, the cosmic womb, a place for re-birth and renewal. When it is seen something beginning is opening, is coming. Apparently, in icons of the Eastern Orthodox Church, the mandorla (referring to the central "eye" almond shape) is used to depict sacred moments that transcend time and space, such as the Resurrection and the Transfiguration of Jesus Christ. It also symbolizes the marriage of the divine and the human. In medieval times the two interconnecting circles were symbolic of encompassing the realms of heaven and earth or the macrocosm and microcosm. The meeting point in the centre is a holy space between the two realms and a mystical convergence of them. Inside the mandorla is the portal through which the divine is made incarnate, a doorway from the mundane to the sacred. There is a connection to the feminine, to the anima mundi, the world soul. Adler points out in Morrissey and Sager (2022, p. 109) that the mandorla is home to the Discipline of Authentic Movement.

Summary

This chapter has presented some illustrations of the ground form and group formats. It has emphasized speaking in the present tense, percept and self-referential language, witness offerings only on the movements spoken by the mover, containment of those not mentioned, and owning of judgement, projection and interpretation. Finally, a brief encounter with the transpersonal element was reported. These transpersonal experiences may arise at any time during this practice.

References

Adler, J. (1995). *Arching backwards*. Inner Traditions. https://www.britannica.com/topic/Sufism/The-path

Adler, J. (1999). Body and soul. In P. Pallaro (Ed.), *Authentic movement: Essays by Mary Starks Whitehouse, Janet Adler and Joan Chodorow*. Jessica Kingsley.

Adler, J. (2002). *The discipline of authentic movement*. Inner Traditions.

Morrissey, B., & Sager, P. (Eds.). (2022). *Intimacy in emptiness: An evolution of embodied consciousness: Collected writing of Janet Adler*. Inner Traditions.

Weir, J. (1975). The personal growth laboratory. In K. Benne, L. P. Bradford, J. R. Gibb, & R. D. Lippitt (Eds.), *The laboratory method of changing and learning: Theory and application* (Chapter 13). Science and Behavior Books.

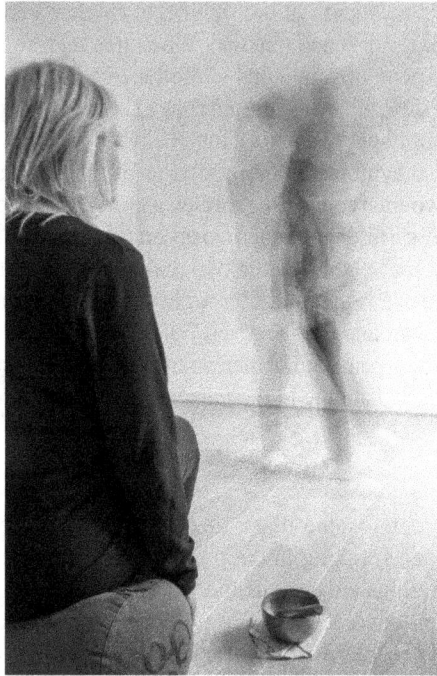

Photograph 2.1 One mover and one witness

Credit: Photography by Lucie Payne

Chapter 2

Authentic Movement and Clinical Supervision

Abstract

This chapter explores the ways in which the Discipline of Authentic Movement (Adler, 2002; Pallaro, 1999) might be used as an avenue for developing the "wise inner teacher/ higher self" (Rowan, 1993) or the "internal supervisor" (Casement, 1985, 1990). In the process of practising authentic movement there is an experience of being both a "mover" and a "witness". The chapter is proposing the witness may be similar to the benign "observing other" of the individuated internal supervisor.

The Witness as Internalised Clinical Supervisor

Casement (1985) speaks of the external support for the beginning therapist being like the baby experiencing the mother's holding (Winnicott, 1965), that is, from the outside, by the clinical supervisor. This then transitionally becomes internalized, during which the therapist hears the voice of the supervisor and uses their thinking, superimposed upon what is actually going on in the session. Finally, this internal support becomes "autonomous and separate from the internalised supervisor" (Casement, 1985, p. 24). It is more responsive to the moment in ways that are more appropriate to it (Casement, 1990).

He argues that the therapist's presence needs to be a transitional or potential presence (like that of a mother who is non-intrusively present with her playing child). In this way there is potential for the client to invoke the therapist as representing an absence or a presence. This space or freedom is possible because the therapist does not attempt to understand or empathize from a place of knowledge or theory, but from a place of "not knowing". Resisting the temptation to prompt or direct the client the therapist leaves space for new understanding to emerge. During the process of therapy Casement says therapists may learn to watch themselves within the session, in their developing capacity for spontaneous reflection, alongside the internalized supervisor. He claims they can do this using an "island of intellectual contemplation as the mental space" (Casement, 1990, p. 32). During their

(Original first published in E-MOTION, Newsletter for ADMT.UK, Winter, 13, 4, 2001. This is an updated and amended version)

DOI: 10.4324/9781003479413-3

development as therapists Casement believes they develop a dialogue between the external supervisor and the internal supervisor whereby there is more of the independent capacity required of a qualified therapist in the process of becoming. Part of this capacity involves a deep empathic understanding of the client. That is being able to share in the experience of the client as if it were our own, partially identifying with the client by introjection before reflecting back by re-projection. The therapist's experiencing ego has to shift "between herself and the client, between thinking and feeling" (Casement, 1990, p. 34). The boundary between conscious, rational thought is crossed and she enters the primary process of irrational thoughts and feelings, in which a free "reverie, alongside the client", is entered into where it becomes easier to monitor what it feels like to be the client.

Active Imagination

This ability to be in two places at once is an aspect of authentic movement training. In authentic movement the two roles of mover and witness are crucial. It is a meditative, contemplative process whereby the place of not knowing can be entered into in response to impulses at a primary level from deep within the body. The resulting movement (or stillness) is the guide for the mover to enter her imagination and to follow. Ego is dropped and she enters an active imagination in movement (Jung, 1916). The fact that movement cannot easily be fixed in the mind or repeated may be advantageous to the process of "letting go" into the experience. Jung (1968) claimed active imagination was a process in which, while the consciousness looks on, participating but not directing, co-operating but not choosing, the unconscious is allowed to appear in whatever form it likes. Something much deeper than personal ego is represented, sometimes connecting with universal human phenomena (Adler, 1992, 1996).

Adler (1948) defines active imagination as:

> A definite attitude towards the contents of the unconscious whereby we seek to isolate them and thus observe their autonomous development. We may also say that "we make them come to life", but this is incorrect in as far as we merely observe what is happening . . . it is not unlike watching a film or listening to music, where in each case one sits back and "takes in" something which one has not made but which happens, with a concentration which is a definite kind of activity. Only the difference is that in active imagination the "film" is being unrolled inside.

> (Adler, 1948, p. 43)

The Witness and Mover in Authentic Movement

The witness in authentic movement acts as a container, noticing her judgements, interpretations, projections, thoughts, feelings, kinaesthetic impulses, bodily sensations, images, thoughts, and kinaesthetic and proprioceptive responses in the presence of the mover. She has her eyes open; the mover has her eyes closed. After the mover has completed her experience, she returns to the witness and shares this direct experience of the unconscious. Immediately she speaks that experience becomes one step removed from her. She may choose other arts media instead of speaking, for example to draw or write poetry; later she may wish to speak as well. Then, if invited by the mover, the witness shares her experiences whilst in the presence of this mover. She owns all her projections, judgements and interpretations. The dyad journey together with this practice and their stories unfold within a deep respect and empathy for each other. The mover may choose to incorporate into her meaning-making her witness's perceptions or not. It can be profoundly important for movers to be "seen" at times.

Movement-in-depth was conceived in America in the 1970s (Frantz, 1972) by Mary Starks Whitehouse (1977, 1979) who was a dance teacher with an interest in Jungian thought emerging from her Jungian analysis. She described her use of the term "authentic" as referring to unlearned truth, genuineness belonging to that person. The movement is not a set of exercises or a choice to move. Neither is it improvisation or creative movement, which takes place in a different context and for another purpose entirely. Rather in refraining from exerting any demand on the self to move it employs the opposite in the sense of "I am moved". It is a unique and powerfully awesome moment when this happens. In that moment the ego gives up control and stops choosing, allowing the self to embody the physical body as it will, in a kind of "indwelling". This cannot be sought, repeated, nor explained. It is unpredictable, unpremeditated, spontaneous and freeing. It is this process which leads the mover into that "place of not knowing" which is of profound importance.

Often the mover speaks of not doing it herself, or knowing what she is doing, and yet something is done. This experience brings both mover and witness into a balance between action and non-action (Whitehouse, 1979) allowing them to live from a different awareness. That place where experiencing themselves can be viewed with a detachment, having these two qualities at the same time. They may be aware of, and contain, the opposites of say, suffering and enjoyment at the same time. From this, something else emerges, something new is discovered. Janet Adler, one of Mary's students, built on this approach to coin the term discipline of authentic movement (Adler, 2002).

Training Potential

During their training in authentic movement the therapist can begin to learn from her experience about the detachment required of the mover in order to be free from ego control and develop the capacity to "dream" alongside her client. Eventually the experience of being seen by the witness outside her helps the evolving inner witness. Adler (1987) discusses the process of developing the internal witness. It begins with being seen by another, says Adler. Following this one begins to see oneself, here the internal witness is developing, and the student of authentic movement can begin to witness another. From this witnessing of another develops a new ability to see oneself, as one is. As a result, the witness becomes more highly tuned inside her, promoting the development of the internal supervisor Casement describes. By developing this ability to tune in to one's experiencing whilst experiencing, the therapist can learn to listen to her internal supervisor whilst practising therapy. Witnessing both self and other in a compassionate, non-judgemental manner is a skill referred to in authentic movement both for groups and individual work. As the student develops the internal supervisor/witness her access to images, memories and her own inner life is seen to be quite relevant to the process of therapy. In this way transferences and counter-transferences can be identified more easily.

Chodorow (1991), also a student of Mary Starks Whitehouse, built on the Jungian trajectory of active imagination (Chodorow, 1978, 1982, 1984, 1986). She emphasizes the nature of the witness experience as subjective and the fact that one of the ground rules is that each mover and witness contains part of the experience. In the "play" between curiosity and imagination, Chodorow (1991) says, the witness fluctuates between differentiated, objective, defined ways of seeing and subjective, imaginative ways of seeing. That is, the same movement event can be seen and described in a number of ways. So, as well as describing what actually was seen in terms of body parts moving and how, at the same time, there is an empathic relatedness, such as wanting to comfort a sad child. Rejecting feelings may also arise if, in this case for example, either the witness or the mover had a neglected childhood. Chodorow states the mover-witness relationship, which serves as container and process, offers a valuable resource for the training of psychotherapists and analysts.

The importance of "inner listening" is at the heart of counselling/psychotherapy and authentic movement. Adler (1987) describes it as "[the witness] responding to a sensation, to an inner impulse, to energy coming from the personal unconscious, collective unconsciousness or super-conscious. Her response to this energy creates movement that may be visible or invisible to the witness" (Adler, 1987, p. 2). Casement (1985) refers to "unfocussed listening" as the "first step beyond that of familiar evenly suspended attention, with which analysts are encouraged to listen to the over-all drift of a patient's communication" (Casement, 1985, p. 38). The therapist's capacity to stay with the "stream of free-floating attention" during the therapy sessions, he says, provides valuable material to use in the service of the client when in supervision reflecting upon sessions as well as during the sessions themselves. This form of "listening" or "responding to the inner impulse" has a special quality and is one of the fundamental processes and skills developed through authentic movement.

In addition, the repeated experiences of entering the place of not knowing through authentic movement as both mover and witness enable the therapist to learn a deep empathy and respect for herself and the mover. This can be generalized to working with clients where empathic capabilities are crucial.

Summary

This chapter has introduced the concept of the internal clinical supervisor drawing extensively on Casement's writings. It is proposed here that the witness in authentic movement and the inner witness in the mover may be similar to the benign "observing other" of the individuated internal supervisor.

References

Adler, G. (1948). *Studies in analytical psychology*. Routledge and Kegan Paul.
Adler, J. (1987, Winter). Who is the witness? *Contact Quarterly*, *7*(1), 20–29.
Adler, J. (1992). Body and soul. *American Journal of Dance Therapy*, *14*, 73–94.
Adler, J. (1996). The collective body. *American Journal of Dance Therapy*, *18*(2), 81–94.
Adler, J. (2002). *The discipline of authentic movement*. Inner Traditions Press.
Casement, P. (1985). *Learning from the patient*. Routledge.
Casement, P. (1990). *Further learning from the patient*. Routledge.
Chodorow, J. (1978). Dance therapy and the transcendent function. *American Journal of Dance Therapy, 2*(1), 16–23.
Chodorow, J. (1982). Dance/movement and body experience in analysis. In M. Stein (Ed.) (1995), *Jungian analysis* (2nd ed.). Open Court. Shambhala, paperback 1984.
Chodorow, J. (1984). To move and be moved. *Quadrant Journal of the C.G. Jung Foundation for Analytical Psychology*, *17*(2), 39–48.
Chodorow, J. (1986). The body as symbol: Dance/movement in analysis. In N. Schwartz-Salant & M. Stein (Eds.), *The body in analysis* (pp. 87–108). Chiron Publications.
Chodorow, J. (1991). *Dance therapy and depth psychology; the moving imagination*. Routledge.
Frantz, G. (1972). An approach to the center: An interview with Mary Whitehouse. *Psychological Perspectives*, *3*(1).
Jung, C. G. (1916). The transcendent function. In *Collected works of C. G. Jung (1969)* (Vol. 8). Princeton Universities Press.
Jung, C. G. (1968). *Analytical psychology: Its theory and practice*. Pantheon Books, Random House.
Pallaro, P. (Ed.). (1999). *Authentic movement: Essays by Mary Starks Whitehouse, Joan Chodorow and Janet Adler*. Jessica Kingsley Publications.
Rowan, J. (1993). *The transpersonal: Psychotherapy and counselling*. Routledge.
Whitehouse, M. S. (1977). The transference and dance therapy. *American Journal of Dance Therapy*, *1*(1), 3–7.
Whitehouse, M. S. (1979). CG Jung and dance therapy: Two major principles. In P. Bernstein (Ed.), *Eight theoretical approaches to dance movement therapy*. Kendall/Hunt.
Winnicott, D. W. (1965). *Maturational processes and the facilitating environment*. Hogarth Press.

Photograph 3.1 Two witnesses and one mover

Credit: Photography by Lucie Payne

Chapter 3

The Discipline of Authentic Movement, Group Process and Transpersonal Psychotherapy

Abstract

This chapter provides an overview of the group process in relation to transpersonal states in the practice of authentic movement as psychotherapy. Movers and witnesses are discussed in relation to the various group structures: whole group move, breathing circle and long circle. The collective body is highlighted in view of the importance of the concept underpinning the active imagination proposed by Carl Jung.

Introduction

Authentic movement excited me when I discovered its powerful way of speaking to me within an empathic, non-judgemental and non-interpretative framework. Authentic movement is a newly emerging discipline employing a sort of kinetic meditation through which the participant can learn to engage with a direct experience of herself, the group process and the transpersonal realm. This can be recognized as an experience beyond words and concepts. It can assist in developing body awareness and bodymindspirit connections. By gaining access and giving creative expression to inner worlds the invisible becomes visible or "authentic" (Whitehouse, 1979).

Originally termed movement-in-depth by Starks Whitehouse in the 1970s the method grew from its roots in dance and Jungian thought, mystical practice and pioneering work in dance movement therapy (Frantz, 1972). Building on Jung's method of active imagination (Jung, 1968) symbolic meaning is seen in physical expression.

Authentic movement is not a set of exercises, creative movement (Payne, 1990, 2020) or dance movement psychotherapy (Payne, 1992), although it may contribute as one method to the latter (Musicant, 2001). In authentic movement cognitive thought often stops. Normally there is no plan or intention to organize the movement

(This chapter is based on an integration of a) an unpublished paper linking transpersonal experiences with the theory of group process within the context of practising the discipline of authentic movement and b) an article published *in Self and Society – Forum for Contemporary Psychology*, Summer 2003, 31, 2, 32–36 titled Authentic Movement, Groups and Psychotherapy)

DOI: 10.4324/9781003479413-4

as in improvisation for choreography. It is a completely self-directed approach in which participants may discover a movement pathway that offers a bridge between the conscious and the unconscious and between the group, the individual and the universal. In this way it fulfils the notion of "authentic", becoming one with the authentic self through exploring embodied consciousness. It is the movement form of active imagination and is particularly powerful because sometimes one moves before one knows it, cannot easily be edited or stopped, and is sometimes referred to as "I am being moved" directly from the unconscious (Chodorow, 1991, p. 28). Its uniqueness lies in the way movement is ephemeral; like a dream, it cannot be held onto, pinned down or repeated exactly.

It has some similarity to group analysis in the way the "conductor" or meta-witness/ facilitator waits without overt action/participation, empathetically facilitating through verbal communication and presence to the group, and individual participants at times. The relationship between participants, including the conductor, is made clear and patterns begin to emerge. In authentic movement relationships of movers with other movers, witnesses with witnesses, and movers with witnesses provide opportunities for raising awareness of group-held issues and differing parts of the group. In this way individuals may come face-to-face with their projections.

Active imagination and symbolism link to transpersonal psychotherapy and Jungian depth psychology and are methods to engage the unconscious to liberally express itself whilst the inner observing-self witnesses the process. According to Whitehouse, active imagination "is Jung's term for a process in which, while consciousness looks on, participating but not directing, co-operating but not choosing, the unconscious is allowed to speak whatever and however it likes" (1999a, p. 83). Active imagination is a personal process that may operate differently according to the person; there may be visual images or voices and "anyone with a motor imagination could make a very beautiful dance out of that motif" (Chodorow, 2006 citing Jung, 1938, p. 474). There have also been developments of active imagination in visual art, drama, movement, music and sand play.

As Payne (2024) highlights, groupwork in the practice of the discipline of authentic movement can offer a richness to movers and witnesses since there are so many more opportunities to see and be seen. The group requires an experienced conductor and clear ground rules to practise safely together, such as ensuring any previous/current relationships between group members are acknowledged and making sure confidentiality is guaranteed. Another example is ensuring that no identifying features or names of group members are shared with others outside of the group. If clients wish to share with others their own experience in the group, then this is acceptable, however they need to abide by these guidelines to protect the confidentiality of all group members. It will need confirming by all members that any leakage about the group by any member comes back to the group the following week to secure group boundaries.

There may be pairing (Bion, 1969) and other patterns of relationships developing in the group. However, the therapist/witness can treat the group as one entity identifying common themes and patterns of relationships such as sub-groups, supporting their capacity to cope with discontent, and offering interpretations of the group process as required. There may be physical contact in authentic movement groupwork, sometimes spontaneously or intentionally. The group need to agree any touch between members is non-sexual and non-violent. Eyes need to be half opened if a member wishes to move quickly or strongly to avoid potential injury to themselves or others.

The group structures, based on the ground form mentioned earlier of mover and witness, include "whole group move" with the therapist as witness, the "breathing circle" and the "long circle". Each are described again separately and as a reminder in the following sections.

The Whole Group Move

The whole group move is where all group members make eye contact with each other and the witness/therapist. They are all in the role of movers in the presence of the therapist as witness. The group normally return from moving for the previously agreed set time duration and enter what is termed a "transition period" (Bracegirdle, 2023) which can be as much as 20 minutes or as little as five minutes. This can include individuals whether movers or witnesses reflecting on their experiences by writing, making clay models or making marks on paper. This is then followed by each member being invited to share two or three significant moments, ensuring they recall the movement contact/action/posture/sound. They can then request witnessing. If the witness/therapist has seen the movement, they can speak of their experience in its presence and in the present tense. If not, they cannot speak from it, saying unfortunately that movement etc., was not seen. There may be others in the group who witnessed the movement, heard the sound or felt the touch who can offer something as a "moving witness".

The Breathing Circle

To reiterate and expand on this format, in the breathing circle half of the group act as witnesses with the therapist as a meta witness. After the time duration is agreed, half the members enter the centre of a circle as movers with the other half as witnesses sitting or standing on the boundary. Movers may go outside the boundary if they wish. They may request a designated witness who only witnesses that mover. One witness may wish to be a silent, non-speaking witness. Eye contact is between movers and witnesses and between the movers themselves, and arms reach out (sprouting) between members of the witness circle in a sort of "holding" of the circle. This can also be instigated by any witness at any time if they are feeling they cannot be fully present for whatever reason.

In this circle, on finishing their movement (or non-movement), movers return to their seats. Witnesses "sprout" to welcome them back. Successively the other half become movers. The same eye contact is performed. Then, following these movers returning to the circle, there is transition time. Thereafter, the first "breath" of movers is invited to speak in the present tense in turn. Each one may share up to three significant moments noting the movement/sound/posture/touch and can request witnessing if they wish. Speaking and designated witnesses who have seen those movements etc., make their offering to each mover if they saw those events. A moving witness from that group of movers who recognizes an event can also offer moving witnessing again in the present tense.

The following section elaborates on the long circle protocol once again as a reminder.

The Long Circle

The Unseen Rhythm Within

On my back flat on the floor mostly still
but gently tapping tapping with
my memoried ring
following
the unseen rhythm within;
another touches
not refused not taken in
for there's a waiting while following
the unseen rhythm within;
there's a call unheard
but felt without for this long circle is waiting for
the unseen rhythm
within;
responses chant
with softened waves.
    (Extract from the personal journal of Christina
        Bracegirdle, open training circle, 2023)

The long circle takes a long time, from 30 minutes to two hours or more depending on the number of participants in the group. This is where the group members sit on the boundaries of a circle and make eye contact and outstretch arms to each other. A member at the outset can voice the option to remain a silent witness throughout, being fully present for the duration including transition, but a non-speaking outer witness when it comes to languaging experiences. This can enhance their capacity for containment although transition can support their self-reflective journalling etc., of the experience of silently witnessing movers moving and witnesses speaking. Another may choose not to move for the whole duration. Any witness can then select a time to go into the circle to move for as long as they wish and at any time during the time allocated to the long circle. They can go in as many times as they wish. There is no requirement for eye contact before or after moving. They can also choose not to go in at all. They can request a designated witness for themselves who cannot enter the space if their mover is moving. All movers need to ensure there are at least three outer witnesses including the meta witness present on the circle boundary before entering the space. On returning to the boundary of the circle witnesses sprout to welcome them back and movers make eye contact with witnesses if they choose. Speaking is conducted in a chronological order with the first member to enter the circle speaking of their significant moments. They can request witnessing, and moving witnesses can speak too, all in the present tense.

These structures for working in an experiential group therapy setting enable the meta witness/therapist to remain available to the whole group constantly and consistently. However, in training circles other structures can be introduced. For example, there is working in threes or fours, or more, with two or more speaking witnesses and/or the role of the silent witness.

The Transpersonal in Group Process

When authentic movement is viewed as an opening to mystical practice (Adler, 1995; Morrissey & Sager, 2022) transpersonal ideas/perspectives come to mind. These are formulations within a particular approach or philosophical worldview rather than a generally established, recognized phenomena or scientific term. The mystical, transpersonal, divine or archetypal wisdom (Stromsted, 2000, 2001, 2009, 2015) has supported, for example, visual artists, musicians, choreographers, sculptors and poets. Transpersonal experiences can be defined as those in which the sense of identity or self extends beyond (trans) the individual to encompass wider aspects of humankind, life, psyche or cosmos. They can be described as beyond words – numinous encounters in altered states of consciousness – shifting aware- ness to something beyond, more than the self. In authentic movement, movers may disidentify from the personal and experience states of "being moved" as noted by Whitehouse (1999b, p. 47) by impulses from the cultural and/or collective uncon- scious (Chodorow, 1999, 2010, 2013, 2015; Stromsted, 2009, 2019). Whitehouse (1999c) reports "each contact was an existential moment . . . consisting of I and Thou and a third element – that which is between us, that which is not mine, though I am in it, and not yours, though you are in it" (p. 62).

These transpersonal states have also been described as emerging from, and within, the relational connections between mover and witness as well as between movers (in groupwork) – any separation between self and other dissolves (Adler, 1999a; Chodorow, 1999; Bull, 2007). Within existential and hermeneutic philoso- phy, the focus is on making sense of the meaning structures of the lived experience of the client. Solowoniuk and Nixon (2009) make links between the transpersonal and phenomenology whereby the individual accepts a non-dual reality, uncondi- tionally accepting many phenomenological states, conditions, experiences and modes of Being and non-Being. Transpersonal phenomenology is supported by undiluted awareness independent of an interrelationship between perceiver and object. Valle (1998) suggests this is a noumenal space from which both intentional- ity and phenomenology come into our awareness.

Transpersonal phenomenology is an approach that invites the witnessing of one's lifeworld in a radically different fashion, going beyond the embodied ego to reveal a re-remembering of, for example, a primordial existence. This phenomenological understanding offers a philosophical perspective of the possible transpersonal nature of moving and witnessing in authentic movement.

Movers and Witnesses

In exploring the relationship between a mover and a witness, being seen and seeing, the hidden becomes visible from a connection between perspectives. Sometimes this meeting moment becomes a unitive experience (Adler, 1999a) as the internal witness within each evolves. With eyes closed, and in the presence of one or many witnesses on the edge of the circle, the mover listens inwardly to find a movement arising from a cellular impulse.

To begin with, the mover may feel they did not know what they were doing, similar to the experience of unconscious non-duality (Horrocks, 2002). Daydreaming is also a non-ego-controlled experience, in which the mind lets go of the separateness normally experienced between the self and other. Authentic movement however is more frequently like lucid dreaming where there is interplay between the dreamer and the dreamed. The creativity is in the interplay. It can also connect the mover to the numinous, the universal "I" or "big me" rarely found in everyday life. In this experience the freedom from/loss of ego or "little i" with attachments such as personal history, identity and so on enables a greater connection with the collective body (Adler, 1999[b]).

Although the witness has chosen not to move, she is not a watcher or an observer of the mover, but an empathic and receptive external part of the mover, regarding the mover. From this co-creation of reality results safety and a deep respect for each other. The witness acts in the role of container for the mover's immersion in unconscious material. After being seen clearly by a witness, the mover begins to see herself and her inner witness can develop further. The outer speaking witness after seeing another also discovers a new ability to see herself. From these experiences both self-witnessing and ways of "being" in relationship, in the here and now, are learned. The witness engages in a process of somatic indwelling or waiting (Musicant, 1994), containing her projections and impulse to move, with the intention of feeling what it may be like for that mover, without preconceived ideas. This is akin to aspects of humanistic therapies; for example, Rogers (1957) stressed the role of empathy and unconditional positive regard as necessary and sufficient conditions for therapeutic change. A deep respect for self and others grows out of the process whereby an internal locus of control is fostered, each person being all that is right and true for them.

As the internal witness develops the mover often returns after the "dream state" to recall, in the presence of a witness, a significant event in the movement. This is a conscious experience (conscious non-duality) because it has been remembered. The non-dual experience is both subjective and objective at the same time; both knowing and not knowing; doing and not doing. Although the emphasis is on the "here and now", recalling an event when languaging in the present tense from the movement experience can add another dimension when shared verbally with witnesses. If witnesses saw the event described, the mover may then request they share their experiences. As an example, I offer next one of my experiences as a witness: "I see a windmill, its sails turning in a wind. The base was firmly in the ground and held in place by a root or chain or some sort. I feel like a mediator between the sky and the earth, a connector".

In speaking of an embodied event, the mover may describe the movement together with associated feelings, sensations, images, body-felt senses and thoughts. Drawing and creative writing may also be used in the transition period between moving and witnessing to bring form and meaning to the experiences. Witnesses, by owning their experience, their projections, interpretations and judgements, give space to the mover to accept or reject their perceptions.

The Collective Body

Moving, witnessing and sharing can enable connections between the individual, the group and the collective/universal body. For example, archetypal beings/figures may be seen, which have lived throughout time (such as Magician, Priestess, King, Grim Reaper, Jester, Warrior or Shaman or an underwater seascape may be revealed), and which are lived again in the mover or witness or both. They are reborn through embodied participants. They can provide a link from the personal to the collective body giving images from which to give meaning to individual lives and communities. The stimuli in our environment such as movers' contact with others or birds singing can have a deep presence inside the mover/witness as if they are part of them. Participants can become at one with their direct experience and feel no separation between themselves and aspects in their imagination or the environment. They experience unity and compassion when personal themes manifest out of, and connect to, a collective body of matter as each mover speaks and receives witnessing in the group.

This altered reality experience may help participants to make sense of life and personal themes. Spiritual questions may be explored at the same time as group dynamics. For example, during the breathing circle (one group structure) if movers leave the space to return to the circle of witnesses the centre becomes empty once again, as in the beginning. Contemplation of this space can bring up, for example, issues of loss, enrichment, mortality, birth and re-birth. Everything and nothing are in the space at the same time, and all participants surrender to this. These issues may be processed in the large group or in two separate groups of movers and witnesses.

The concept of the "wise observer/higher self" (Rowan, 1993) in transpersonal psychotherapy is also relevant. For instance, by waiting for, and listening to, an inner prompt, the mover rediscovers a consciousness of the "wise observer". By "seeing" the mover clearly, the witness regains a similar embodied consciousness. I have discussed elsewhere (Payne, 2001) the links between the process of witnessing in authentic movement and the internal supervisor as portrayed by Casement (1985, 1990) in clinical supervision (see Chapter 2).

The authentic movement experience can be compelling and awesome. It draws participants from a range of backgrounds including the arts, caring/helping professions and psychotherapy. Untrained movers are at an advantage over dancers who may need to unlearn technique. The non-judgemental environment promotes a safe, warm climate for moving in the presence of others. It is a good way to re-energize and make timeless, deeper connections with others.

Summary

This chapter has provided an overview of how the discipline of authentic movement can be practised as a method for group process and for transpersonal experiences to the benefit of all group members.

References

Adler, J. (1995). *Arching backward: The mystical initiation of a contemporary woman*. Inner Traditions.

Adler, J. (1999a). Body and soul. In P. Pallaro (Ed.), *Authentic movement: Essays by Mary Starks Whitehouse, Janet Adler and Joan Chodorow* (pp. 160–189). Jessica Kingsley.

Adler, J. (1999b). The collective body. In P. Pallaro (Ed.), *Authentic movement: Essays by Mary Starks Whitehouse, Janet Adler and Joan Chodorow*. Jessica Kingsley.

Bion, W. R. (1969). *Experiences in groups and other papers*. Routledge.

Bracegirdle, C. (2023). A mover's practice of transition in authentic movement: An embodied non-dual lived experience. *Body, Movement and Dance in Psychotherapy*, *19*(4), 381–396. https://doi.org/10.1080/17432979.2023.2254834

Bull, C. A. (2007). The discovery of deep ecology through the body. In P. Pallaro (Ed.), *Authentic movement: Moving the body, moving the self, being moved* (Vol. 2, pp. 361–363). Jessica Kingsley Publishers.

Casement, P. (1985). *On learning from the patient*. Routledge.

Casement, P. (1990). *On further learning from the patient*. Routledge.

Chodorow, J. (1991). *Dance therapy and depth psychology*. Routledge.

Chodorow, J. (1999). To move and be moved. In P. Pallaro (Ed.), *Authentic movement: Essays by Mary Starks Whitehouse, Janet Adler and Joan Chodorow* (pp. 267–278). Jessica Kingsley.

Chodorow, J. (2006). Active imagination. In R. K. Papadopoulos (Ed.), *The handbook of Jungian psychology: Theory, practice and applications* (pp. 215–243). Routledge.

Chodorow, J. (2010). *Multiplicity in the living, moving body: Psyche, nature, culture*. Proceedings from IAAP Montreal: The 17th International Congress for Analytical Psychology, Daimon-Verlag, Switzerland.

Chodorow, J. (2013). *The living, moving body in analysis: Origins, innovations and controversies (1913–2013)*. Proceedings from IAAP Copenhagen: The 17th International Congress for Analytical Psychology, Daimon-Verlag, Switzerland.

Chodorow, J. (2015). Work in progress – Authentic movement: Danced and moving active imagination. *Journal of Dance & Somatic Practices*, *7*(2), 257–272.

Frantz, G. (1972). An approach to the centre: An interview with Mary Whitehouse. *Psychological Perspectives*, *3*(1).

Horrocks, R. (2002). Non-duality. *Self and Society*, 29(6), 7–14.

Jung, C. G. (1938). *Dream analysis*. Ed. W. McGuire. Princeton University Press.

Jung, C. G. (1968). *Analytical psychology: Its theory and practice*. Random House.

Morrissey, B., & Sager, P. (Eds.). (2022). *Intimacy in emptiness: An evolution of embodied consciousness. Collected writings of Janet Adler*. Inner Traditions Press.

Musicant, S. (1994, Winter). Authentic movement and dance therapy. *American Journal of Dance Therapy*, *16*(2), 91–106.

Musicant, S. (2001). Authentic movement: Clinical considerations. *American Journal of Dance Therapy*, *23*(1), 17–26.

Payne, H. (1990). *Creative movement and dance in groupwork*. 1st ed. Speechmark.

Payne, H. (Ed.). (1992). *Dance movement therapy: Theory and practice*. Routledge.

Payne, H. (2001, Winter). Authentic movement and supervision. *E-motion, ADMT.UK Newsletter*, *13*(4).

Payne, H. (2020). *Creative dance and movement in groupwork* (2nd updated ed.). Routledge.

Payne, H. (2024). Relational integrative psychotherapy and the discipline of authentic movement. *American Journal of Dance Therapy*, *46*, 34–51. https://doi.org/10.1007/s10465-023-09394-5

Rogers, C. (1957). The necessary and sufficient conditions for therapeutic personality change. *Journal of Consulting Psychology*, *21*(2), 95–103.

Rowan, J. (1993). *The transpersonal: Psychotherapy and counselling*. Routledge.

Solowoniuk, J., & Nixon, G. (2009). Introducing transpersonal phenomenology: The direct experience of a sudden awakening. *Paradoxica: Nondual Psychology*, 1.

Stromsted, T. (2000). *Re-inhabiting the female body: Authentic movement as a gateway to transformation* [Unpublished doctoral dissertation, California Institute of Integral Studies].

Stromsted, T. (2001). Re-inhabiting the female body: Authentic movement as a gateway to transformation. *The Arts in Psychotherapy*, *28*(1), 39–55.

Stromsted, T. (2009). Authentic movement: A dance with the divine. *Body, Movement and Dance in Psychotherapy*, *4*(3), 201–213.

Stromsted, T. (2015). Authentic movement & the evolution of Soul's Body® work. *Journal of Dance and Somatic Practices: Authentic Movement: Defining the Field, Intellect*, *7*(2).

Stromsted, T. (2019). Witnessing practice: In the eyes of the beholder. In H. Payne, S. Koch, J. Tantia, with T. Fuchs (Eds.), *The Routledge international handbook: Embodied perspectives in psychotherapy: Approaches from dance movement and body psychotherapies* (pp. 95–103). Routledge.

Valle, R. S. (1998). Transpersonal awareness: Implications for phenomenological research. In R. S. Valle (Ed.), *Phenomenological inquiry in psychology: Existential and transpersonal dimensions* (pp. 270–280). Plenum Press.

Whitehouse, M. S. (1979). Jung and dance therapy: Two major principles. In P. Bernstein (Ed.), *Eight theoretical approaches to dance movement therapy*. Kendall/Hunt.

Whitehouse, M. S. (1999a). C. G. Jung and dance therapy: Two major principles. In P. Pallaro (Ed.), *Authentic movement: Essays by Mary Starks Whitehouse, Janet Adler and Joan Chodorow* (pp. 73–101). Jessica Kingsley.

Whitehouse, M. S. (1999b). The Tao of the body. In P. Pallaro (Ed.), *Authentic movement: Essays by Mary Starks Whitehouse, Janet Adler and Joan Chodorow* (pp. 41–50). Jessica Kingsley.

Whitehouse, M. S. (1999c). Reflections on a metamorphosis. In P. Pallaro (Ed.), *Authentic movement: Essays by Mary Starks Whitehouse, Janet Adler and Joan Chodorow* (pp. 58–62). Jessica Kingsley.

Wild Geese

You do not have to be good.
You do not have to walk on your knees
for a hundred miles through the desert, repenting.
You only have to let the soft animal of your body love
what it loves.
Tell me about despair, yours, and I will tell you mine.
Meanwhile, the world goes on.
Meanwhile the sun and the clear pebbles of the rain
are moving across landscapes,
over the prairies and deep trees,
the mountains and the rivers.
Meanwhile the wild geese, high in the clean blue air
are heading home again.
Whoever you are, no matter how lonely,
the world offers itself to your imagination,
calls to you like the wild geese, harsh and exciting–
over and over announcing your place
in the family of things.

Oliver, M. (1986). *Dream Work* (p. 16).
The Atlantic Monthly Press

Chapter 4

The Body as Container and Expresser

Authentic Movement in the Development of Wellbeing in Our Bodymindspirit

Abstract

This chapter examines the discipline of authentic movement, which is one method of an approach used to promote emotional wellbeing and health in the practice of dance movement psychotherapy. It begins with an overview of authentic movement, its history, why it is used and with whom, and followed with sections describing authentic movement from both a practical and a theoretical basis. A focus group was conducted to elicit trainees' reflections for inclusion in the narrative.

Introduction

In brief, the discipline of authentic movement (AM) can be described as aiming to increase connections between body, mind and spirit in the context of a group approach to health and healing, embodiment and wellbeing. It has been adapted for use with those with organic and non-organic medical conditions, dancers, artists and health practitioners and in the training of counsellors and psychotherapists.

Authentic movement is a powerful way of developing personal wellbeing using a unique form of free association in movement, to bring mindfulness through kinetic meditation (in other words, contemplation through spontaneous, expressive movement of the body). The participant can learn to engage with a direct experience of themselves, of the group and of the transpersonal, an experience often beyond words and concepts. It can assist, for example, in developing emotional literacy (intrapersonal intelligence), interpersonal skills and processes, body awareness, somatic intelligence, leading to bodymindspirit connections. By gaining access and giving creative expression to inner worlds the invisible becomes visible or "authentic", claims Californian founder Mary Starks Whitehouse (1979), although the term "authentic" in dance movement therapy was coined prior to this by US dance therapist Dosamantes-Alperson (1974) in describing her approach. Authenticity encompasses darkness as well as light: respecting the shadow while

(Updated version. First published in: Corrigall, J., Payne, H., & Wilkinson, H. (Eds.). (2006). *About a body: Working with the embodied mind in psychotherapy* (Chapter 11, pp. 162–180). Routledge)

DOI: 10.4324/9781003479413-5

learning to hold the tension between these opposites in each one of us, and which is part of the process in authentic movement.

The term "authentic" might appear confusing in this practice. However, it could be likened to the concept of congruence in person-centred psychotherapy (Rogers, 1961; Kirschenbaum, 1979). This emphasizes the need for the feeling state in the therapist, as provoked by the client, to be maintained as truthfully as possible, whether or not this is disclosed to the client. It is often difficult to "know" what is or is not congruent or authentic, though, from an outer perspective. Perhaps it is the impact of a movement, a stillness or an interaction with another mover and/or the environment which the mover recalls with much significance and/or a witness who experiences it as a powerful moment, which denotes a degree of authenticity.

In some ways the term authentic movement belies the practice. It limits the description since, as well as a mover, there is also a witness involved and verbal exchange together with a transition period in which mark-making, clay sculpting and reflective writing are all options. However, another more accurate term to describe the discipline has yet to be put forward.

History

Mary Starks Whitehouse was a dancer and a dance teacher with an interest in Jungian analysis and co-opted the notion of active imagination from Jung's approach. Her papers explore such issues as the role and experience of spontaneous and creative movement (Whitehouse, 1958); following an inner impulse, to the nature of embodiment in the process of change and transference (Whitehouse, 1970, 1977); and the complexity of Jungian thought in relation to dance therapy (Whitehouse, 1979). Two of her students, Joan Chodorow (1991, 1997, 1999) and Janet Adler (1995, 1999, 2002) (and Adler in Morrissey & Sager, 2022), have each developed AM further incorporating understanding from analytical psychotherapy and the mystical disciplines respectively. Adler, coined the term the "discipline" of authentic movement (Adler, 2002). Stromsted (2015, 2025a, 2025b), a student of Chodorow, has built on Chodorow's efforts of authentic movement as active imagination in the USA and has taught internationally. In Europe AM has absorbed elements from other disciplines besides dance movement therapy, for example, from the arts (Goldhahn, 2022), somatic practices (Hartley, 2022), research methodology, dance performance, and individual psychoanalytic psychotherapy (Penfield, 2006).

The Group

Authentic movement is frequently employed one to one with individuals and may involve working directly with the transference relationship as well as in groups with dance movement psychotherapists. Other teacher practitioners work with adults who seek wellbeing, somatic or contemplative practice through embodiment in a body-based discipline, also individually or in a group. Registered dance movement psychotherapists will have extensive personal development experiences and an in-depth training in authentic movement and groupwork. Authentic movement is entirely suited to group psychotherapy, where the holding capacity of the circle of external, conscious witnesses extends beyond that of any one therapist. Groups are normally self-selecting, although the therapist would probably interview participants to assess their suitability prior to starting in an ongoing group.

As with dance and dance movement therapy (and for that matter counselling and psychotherapy), men participate far less often than women, which is a pity as more of a balance between male and female would nourish the masculine and feminine in each of us more richly. Perhaps men are more likely to feel inhibited using movement in such a receptive way in the presence of other men and women. This phenomenon may connect to society's marginalization of the use of the body as an art form resulting in women, for whom cultural stereotypes may allow greater interest in dance and in connectivity, taking more of a lead in this discipline. The composition of authentic movement groups is mostly middle class, drawn from socioeconomic groups one and two, like participants found both in group and individual psychotherapy and counselling, and in training programmes. Much more attention needs to be given to encouraging participation from minorities, including those from ethnic groups.

Groups using authentic movement are certainly suitable for anyone interested in wellbeing, regardless of gender, ethnicity or class. However, in my view groups would be unsuitable for those suffering from mental health problems such as clinical depression, psychosis or borderline conditions or those needing ego strength building as authentic movement groupwork demands so much self-direction.

Another way in which authentic movement groups are being used is to provide continuing professional development for dance movement therapists, counsellors, psychotherapists and psychoanalysts, dancers and other artists. Indeed, anyone, from any profession or none, and especially anyone interested in spiritual growth can benefit from participating in an AM group. Those untrained in dance as an art form could be at an advantage over professionals who may firstly need to unlearn their dance technique.

When offered in a non-judgemental environment, with unconditional positive regard (Rogers, 1957), authentic movement provides a safe climate for moving in the presence of others. It is a good way to heal a trauma, to become your own person, to re-energize and to make timeless, deeper connections with others. It is the therapist/facilitator's task to prepare participants for an authentic movement group in the usual way, by negotiating, clarifying and maintaining the ground rules. It is also important in setting up a group to describe the intention/purpose, the different roles and forms taken in the group structure and the nature and role of moving from within. My own style is to collaborate fully with the group, for example, on setting ground rules and planning any breaks in the session. Sessions might range from a couple of hours to ongoing/intensive weekends, to residentials. As with any personal development group safety is essential (Payne, 2001).

The group participants need to be offered the "good enough" relaxed environment of which Winnicott (1971) speaks, to be able to relax into/release their movement impulses, thoughts, sensations, images. Reciprocal free association, as in Winnicott's Squiggle game of "no rules" (Winnicott, 1971, p. 16) (where the therapist makes an impulsive mark on paper, then invites the client to turn it into something, after which the client takes a turn), simply cannot take place if the group members feel too much anxiety. This is of particular importance when starting in authentic movement, as the work is done in ways usually unfamiliar to the participants, such as moving with closed eyes, only half opening them if moving quickly and strongly to ensure safety for the mover and other movers. Having said that, eyes can be opened at any time although this can engage an outer focus as the visual pulls us into our environment.

Some problems are encountered from time to time as illustrated by the following participants' comments:

> I would say difficulties revolved around adjusting to the changes in structures. Because [the] work is structured, I feel safety in that, then, when ways of using the form are changed or altered it can feel quite challenging yet also very important (a group participant).

And

> When new members join an established group {in an open group format} it is good, because it helps remind me of the ground form and makes me realize what I have understood and gained. However, it can feel unsafe when perhaps I have been at a different level in my own journey with authentic movement and again, brings up issues of trust and safety (another participant).

Roles Taken in Authentic Movement Groups

Participants are invited to enter one of two distinct roles during an AM group as described by this group member:

> Authentic movement groups enable the work to be broken up into component parts to explore, for example being the witness (silent, verbal or collective) and being mover. By exploring how the roles of witness and mover can be used by initially almost exaggerating separateness between them I am becoming skilled at experiencing them (another group participant).

The primary structure in authentic movement is the dyad (a mover and her witness) which is referred to as the "ground form".

Sometimes group members new to authentic movement resist closing eyes to begin with:

> When I found out that the practice of authentic movement included moving with eyes closed, I had an immediate negative reaction. To see is one of the main

vehicles of communication between people (eye contact). I need to see, I need to look if I am looked at, and I need to look where I go and what I do. When I close my eyes, I lose control of me, of others, of the environment. Now I know that when I move with my eyes closed in a trusted environment created by the facilitator, I go with my sight . . . inside, and there I see more (a participant).

The mover endeavours to maintain an awareness of "immediacy" and to respond to their inner experience with expressions such as stillness or non-directive movement. They are the first to be invited to speak about their experience, particularly the action involved in any significant moment during it. They may or may not request witnessing either from the witness if in a dyad or from a designated witness or the witness circle as a whole (if in a circle format).

The mover learns to track their movements and the inner experience accompanying them. They learn to wait for the next movement impulse and in this process recognize truthful, or authentic, movement. In the presence of one or many witnesses on the edge of the circle, the mover beings this process by listening inwardly in stillness to find a movement arising from a deep, cellular impulse.

After their movement experience the mover returns to their witness. In speaking of their story, an embodied event or "significant moment", the mover may describe the movement together with associated feelings, sensations, images, body-felt senses and thoughts. At first the mover, when reflecting on the experience, may feel they did not know what they were doing, in a way similar to the experience of unconscious non-duality (Horrocks, 2002). This dream state, like daydreaming, is a non-ego-controlled experience, in which the mind lets go of the separateness normally experienced between the self and other, resulting in a third dimension, a non-duality. In the early stages of AM work, the mover's experience remains unconscious and thus unremembered when they try to recall it. I suggest this lack of recall is pertinent to their learning, but by working with solely that which is recalled (even if that is nothing at all, not even the physical movements), the material emerging will still be that which is ready to be processed. Both witness and mover trusting in the mover remembering when the time is right is crucial here. This is in the same way as a person-centred psychotherapist would only speak/reflect the material a client has brought to a session, rather than bringing in their own recalling of their story etc. Similarly, a dreamer can recall a dream or only parts of a dream as material to be worked with.

Later on, the moving experience is more frequently like lucid dreaming where there is interplay between the dreamer and the dreamed. The creativity is in the interplay. It can also connect the mover to the numinous, the universal "I" or "big me" rarely found in everyday life. In this experience the freedom from, or loss of, ego or "little i" (with attachments such as personal history, identity and so on) enables a greater connection with the collective body (Adler, 1999) and a feeling of immense wellbeing.

Witnesses

The witness, the one who has chosen not to move, is an empathic conscious, present and receptive co-participant. From this co-creation of reality, safety and a deep respect for each other ensue. The witness acts in the role of container for the mover's embodied immersion in unconscious material, an unconscious which unfolds whatever, and however it likes.

The witness endeavours to be "present" in the mover's movement and, while attending to her own thoughts, sensations, feelings, images and impulses to allow these to be influenced by what she sees in the presence of the mover. She is in a state of "being" rather than "doing" although still active in tracking her inner attitude. This inner embodied conscious tracking is similar to the phenomenon of countertransference in the therapist found in psychodynamic psychotherapy. The tracking can include noticing, for example, bodily sensations, images, feelings, kinaesthetic impulses to move, sensations or the need to move/act, thoughts and judgements.

The witness is encouraged by the facilitator to speak only of those elements of her experience which link to aspects of the mover's already spoken journey or "significant moment/event", preferably in the present tense to keep the experience in the "here and now".

As the inner witness develops in the mover, so the mover too desires to be a witness, to track another's movements whilst she sits in stillness, being conscious of her own inner experiences of thoughts, sensations, images, feelings and movement impulses although refraining from enacting them. Rizzolatti et al. (1996) found that when a primate watched another perform an action that was within their own movement repertoire, the frontal cortex's mirror neurones fired up in a form of kinaesthetic empathy (Moore & Yamamoto, 1988). Thus, while witnessing another move, we can often make an informed guess about what the mover is feeling, imagining or even thinking (see Chapter 6).

The concept of the "wise observer/higher self" (Rowan, 1993) in transpersonal psychotherapy is relevant here. For instance, by waiting for, and listening to, an inner prompt the mover (re)discovers a consciousness of the "wise observer" termed the "inner witness". By "seeing" the mover clearly the witness (re)gains a similar consciousness. This consciousness reminds me of that of a mother who sits with her child at play, aware but without intervening in the play. The child is making use of the "potential space" or "space between" which Winnicott (1971) discusses, which is the place where inner and outer reality are separate yet interrelated, the intermediate area of experience.

Movers and Witnesses

"I like authentic movement because it develops 'presence of the body', presence and attention to others and integration between body/emotion and awareness" (a participant).

To continue with delineating the process of a dyad or group, the stage after the mover moves is that of "transition". This is when movers and witnesses are usually invited to be alone in "transition time" to allow them, if they wish, to begin to process their experience. It is here that drawing, writing or clay modelling may be used as expressive forms prior to coming to a circle and languaging the experience as either witness or mover. Bracegirdle (2023) speaks to transition as a non-dual experience highlighting how the writing process for her, in transition, stimulates poetry.

The dyads which can take place in the early stages of a group might be considered to emphasize individual self-awareness rather than the group process. However, this format is usually both preceded and followed by the facilitator acting in the role of witness for the whole group as they move in the space. Other roles in the groups I facilitate include that of the non-witness – non-mover role, that is, the one who stays in the space outside the circle; the silent witness role that is the one who does not offer witnessing; and the non-mover role, the one who elects not to move. Consequently, no role is marginalized – all are included.

In exploring the relationship between a mover and a witness (being seen or not seen, fearing being seen, and seeing/not seeing), the hidden becomes clearer as different people's perspectives intersect. Here a participant acknowledges that the two roles entered into, in turn, can help to clarify processes: "Experimenting with witness and mover roles, as and when uncertainties arise, is useful".

Sometimes this meeting-moment between witness and mover becomes a unitive experience (Adler, 1999) as the internal witness within each evolves. This is a moment when the "witness consciously knows the experience of the mover because it is her experience at the same moment" (Adler, 2002, p. 89). It is not a moment of merging but of a presence in both their internal witnesses. In this moment the mover's witness is completely aware of what the mover is doing and of her inner response to it. "Her boundaries are porous as she consciously experiences her mover and herself as the same" (Adler, 2002), that is, experiencing this unity in a non-duality state of wholeness. Both the mover and the witness may later speak of being in a unitive state – a clear way of knowing.

After repeatedly being seen clearly by a witness (at first this is mainly by the group facilitator) the mover begins to see herself, with the result that her own inner witness develops further. Then, when in the role of witness, after seeing another, the mover discovers a new ability to see herself. From these experiences, group members learn both self-witnessing and ways of "being" in relationship, in the here and now. The learning is supported by fully engaging organically, at different times, with both the roles of mover and witness.

The witness engages in a process of somatic-indwelling or waiting (Musicant, 1994, 2001), containing her projections and her impulse to move, so that she may, without preconceived ideas, feel what it may be like for that mover. A deep respect for self and others can grow out of learning these conditions through the discipline of AM.

As the mover's own internal witness develops, the mover often returns after the "dream state" to recall, in the presence of a witness, a significant event experienced through the movement. This is a conscious experience, as it is consciously brought to mind. It could be called a conscious non-duality. Non-dual experiences normally occur where a constellation of the opposites results in a third element in which a union or synthesis occurs. The opposite or counterparts within us are in contrast to the known (conscious) aspects of our personality. This unknown "other" (sometimes equated with Jung's concept of the "Shadow") is extremely afraid of consciousness and is therefore difficult to access in normal life. For example, the corresponding vice to the positive characteristic of compassion would not present itself to the conscious mind voluntarily. Yet without its counterpart the victory of compassion over the negative, or vice, would be unreal. This exerts a necessary psychic tension. The threat from this counterpart is mediated by complementary processes in the unconscious.

Authentic movement aims to help each participant's consciousness to produce a uniting symbol and, through experiencing and working with this in movement, to own the menacing "other" by recalling it and verbalizing it. Once the "other" has been expressed verbally, integration can occur. Outcomes from this process in AM work have included increases in emotional wellbeing, inner confidence and self-reliance, together with an increasing capability both to separate self from other and to join with the other.

Witnesses, by learning to own which of their experiences are their own projections, interpretations and judgements, can give the opportunity to the mover to accept or reject their perceptions. Here, a mover speaks of her difficulty when a witness fails to manage this:

> I find it particularly difficult when being witnessed by someone when interpretations are made, and the content of the language not owned. Maybe this is difficult for me because in authentic movement as a mover I am inviting myself to become potentially more open than I otherwise would be.

> (a participant)

Issues concerned with attachment (Fonagy, 2001) can become evident from the relationship between witness and mover, or participant and facilitator. Within the AM form the prominence of reflexivity, the capacity for verbal narratives from recalled direct experience of the self, together with the possibility of clear seeing from a witness, all held within a secure environment, gives the opportunity for healing insecure or anxious/avoidant attachments.

Normally I tend not to interpret or probe into what is perhaps behind a mover's expression (whether verbal or nonverbal). If interpretations, or positive and negative expressions, are made they need to be recognized and owned, so that each participant is encouraged to move towards a fuller acceptance of their total being (Rogers, 1970). As participants start to feel less threatened, defensive and resistant in the group, they learn to hear and see each other and themselves more clearly. This greater capacity to witness results in increased learning from themselves and each other, as this comment illuminates:

Having time to talk about experiences with group members makes links and meaning in the work for me, as does having space to integrate personal meanings to make sense of the work, such as keeping a personal journal, circle reflection time and relating to more universal stories and concepts.

(a participant)

Communication is thereby enhanced and the desire for creative expression deepened rather than resisted or inhibited. Participants develop the capacity to offer witnessing in a congruent, healing and empathic manner. The facilitator encourages both story making and story breaking whereby participants learn to tell a story coherently and also allow for the story to be told in a different way by engaging the participant in a dialogue in the light of a new experience.

The Collective Body

The term collective body describes an experience which movers or witnesses may have in the group and are invited to speak about as a collective witness. A desire arises in the group members to participate in the gestalt experience, to explore ways of relating to the many, rather than the one without losing consciousness of the self. The phrase collective body contains an implicit reference to Jung's term the collective unconscious. Here I mean the experience that arises from the group's embodiment of unconscious material. For example, participants may experience powerful relationships, meetings and synchronicities within a group movement, which go beyond the individual and which encompass a greater sense of belonging. This concerns the collective desire for consciousness – the conscious body – which Adler conceives of as mysticism (Adler, 2002). Indeed, one form of this state can be a greater awareness of the spiritual. Part of the facilitator's role here is to guide the conscious development of relationships such as that between the individual body and the collective body. Moving, witnessing and sharing can enable connections to form between the individual, the group and the collective or universal body (that is, movers, embodying archetypes experienced by witnesses and/or movers as living again in the mover). They can provide a link from the personal to the collective body, giving images from which to give meaning to individual lives and communities. Jung reminds us that "fantasies guided by unconscious regulators coincide with the records of man's mental activity as known to us from tradition and ethnological research" (Jung, 1947, p. 402).

He wrote of a dark impulse which is the "arbiter of the pattern created when the foot makes a dance step, or the hand guides the crayon" (Jung, 1947, p. 402). At the very moment we feel vulnerable to chance, we do not know that someone else's consciousness is being shown the way by the very same impulse. From these and other reflections Jung surmised that there are certain collective unconscious conditions which "behave like the motive forces of dream" and "act as regulators and stimulators of creative fantasy-activity and call forth corresponding formations by availing themselves of existing conscious material" (Jung, 1947, p. 403). Jung based his theory of the impersonal collective unconscious on these unconscious regulators, which he saw as a synthesis of passive conscious material and of unconscious influences, resulting in a spontaneous amplification of the archetypes.

The stimuli in our environment (including movers' chance encounters with others in the container of the group or movers' hearing, for example, the birds singing outside) can have a deep presence inside the mover/witness and be incorporated into their experience.

Participants can then feel in direct contact with aspects in their imagination and in the real environment of consensus real-time. Movers can feel unity and compassion when personal themes connect to a collective body of experience revealed by that which is spoken of within the group. This experience of an altered reality may increase a sense of wellbeing and help participants to understand their personal themes.

For some participants the creativity experienced in the movement process is another pathway to spirituality. In groups, spiritual matters, as well as group dynamics, may be explored. For example, during the breathing circle (one group structure) if movers leave the space within the circle to return to the circle of witnesses the receptacle becomes empty once again. Contemplation of this empty space can bring up, for example, issues of loss and enrichment, but also of mortality, birth and re-birth. These may be articulated and processed in the large group, or in two groups of movers and witnesses.

Authentic Movement Group Formats

I become interested in authentic movement because by comparison to other body-oriented therapy groups it has a strong, complex and flexible structure. The structure of authentic movement provides rules about time, organisation of different kinds and boundaries. In this way safety, respect, holding are ensured to support the individual and the group process.

(another participant)

Specific structures/formats or rituals are crucial to the practice, including the specific language adopted. It is significant that the facilitator also acts as witness throughout and contributes to group experience. For example, a session may begin with the facilitator witnessing all movers. In her witnessing of the ground form (the dyadic structure) where one witness and mover work together, changing roles after their sharing dialogue, she acts as a silent witness to all dyads at once, bringing the movers' experience to a close after a time period. This might be followed with triads (the dyad with an additional "silent" witness – one who does not offer witnessing at all) and thereafter by working in fours before the basic circle format in which each mover has a designated witness. At all times in all these structures the facilitator takes the role of a free-floating witness, to all movers.

To further help participants to develop their capabilities as witnesses, a circle of free-floating witnesses is formed in which all who witnessed a mover inside the circle can offer witnessing if asked to by a mover. The psychic elements are contained within the circle, the witness's attention is drawn towards a mover, and an opportunity is given for all the varying aspects of the individual body (participant) and the collective body (group), to be witnessed. A comparison can be drawn here with psychodrama whereby different parts of one protagonist are played out by several individuals in the group. The facilitator would again be a witness throughout, sitting on the edge of the circle with the other witnesses, offering witnessing when invited by a mover to do so. This role could be seen as synonymous with Rogers' (1970) view of the facilitator being less directive and interpretive in the development of the group process. During the transitional phase, which is between moving/witnessing and receiving/offering witnessing (sharing), the facilitator may provide opportunities for artwork, writing, poetry and clay work as a connection between the moving and witnessing experience and the verbal dialogue. Sometimes participants offer these symbols or writings as movers or witnesses where they feel there is a direct relationship between with their own experience and the mover's story. Drawing and creative journal writing may bring further form and meaning to experiences, as expressed by this participant: "The facilitator encouraging the use of image-making, writing and other creative media is helpful to me as well her clarifying the language used and continually acting as collective witness". For example, a mover returned to her place at the edge of the circle to ask if any witness saw a particular frozen moment of stillness as she sat on the floor with a turned head. One of the witnesses responded by speaking from her journal about seeing a Medusa, who had turned her (the mover) into stone and wrote a story in her journal that about this moment of "turning into stone" which could be heard as collective witnessing. She told the group that at that very moment at which she was watching the mover she saw another mover who appeared to be embodying a Medusa's head, flailing, with hissing and squirming snakes. She wrote of her fear, of a chill going down her spine. The mover was relieved to have heard this witnessing as she too had felt and heard a terrifying presence in the room and was petrified by it. Later another mover spoke of one of her significant moments where she had feelings of rage and power as she stood tall, hissing and spitting venom at the world. A connection was made in the group to the experience of terrifying rage, the Medusa and being turned to stone by fear.

In another example, following another mover's story, two witnesses commented on how they saw the very young baby this mover had described herself as being. Both witnesses saw the baby enjoying suckling and making noises with her lips. Another mover spoke as a moving witness. She had heard the sounds and sensed a baby nearby, happily gurgling, and had painted this in her journal. Yet another witness said she had felt motherly towards this baby, wanting to cuddle her. She felt warmed by the infant. Later in that same group experience a mover described a particular moment in which her struggle to attain something precious was just too difficult, she requested witnessing. I (as a witness) recalled seeing a figure struggling to reach something high up. She was quite close to me at the edge of the circle. I had written in my journal:

I looked up, and to my right to catch sight of a woman's face emerging from behind hands (I had drawn this image). She appeared distressed. I felt sad. Her eyes opened and, at that precise moment, on hearing the bell to bring the group experience to an end, I felt seen in my sadness.

In the mover's reflections later in the group she told of how frustrated and disappointed she had been, unable successfully to resolve her desire for a baby. She said she had felt seen in her sadness by her witness and that being seen at that moment meant a great deal to her. It was then that I spoke from my journal (written and drawn in during the transition phase) of my experience in her presence. This illustrates the importance of the procedure that the witness speaks only after the mover has spoken and then only on movement and elements aligned with it that the mover has herself mentioned.

Authentic Movement and Play

Authentic movement and DMP draw to some extent from the same spontaneous and creative well as is enacted in play. Both foster personal growth by building upon our natural, dynamic, creative, spontaneous and self-expressive capabilities in an interplay of inner and outer worlds. Like play, both permit the participant to express themselves, be themselves, accept themselves and be accepted by others without an outer task to perform. The process of play is one without an extrinsic goal conscious to the player at the time (Garvey, 1986). The same could be said for DMP and AM. In play therapy, children are encouraged to play out problems, events, feelings and attitudes (Axline, 1969). In this approach the cathartic element is emphasized whereby the child symbolizes a traumatic experience (such as sexual abuse) using dolls or other objects. By revisiting it with all the accompanying feeling states in the presence of a therapist, the child may move to a better integration of the experience. Authentic movement draws upon the same powerful capacities of play and self-expression but in movement enacted in the presence of another, the witness, and within a specific protocol. It similarly enables experiences to be enacted, often through the use of metaphor, even when they cannot be verbalized explicitly. The embodiment of a creative metaphor may enable regression and an integration and capacity to be oneself which was previously not possible. Winnicott (1971) suggests: "It is only in play that the individual is able to be creative and to use the whole personality, and it is only in being creative that the individual discovers the self" (Winnicott, 1971, p. 54).

Authentic Movement and Jung

Building on creativity and play and on Jung's method of active imagination (Jung, 1968) authentic movement uses symbolic meaning, seen in physical expression as another road to a descent into the unknown. The process of the mover (who cannot see the witness or facilitator) might be likened to Jung's concept of "trancing" in an "active fantasy" (Chodorow, 1997, p. 3). Jung (1935) states in his Tavistock lectures:

[the patient] can see their [archetypal images produced by active imagination techniques] real meaning only when they are not just a queer subjective experience with no external connections, but a typical, ever-recurring expression of the objective facts and processes of the human psyche. By objectifying his impersonal images, and understanding their inherent ideas, the patient is able to work out all the values of his archetypal material. That is, he can really see it and his unconscious becomes understandable to him.

(Jung, cited in Chodorow, 1997, p. 146)

Jung uses the term archetype to describe images from the collective unconscious (as opposed to the first layer of the personal unconscious) that have existed from the remotest of times. Archaic, primordial images charged with psychic energy (the numinous) he thought were a piece of life itself, connected with the living individual by the bridge of emotion. The archetypal experience consists of imagery and affect (instinct/somatic and psychic). Jung emphasized the universal character of the collective unconscious and thought that instincts (inborn, unlearned tendencies) and mythological motifs were already laid down in our brain in their pre-conscious form as invisible ground plans, inherited from our ancestors. These then interact with our consciousness which has available to it all the history of rituals, symbols, stories and so on from our own cultural sources. Movement arising from the collective unconscious may have a foreign, chaotic quality in a form outside recognizable human culture. Some images witnessed in AM do seem to emerge from the primitive depths of life itself as though the mover is possessed, for example, by terror (the one who is shaking holds onto another for comfort), anguish (the never-ending sobbing and wailing of a woman) or rage (the monstrous one kicking and biting, nostrils flared, fingers like claws ready to scratch). This cathartic expression is held by the imaginative movement process inside the mover and by the witness outside. At other times the movement has parallels with the characteristics of nature, animals or mythological creatures (such as huge dragons breathing fire) and are less chaotic but equally trance-like. It is as though these life-forms are being danced (Chodorow, 1999) or metamorphosed as in the shape shifting of the Shaman, for example. It is the facilitator and/or witness who offers the necessary parallels to the mover, as a context for the individual and/or collective images experienced.

Authentic Movement and Group Process

Verbal groups sometimes develop a breakdown in communication. However, authentic movement groups, by using an approach which focuses on the content of the movement expression, rather than directly on the person or group, can enrich mutual communication, each one understanding the other from the other's point of view. The greater the authenticity in the mover's experience, awareness and expression, the more likely it is that the witness will see it clearly thus fostering clearer communication. This element links strongly with Carl Rogers' approach to group-work: "If the cues from speech, tone and gesture are unified because they spring from a place of congruence and unity, then there is much less likelihood that these cues will have an ambiguous or unclear meaning" (Rogers, 1961, p. 342). Similarly, if the expressed movement (or sound) arising in the mover stems from a place where the feeling/sensation/image and so on is truly connected to the self then the movement (or contact etc.) is authentic and consequently is clearer to the witness.

Rogers (1970) refers to a 15-process model of groupwork which offers another way of describing some of the experiences in the authentic movement group. The formative stages in authentic movement groups may well consist of difficulties such as participants not being able to close their eyes, take the role of witness or move authentically. Despite several hours of educational work during which the basic dyadic structure of the mover and witness roles are experienced, participants may continue to feel they do not know what to do, in movement for example, for a while. This together with the reluctance, even shyness, is commensurate with Rogers' stages of milling around and resistance to personal exploration. Fears usually revolve around an assumption there will be a critical judge.

An exercise to bring out the critic and acknowledge the power it has is normally helpful at this point. The participants are encouraged by the facilitator to express negative feelings or thoughts (similar to Rogers' identified trend of expressing negative feelings). A more meaningful trend usually follows, whereby participants are willing to take the risk of exploring personal and interpersonal material within the group and tolerate the not knowing in their movement process. Both movers and witnesses then start to show a greater openness and receptivity. The ability to respond to immediate feelings, thoughts, images and sensations becomes the norm. Safety has been established by the facilitator "holding" the group through the first two stages, and this, together with a clearer understanding of the ground rules, language use and structures, usually lead, in Rogers' term to the cracking of facades whereby participants reveal congruence (or authenticity, see Chapter 8) in reclaiming their projections (Payne, 2004). In this way the need for defensiveness with a safe persona is dropped and a more real, honest, accepting process is engaged with, leading to greater empathic connection between participants. At times the facilitator might be confronted as the group develops. After processing, the group and sometimes the form itself may evolve as a result. A growing acceptance of each other, built on a deep respect that each is doing the best they can, is demonstrated by a caring and sharing inside the group and an increasing awareness of each person's inner witness. The group process continues to move in and out of different patterns, depending on the levels of felt safety. Some of this clearly connects with the model described by Rogers contrasting to the linear one proposed by Tuckman (1965) where all groups follow a number of predictable, orderly stages (norming, storming, forming, performing).

Regression to previously experienced trends is noticeable just as in the individual client-therapist process. This may echo relationship phases between group members and/or intrapsychic processes. Authentic movement enables a deep regression at a personal level resulting in a truly embodied integration which leads to an increase in the felt sense of wellbeing.

Summary

Participating in an AM group can be a compelling and awesome experience. It draws participants from a range of backgrounds including the arts, the caring professions and from psychotherapy who are willing to open up to the power of the unconscious, as contained, expressed and experienced through stillness and movement.

References

Adler, J. (1995). *Arching backward*. Inner Traditions.
Adler, J. (1999). The collective body. In P. Pallaro (Ed.), *Authentic movement: Essays by Mary Starks Whitehouse, Janet Adler and Joan Chodorow*. Jessica Kingsley.
Adler, J. (2002). *Offering from the conscious body*. Inner Traditions.
Axline, V. (1969). *Play therapy*. Ballantine Books.
Bracegirdle, C. (2023). A mover's practice of transition in authentic movement: An embodied non-dual lived experience. *Body, Movement and Dance in Psychotherapy, 19*(4), 381–396. https://doi.org/10.1080/17432979.2023.2254834
Chodorow, J. (1991). *Dance therapy and depth psychology: The moving imagination*. Routledge.
Chodorow, J. (1997). *Jung on active imagination*. Princetown University Press.
Chodorow, J. (1999). Her papers. In P. Pallaro (Ed.), *Authentic movement: Essays by Mary Starks Whitehouse, Janet Adler and Joan Chodorow*. Jessica Kingsley.
Dosamantes-Alperson, I. (1974). Carrying experiencing forward through authentic body movement. *Psychotherapy: Theory, Research, and Practice, 11*(3), 211–214.
Fonagy, P. (2001). *Attachment theory and psychoanalysis*. Other Press.
Garvey, C. (1986). *Play: The developing child*. Fontana Press.
Goldhahn, E. (2022). *Reflections on authentic movement: Theory, practice and arts-led research*. Routledge. https://doi.org/10.4324/9781003222309
Hartley, L. (Ed.). (2022). *The fluid nature of being: Embodied practices for healing and wholeness*. Hardspring Publishing.
Horrocks, R. (2002). Non-duality. *Self and Society, 29*(6), 7–14.
Jung, C. G. (1935). *The symbolic life*. Tavistock lectures. Collected Works (Vol. 18).
Jung, C. G. (1947). *The structure and dynamics of the psyche*. Collected Works (Vol. 8).
Jung, C. G. (1968). *Analytical psychology: Its theory and practice*. Random House.
Kirschenbaum, H. (1979). *On becoming Carl Rogers*. Delacorte Press.
Moore, C.-L., & Yamamoto, K. (1988). *Beyond words: Movement observation and analysis*. Gordon Breach.
Morrissey, B., & Sager, P. (Eds.). (2022). *Intimacy in emptiness: An evolution of embodied consciousness: Collected writings of Janet Adler*. Inner Traditions.
Musicant, S. (1994, Winter). Authentic movement and dance therapy. *American Journal of Dance Therapy, 16*(2), 91–106.
Musicant, S. (2001). Authentic movement: Clinical considerations. *American Journal of Dance Therapy, 23*(1), 17–26.
Payne, H. (2001). Student experiences in a personal development group: the question of safety. *European Journal of Psychotherapy, Counselling and Health, 4*(2), 267–292.
Payne, H. (2004). *Notes on authentic movement and congruence*. Unpublished paper prepared for Retreat in Authentic Movement Nov 2004.
Penfield, K. (2006). Another royal road to consciousness: The application of Freudian thought to authentic movement. In H. Payne (Ed.), *Dance movement therapy: Theory, research and practice*. Routledge.

Rizzolatti, G., Fadiga, L., Gallese, V., & Fogassi, L. (1996). Premotor cortex and the recognition of motor actions. *Cognitive Brain Research, 3*, 131–141.

Rogers, C. (1957). The necessary and sufficient conditions for therapeutic personality change. *Journal of Consulting Psychology, 21*(2), 95–103.

Rogers, C. (1961). *A therapist's view of psychotherapy*. Constable and Co Ltd.

Rogers, C. (1970). *Encounter groups*. Pelican.

Rowan, J. (1993). *The transpersonal: Psychotherapy and counselling*. Routledge.

Stromsted, T. (2015). Authentic movement & The evolution of Soul's Body® Work. *Journal of Dance and Somatic Practices: Authentic Movement: Defining the Field, Intellect, 7*(2).

Stromsted, T. (2025a, January). Psyche's body: A brief history of engaging the body in analysis and psychotherapy. *IAAP News Bulletin*, (36).

Stromsted, T. (2025b). *Soul's Body: Active Imagination, Authentic Movement, and Embodiment in Psychotherapy*. Routledge.

Tuckman, B. W. (1965). Developmental sequence in small groups. *Psychological Bulletin, 63*, 384–399.

Whitehouse, M. S. (1958). The Tao of the body. Reprinted in: D. H. Johnson (Ed., 1995), *Bone, breath and gesture: Practices of embodiment*. North Atlantic Books.

Whitehouse, M. S. (1970). Reflections on a metamorphosis. Impulse Publishing. Reprinted in: R. Head, R. E. Rothenberg, & D. Wesley (Eds.). (1977), *A well of living waters: Festschrift for Hilde Kirsch*. CG Jung Institute. Reprinted in: P. Pallero (Ed.). (1999), *Authentic movement: Essays by Mary Starks Whitehouse, Janet Adler and Joan Chodorow*. Jessica Kingsley.

Whitehouse, M. S. (1977). The transference and dance therapy. *American Journal of Dance Therapy, 1*(1), 3–7.

Whitehouse, M. S. (1979). Jung and dance therapy: Two major principles. In P. Bernstein (Ed.), *Eight theoretical approaches to dance movement therapy*. Kendall/Hunt.

Winnicott, D. W. (1971). *Playing and reality*. Tavistock.

Photograph 5.1 One witness and two movers

Credit: Photography by Lucie Payne

Chapter 5

Bodies Becoming Conscious

Body Mind Experience in Authentic Movement

Abstract

The re-discovery and integration of body and bodily felt experience, as well as the connection between different levels of processing are essential parts of the practice of authentic movement. Memories and regression can be experienced as more "whole" by adding formerly unconscious or forgotten bodily felt aspects. Embodying metaphors may lead to a direct experience of their structure. The integration of different levels of experience can be furthered through metaphors which support a holistic understanding of the body-mind process as well as the communication between mover and witness.

Introduction: Invisible Bodies

When Johnson (2007) is talking about "bodily disappearance", the "recessive body" or "background disappearance", he is arguing that many of our bodily processes, our perceptive organs, much of our sensory-motor system and our internal organs, are vital to making experience possible, consciously accessible. Thus, we rely on the body functioning without necessarily feeling how this function is taking place. Johnson concludes, "The principal result of these forms of bodily disappearance is our sense that our thoughts, and even our feelings, go on somehow independent of our bodily process" (Johnson, 2007, p. 6).

Zitt (2008) describes another kind of body disappearance contrasted by the ever-growing attention on body appearance in the media and personal lives. "The body . . . is getting a great amount of attention in Western society and culture . . . while at the same time the sensual perception of body sensations and basic bodily needs seem to disappear" (Zitt, 2008, p. 39, translated by author).

Under this influence, the body is presented with a new set of expectations to fit the standards of health and beauty promoted by mass media. At the same time, it appears to have lost its meaning as a working body, and the awareness of one's physical wellbeing is increasingly ignored. The sensitive, feeling and knowing body

(First published together with my authentic movement trainee Ilka Konopatsch in "Body Memory, Metaphor and Movement" Edited by Sabine C. Koch, Thomas Fuchs, Michela Summa and Cornelia Müller. John Benjamins Publishing Company, 2011)

DOI: 10.4324/9781003479413-6

is rarely taken into account on either the grounds of natural condition or cultural reality. Nevertheless, a large number of people are seeking a different approach to their bodies through sports, yoga, meditation etc. In the therapies, this seeking is reflected by a growing attention paid to the arts and body-based therapies.

There, the feeling and sensing body returns to the focus of attention. We are eager to re-learn focussing and relying on the resource of the body's natural knowledge.

> Trusting the experience of the body is the hardest because most of us don't feel the body. I think that's why we keep being more and more removed from the body because it's not seeable in a way that is valued in our culture. We need to trust that the body has its own wisdom, that it is enough for the experience just to stay in the body. The body wants to tell its own story by moving. Movement is the body's story.
>
> (Sullwold with Ramsay, 2007, p. 49)

Authentic movement as an approach to self-exploration intends to create a space for hidden, unconscious and sensitive personal themes to be explored. By being movement-based, it is creating a space for the "hidden" body, making the invisible visible. In the process of allowing the mover to connect to body sensations, thoughts, feelings and needs equally, some of the aforementioned effects of the "appearance emphasized" pre-occupation with the body might be reduced.

Authentic Movement

As previously described, the role of the mover is to descend into a process that is comparable to active imagination or free association. After a warm-up and agreement on time frame, she closes eyes and turns the focus inward to any bodily sensation, feeling, thought or image that arises. There is no instruction or thematic aim to a movement sequence. On the contrary, movers are encouraged to stay congruent to their experience and let the body take the lead in exploring upcoming themes. These threads can then be followed or dismissed whenever it feels appropriate, in movement or stillness with the eyes kept closed. Stillness can be experienced just as meaningfully as movement in this context, dismissing an impulse as important as following it.

One mover describes her descent into the process like this:

> Hm . . . it's always different. Sometimes I have reacted to inner images, sometimes there was nothing, just emptiness. Sometimes there was a twitch of muscles, or the arm just suddenly started to move. That can be very different.
>
> (Interviewee FC, Konopatsch, 2005,
> p. 56, translation by first author)

A movement sequence can last between just a few minutes, up to half an hour or more. In group settings, longer sequences are used frequently. Consequently, usually more than one theme emerges in a session. As the process is not shaped by expectation or direction, it could be best described as an ongoing stream of sensations and ideas that, just like in active imagination, might lead to unexpected insights described as follows: "that means, I embody these images, then this is not right anymore. Then I let go. It's an ongoing trying 'Where am I' without losing myself" (Interviewee FA, Konopatsch, 2005, p. 58, translation by first author).

The role of the witness is usually taken by the facilitator/teacher. In a group setting participants also act as witnesses for other group members. The witness sits in stillness in the presence of the mover's experience. She follows the mover's physical movements as well as her own inner process in response to what she is seeing. She is also keeping the time, signalling the beginning and end of a movement sequence, so that the mover can slowly return and open her eyes. From a witness's notes: "One mover is on her belly, tapping a rhythm with her hands. Clicking a rhythm with her fingers. Then she stretches one arm out, directed towards me. I imagine she is saying, come on, join!" (Extract from second author's personal journal).

After moving, mover and witness sit together to speak. The mover can now share significant elements of the movement experience as she speaks first about her specific remembered movements, connecting them then with images, feelings etc. that accompanied the movement.

Then, if invited by the mover, the witness speaks with unconditional positive regard (Rogers, 1973), carefully selecting those aspects of her own experience that respond to the elements of movement already mentioned by the mover. Adler refers to the importance of a witness who is aware of her own personal history and her boundaries (Adler, 2002). Great care is also taken in the way experiences are put into words by a strict discipline regarding the verbal format. Speaking in the present tense and other verbal language structures help to ensure emotional safety for the mover. Consequently, processes of transference and countertransference become transparent for both mover and witness, furthering the understanding of their individual process.

Body with Mind Experience in Authentic Movement

Closing their eyes at the beginning of a movement session, movers exclude visual input and turn their focus inward. By turning away from the dominant levels of conscious everyday experience, space and attention is given to what we may call bodily wisdom to unfold. Beginners in this practice start by learning how to pay attention to their body sensations, images, feelings or thoughts that may eventually turn into an impulse to move.

Authentic movement is suitable for participants with a strong sense of self and probably some former experience of therapy or self-exploration. Cultivating body awareness can be a vital part of the work alongside the mover-witness experience. Practising inner listening is promoting a new focus on body experience. The mover is becoming aware of the body in connection to emotional states. The emerging movement is not restricted by any frame, technique or purpose. Movers are encouraged to follow their own individual impulses, whether these are visible in movement or not. Tracking one's movement without planning or generating it creates a new state of being in the body and the mind while at the same time being aware of one's body in space. While letting go and following free flowing movement, movers are at the same time responsible for ensuring that they move safely for their own benefit and for others in the group. When moving strongly and fast they are asked to open their eyes slightly and briefly to be sure of their position in space and that of others around them. They develop an increasing awareness of spatial boundaries and of the body's natural ability to sense others in the room. In fact, interruption between movers or between mover and object occurs very rarely. By the heightened sensibility to sound, temperature and other senses, participants learn to adjust their movements accordingly. The witness, sitting in stillness, is a constant reference point for the mover's spatial and emotional journey. They are predictable and reliable creating safety for the mover.

Self-exploration and change are sometimes experienced purely in the body, without the need for verbalization. The why and how of an action are not necessarily available to the conscious mind, yet it can clearly be experienced in the body, often accompanied by a feeling of deep satisfaction. The endpoint of a process is often more apparent to mover and witness. For example, after a long period of heaviness and working on the floor, a mover might get up and jump. After months of activity, another mover may finally lie down. Clearly the body in authentic movement is not a mere pathway to explore a problem or discover hidden conflicts. Much rather, if followed, it may offer pathways and solutions by its own means. The body itself may facilitate change.

While some movement sessions evolve purely around body sensations, more often movers experience a connection between the body and other levels of experience. With practice, following and tracking one's movement becomes easier, and movers become more aware of accompanying thoughts and images. Simultaneously this creates new meaningful experiences, complementing change and contradicting each other.

The surrender to a movement impulse, awareness of different levels of experience and the meta-perspective of tracking one's own movement together result in a state of moving and being moved (Whitehouse, 1979).

Memory and Regression: BodyMind Connections to the Past

"Because of the natural wisdom of the body and its capacity to store every memory at bone level" (Adler, 1999, p. 146). Panhofer (2017) describes six types of body memory referring to Fuchs (2003) who proposed the following form part of the implicit memory: procedural, situational, intercorporeal, intercorporative, traumatic and pain (which he added in 2012).

Learning from the body needs the individual to settle down into forgetting the explicit knowing and dive into the implicit, unconscious knowing (Fuchs, 2003), well, that which is waiting to be known that is as bodily felt lived knowing or enduring recollection. We are entering into authentic movement with a physical history, and we may connect to it through our body. Memories can be triggered through a certain movement, a body position, while at other times a memory can be the initial impulse to move. Either way, the cognitive recollection is connected to the body experience, which points out the body-mind aspect of authentic movement. A memory can even evolve completely around a bodily felt sensation such as in the following example:

> Having lost my great aunt who was very dear to me some months earlier, I moved without the intention to focus on this event. After a while of moving around and searching, I found myself in a position where one of my hands lay in the other. Suddenly and vehemently, I remembered an event that happened two or three years before. I had visited my aunt in hospital for some minor illness and was holding her hand, me sitting in a chair, her sitting on her bed wearing a nightdress. I realised how the hand I was holding now in the movement session, my own, was so similar to the one I was holding then, my great aunt's. At this moment all my held-back grief for the recent loss broke through as well as a deep gratitude for the memory of closeness that I was given in that moment. To this day I have access to the memory of my aunt's hand by recalling the movement session.
>
> (Extract from second author's personal journal)

The mover's memory in this narrative was triggered by a body position, i.e., holding her own hand. Experiencing the recollection in a body-mind-state added an additional, formerly unnoticed aspect to the memorized event, the feeling of her aunt's hand in hers at the event a few years ago. The bodily felt aspect also promoted a new insight, the similarity of the two hands, thus making a connection to the lost person. Emotions of loss and of gratitude were firmly set in the present time, the movement session. The memory, by being directly experienced in the body, is connecting past experience to the present process. By sharing the experience with her witness verbally, this mover was enabled to further process the event, making a connection with the future through the lasting body-mind-memory of her aunt.

The amount of simultaneous input, cognitive recollection, body sensation, insight and emotion may sound much to deal with. Nevertheless, it is usually experienced as a natural flow of impressions and sensations in a state of heightened attentiveness. The complexity of tasks is easily addressed within movement. Unravelling and integrating experiences are happening at the same time, integration furthered and deepened in transition and in verbalization with the witness.

Authentic Movement and Metaphor

The emergence of metaphors and the conscious dealing with them are important factors in the integrative process, and integral parts of authentic movement. Due to their multi-modal nature, metaphors are especially useful in accessing themes otherwise too complex to grasp.

Metaphors and symbols evolve throughout the authentic movement process. During the movement experience they can emerge directly out of the bodily movement or be initiated by a thought or image. Just like the memories described earlier, they are felt and moved in, and by, the body not thought about or reflected upon but directly experienced in movement. Metaphors have different sources: personal, cultural and archetypal according to Samaritter (2009). Personal metaphors, she claims, represent individual body experience that can also be represented in spoken language. Conceptual metaphor theory roots the genesis of metaphorical thinking in body experience so that abstract conceptualizations are linked back to body process (Johnson, 2007). Regarding AM it could be said the mover experiences being both the embodied and the abstract meaning of a metaphor by accessing the physical sensation at the same moment as the abstract idea, thus consciously experiencing the source domain and the target domain connected in the same instance.

Lackoff (2008) describes the emergence of primary metaphor through the simultaneous occurrence of experiences. A body sensation, such as warmth, and an emotion, such as affection, can be connected on a neuronal level. He says, "Thus, affection is warmth which arises from experiencing affection while being held by one's parents and simultaneously experiencing their body warmth" (Lackoff, 2008 p. 187).

Those most basic connections, reflecting the structure of some of our metaphorical thinking, can potentially be experienced in movement. Similar to the experience of regression, various levels of processing are active at the same time. A body sensation experienced in authentic movement is receiving metaphorical meaning of affection or positive energy. In the following example, for the mover, the different experiences in the flow of the movement sequence are held together by the metaphoric meaning and the personal sense making resulting from it. A mover reports:

> at some point my hand came to this sun and I felt this warmth and a huge amount of pain swelled up, many tears, but I was THERE, I had arrived. And this was a key moment in Authentic Movement that I would have experienced in a completely different way in verbal therapy. So, this warmth then came through the hand and through the whole body and that was as if, also here, I can receive the sun I need to survive.
>
> (Interviewee FA, Konopatsch, 2005, p. 63, translation by first author)

Just as metaphors have the potential to integrate different levels of processing and connect them to a holistic experience, metaphors can also help to further reflect movement experience thus enhancing the mover's ability for change. In movement metaphors first evolve in their embodied form. The mover can literally "move on" with them, and process and change are facilitated in the body experience, as described earlier. After the movement experience, in transition time, the same metaphor is processed or other, new complementary images may be found.

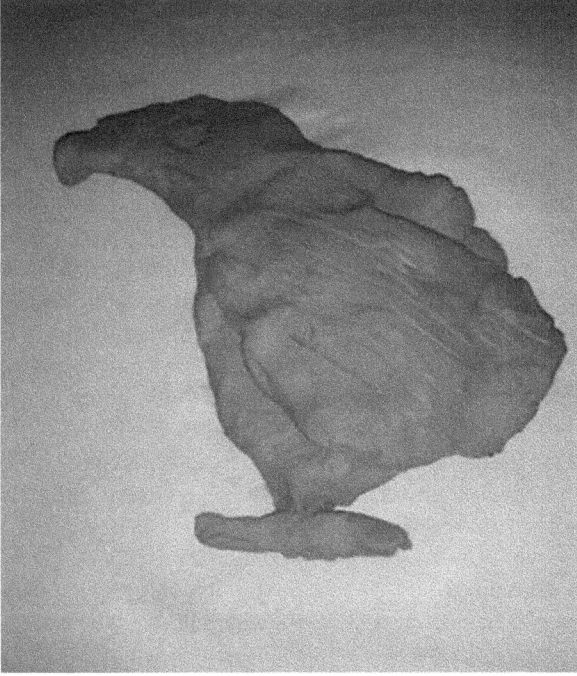

Photograph 5.2 An example of a clay sculpture

In addressing a new level of processing through different media such as writing, drawing and clay work (Photograph 5.2), a different quality or aspect is added to the experience through the different medium, and integration of the movement experience into cognitive awareness may be reached.

In verbal sharing, the communicative value of metaphors becomes especially apparent. The witness may already have perceived the embodied metaphor in sitting with the mover, present with empathy, throughout the movement sequence. Now she could learn about the mover's experience through the words and metaphors offered by the mover. The mover speaks about the experience and names a metaphor or may show a picture etc. If she resonates with it, the witness can respond with an image or metaphor that evolved in the presence of the mover's experience. Both these metaphors are rooted in the body. Firstly, in the mover's body – the one who is expressing the embodied metaphor. Secondly, in the witness's body that is responding to this expression with sensation, image etc. For the understanding and communication between mover and witness this is of particular value. Meekums speaks to the importance of metaphor in the following quotation:

> the importance of metaphor conveying complexity and facilitating a deep understanding between client and therapist or between group members, allowing

those individuals to provide the kind of silent "not-knowing" (yet deeply under-standing) witness that conveys far more than words, and also allowing for the transformative qualities of the metaphor to reveal themselves.

(Meekums, 2008, p. 27)

In the following example, a metaphorical image is guiding the mover through the entire authentic movement process:

A mover is going down on her knees. She is suddenly in a jungle, surrounded by huge plants. A tiger, moving slowly, looking out for prey she is feeling the energy and power in her body. In transition she draws a tiger's head in strong colours with piercing eyes. A sense of satisfaction is present, having put this feeling into a visual expression. In the verbal exchange she talks about the experience and shares the picture with her witness. The witness, in turn reports having seen a big cat moving around the room. She in turn, offers to show her picture drawn in transition time. The mover accepts to see the picture and finds not a tiger's but a leopard's pattern – a rather delicate drawing that she feels connects and adds another quality to her own interpretation of her experience, making it more complete. When mover and witness put the drawings on the wall, they realize their drawings indeed connect in two touching lines at the bottom of the tiger's head and the top of the witness's more abstract drawing.

(extract from second author's personal journal)

A web of connections was made visible in the process described. The mover was fully involved in a body-mind-experience embodying the image of the tiger in move-ment, exploring different qualities of the image such as strength and power. She then transferred some of this experience into drawing and speaking to her witness.

Witness and mover connected through sharing a similar metaphor, then silently reflecting on it individually in transition, and finally by sharing visual and ver-bal references to the experience. Similar or matching metaphors, especially when experienced non-verbally, can be deeply touching for both mover and witness.

This mover continues to report on the experience of being seen:

[It was] such a feeling of inner strengthening and support. To be seen in this moment. And that the image was the same as my witness's image. That was so incredible for me! I felt so much strengthened and supported. In a way I hadn't known before.

(Interviewee FC, Konopatsch, 2005,
p. 71, translation by first author)

Contradicting metaphors may also be shared by the witness, especially since the process is not focused on the mover but on the movement experience. In this way it offers an opportunity to explore differentiation (rather than unity), witness percep-tions and transference in relation to their own individual experience.

Moving in the Collective

Authentic movement is mostly used in group settings. Experience is different from the ground form of the mover-witness dyad. Different themes can be explored as a member of a group. The evolving of memories and metaphors is influenced by other movers' processes. Movers can also change perspective and become witness for another member of the group. By attending to their process in the service of their mover, and in resonance with the other's experience, or the interrelatedness of experiences, transference and compassion become more present and are, again, related to the actual bodily experience during witnessing.

As a mover is in a group of many, people meet. They touch, they hear each other, avoid or welcome each other. Even without contact, movers are aware of being in a group and the individual experience is put into perspective with this reality. Memories and regression can change in so far as other bodies and sounds might be either included in the triggering of the memory, or in the embodiment and "moving with" the memory, for example, when a mover leaning against another mover's leg remembers leaning against her mother as a little child.

Contacting another mover, perhaps through physical touch, often involves images and metaphors. Two movers often share a similar story or image; sometimes they each move within their own individual fantasies. On occasion, an entire group can become involved in a shared story. "I mean, there are other people, there is sound, there are voices, maybe with these voices the fantasy of a choir in Greece, sometime, a thousand years ago emerges" (Interviewee FA, Konopatsch, 2005, p. 57, translated by first author). A witness becoming aware of such a story or image can share this with the group as a piece of "collective witnessing".

Summary

In authentic movement different levels of experience are present at the same time. Thinking, sensing and imagining are related to the body in movement. By making conscious connections, experiences can gain new meaning and further personal insight. Memories recalled in movement may be triggered by thoughts, images, movement or body sensation. The bodily felt aspect of a memory can be added to the recollection of a meaningful event. Integration and understanding are furthered by embodied metaphors. While these can change and "be moved with" further processing takes place in clay work, writing, drawing and verbalization. Metaphors also facilitate communication and understanding between mover and witness and thus support the development of their relationship. The combination of verbal and non-verbal techniques, together with moving and witnessing supplements a participant's sense-making and symptom-management and often lead to the symptom's disappearance or reduction.

Practising authentic movement in a group setting is changing and enriching the mover's experience of herself and others, as is taking on the role of the witness for other group members. This unique way of sharing the process of self-exploration in movement creates a sense of belonging in the group. The basic underlying principle of "both-and" (Whitehouse, 1979), of discovering and connecting, of differentiation, unity and integration is mirrored in the group, where each is attending to their own process whilst being part of the collective. As Janet Adler describes it:

> This unrehearsed, synchronous unfolding of events creates a village story. Movers and witnesses participate within the complexity of their own individual personalities, doing what they each must do. It is the story of a collection of people bringing unconscious material into consciousness, through embodiment, because of each other. It is not unlike a cluster of cells, like the heart, in which each cell is doing what it must do, resulting in a pumping heart.
>
> (Adler, 1999, p. 199)

References

Adler, J. (1999). The collective body. In P. Pallaro (Ed.), *Authentic movement* (pp. 190–204). Jessica Kingsley.

Adler, J. (2002). *Offering from the conscious body*. Rochester.

Fuchs, T. (2003). *The memory of the body*. http://www.klinikum.uni-heidelberg.de/fileadmin/zpm/psychatrie/ppp2004/manuskript/fuchs.pdf

Johnson, M. (2007). *The meaning of the body*. University of Chicago Press.

Konopatsch, I. (2005). *Warum Authentische Bewegung?* [Unpublished Masters' thesis, Technical University, Berlin].

Lackoff, G. (2008). The neuroscience of metaphoric gestures. In A. Cienki & C. Müller (Eds.), *Metaphor and gesture* (pp. 283–289). John Benjamins.

Meekums, M. (2008). Spontaneous symbolism in clinical supervision. In H. Payne (Ed.), *Supervision of dance movement psychotherapy* (pp. 18–32). Routledge.

Panhofer, H., & Payne, H. (2011). Languaging the embodied experience. *Body, Movement and Dance in Psychotherapy*, 6(3), 215–232. https://doi.org/10.1080/17432979.2011.572625

Rogers, C. R. (1973). *Die klient-bezogene Gesprächstherapie*. Kindler.

Samaritter, R. (2009). The use of metaphors in dance movement therapy. *Body, Movement and Dance in Psychotherapy*, 4(1), 33–43.

Sullwold, E., with Ramsay, M. (2007). A dancing spirit: Remembering Mary Starks Whitehouse. In P. Pallaro (Ed.), *Authentic movement* (Vol. 2, pp. 45–49). Jessica Kingsley.

Whitehouse, M. (1979). C. G. Jung and dance therapy. In P. Pallaro (Ed.), *Authentic movement* (pp. 73–101). Jessica Kingsley.

Zitt, C. (2008). *Vom medialen Körperkult zum gesellschaftlichen Krankheitsbild*. Praesens Verlag.

Photograph 6.1 Two witnesses and two movers

Credit: Photography by Lucie Payne

The Psycho-Neurology of Embodiment With Examples From Authentic Movement and Laban Movement Analysis

Abstract

There is widespread agreement that thought is embodied cognition and that our earliest learning is implicit, through the body, and nonverbal expression. This chapter advances the proposition that the integration of thought and emotion is felt through the body. Embodiment and embodied simulation (ES) (Gallese, 2011) represent controversial topics in both the philosophy of mind and cognitive neuroscience (Gallagher, 2015; Gallese & Sinigaglia, 2011a; Gallese, 2014). As a result of advances in these areas of research, there is a need to re-conceptualize our understanding of the mechanisms and processes involved in dance movement psychotherapy. Could ES be applied to the psychology of movement? This chapter attempts to apply this theory of embodiment to authentic movement (AM) and Laban Movement Analysis (LMA). The theory of ES is proposed as one possible explanation of how the witness in authentic movement comes to know her inner experience in the presence of a mover, which may lead to an "offering" to that mover from the witness's conscious body (Adler, 2002). Furthermore, there is an examination of how ES connects to the task of movement observation and how meaning is arrived at from the various movement patterns observed.

Introduction

The concept of embodiment has received a great deal of attention in recent years. This conceptualization, rather than proposing forms of cognitive involvement with movement, stresses the role of the dynamic body (changing movement) in the agent (the individual), and holds that the attribution of movement meaning is action-based and enactive, incorporating the motor-knowing of the observer and performer. The term embodiment could be said to refer to the biological and physical presence of our bodies, which are necessary preconditions for subjectivity, emotion, language, thought and social interaction. The phenomenologist Merleau-Ponty (1962) gave an account of embodiment in which he distinguished between the objective body (the body as a physiological entity) and the phenomenal body referring to my (or your) body as I (or you) experience it. Although there is an experience of our body

(Updated. Originally published in the American Journal of Dance Therapy, 2017, DOI 10.1007/s10465-017-9256-2)

DOI: 10.4324/9781003479413-7

as a physiological entity, the tendency is to experience our body as a unified potential or capacity for doing things or responding to a need via movement. Motor capacities (expressed as bodily confidence) do not depend on an understanding of the physiological processes involved in performing these actions.

Embodiment, therefore, refers to the phenomenal body and to the role it plays in our object-directed experiences. Csordas (1999) speaks of embodiment as an existential condition in which the body is the subjective source of experience. The ground from which it springs is culture and the experience of being-in-the-world. Varela et al. (1991), when speaking on embodiment, refer to an enactive (Thompson, 2007) approach to cognition (a dynamic interaction between an acting organism and its environment) saying that:

> first, cognition depends upon the kinds of experience that come from having a body with various sensorimotor capacities, and second, that these individual sensorimotor capacities are themselves embedded in a more encompassing biological, psychological and cultural context.
>
> (Thompson, 2007, pp. 172–173)

Accordingly, in cognitive science it is claimed that intelligent behaviour emerges from the interplay between brain, body and the world, and that this interplay is termed embodied, embedded cognition. Varela et al. (1991) pioneered the view of embodiment in relation to mind whereby cognition rather than being conceived of as a detached re-construction of the world is seen as a suite of dynamic processes enabling embodied activity (Engel et al., 2013). Action is what enables perception and cognition rather than being in a secondary role to them. One could foresee a third wave of cognitive therapy emerging as a consequence – following behavioural and mindfulness – perhaps to be termed embodied, enactive cognitive therapy. The dynamic nature of the mind (Kelso, 1995; Thelen & Smith, 1994) and the body (which is as plastic as the brain) in action leads to considerations about perception as an embodied activity (Hutto & Myin, 2013). According to a quotation in Kirchhoff (2018), "affect, cognition and sensorimotor contingencies are inseparable given that patterns of affectivity are part and parcel of perception, action, and cognition" (Colombetti, 2013; Gallagher et al., 2013). There are also the related issues of action understanding and mind reading. In the area of philosophy of mind, folk psychology is a name traditionally used to denote our everyday way of understanding, or rationalizing, intentional actions in mentalistic terms. This quotidian competence is known by other names in the philosophical literature: commonsense psychology; naïve psychology. Folk psychology by the observer (Hutto, 2003) refers to the ability to understand others, whereby minds are read by ascribing to them intentions, beliefs and other mental states (Davies, 2005). In cognitive neuroscience this is the main aspect of Theory–Theory and Rationality–Teleological Theory. According to Gallese and Goldman (1998), we understand others because we have developed a common-sense theory of mind consisting of: a set of causal/explanatory laws that relate external stimuli to certain inner states (e.g., perceptions), certain inner states (e.g., desires and beliefs) to other inner states (e.g., decisions), and certain inner states (e.g., decisions) to behaviour (see also Stich & Nichols, 1992; Scholl & Leslie, 1999, p. 496). Dennett (1987) claims that mentalizing has a set of rational principles underlying it which the mind-reader uses to decide which mental state would be embraced by the others, seen as rational agents. However, more recent research has taken us beyond the cognitive and mind-reading propositions. The era of the dominant cognitive paradigm, and the associated cognitive behavioural therapy aiming to change the patient's maladaptive conscious cognitions, has passed. The new acknowledgement of the bodily-based emotions and psychobiological states has been welcomed to centre stage in both research and clinical practice. Gallagher (2005) has underlined the important role of the body in shaping the mind beyond the brain – including the sensorimotor system, the perceptual system and situatedness (the body's interaction with the environment) – in challenging Cartesian dualism.

In dance movement psychotherapy (DMP)[1] as far back as Berrol (1992, 2006), an overview of the neurophysiological and neuroscientific connections has been made; Homann (2010) has presented concepts from embodiment and related them to neurobiology. Affective neuroscience (Gallese & Lakoff, 2005) emphasizes the importance of body-originated information for the formation of neural structures.

Schore (2012) alerts us to the paradigm shift taking place in psychotherapy where there is an integration of nature and nurture, specifically biology/neurology and psychology. It is the duality of thought and emotion that interpersonal neurobiology does not support (Schore, 2012; Siegel, 2012; van der Kolk, 2014). Instead, all thought is now understood as embodied cognition. Our earliest learning is implicit, through the body, and nonverbal.

The aforementioned cognitive model posits a clear-cut separation between sensory perception and motor processes. However, contemporary studies in the neurosciences provide a new perspective of the mind. The proposal that movement is uninvolved in the coding of sensory information and confined only to execution is no longer valid (Gallese et al., 1996). Cortical motor areas traditionally believed to possess functions purely related to movement are now known to be actively involved in processing sensory information too (Rizzolatti & Craighero, 2004). Several investigations have demonstrated that cortical areas involved in the motor control of, for example, a hand grasp, are also activated during the observation of graspable objects, or, in the case of research on mirror neurones (see Photograph 6.1) during the observation of an action performed by another entity (Gallese et al., 1996; Ferrari et al., 2003; Fogassi et al., 2005). This demonstrates that the behaviours, emotions and sensations of others are mapped onto our internal motor representation, which creates a direct connection between self and others.

Through a mirror mechanism we can simulate in ourselves the same emotional and somatosensory experiences that we observe in others. This direct, interpersonal route of knowledge allows us to resonate in synchrony with others and makes it possible to share dimensions of experience at a nonconscious level, i.e., that of implicit intercorporeality. The term nonconscious found in neuroscience and psychology refers to processes experienced and observed in physical actions and feelings without the involvement of language and symbolic thinking (Rustin, 2013).

Established in infancy pre-verbally, Lyons-Ruth (1998) called it implicit relational knowing, however, it may become conscious through bringing attention to the movement and/or feeling (Stern, 2004; Beebe & Lachmann, 2014). The nonconscious is differentiated from Freud's references to the unconscious and to unconscious repressed material. Furthermore, Schore (2003) argues that the nonconscious survival functions of the right brain, rather than the language functions of the left, are dominant in development and psychotherapy, as are the most complex, highest human functions such as empathy, stress regulation, intersubjectivity, compassion, creativity and intuition. Implicit relational knowledge lies in the nonverbal communication right to right brain, underneath words (Schore, 2011). This finding connects to Travarthen's research on intersubjectivity in mother-infant communication (Travarthen, 1977; Travarthen & Aitken, 2001). Furthermore, it is accepted that change can happen through transforming implicit memories at nonconscious levels (Lyons-Ruth, 1998; Schore, 2011).

Merleau-Ponty (1968) first coined the term "intercorporeity", which is associated with Travarthen's (1977) term intersubjectivity, the space between two people. Atkins defines intercorporeity as "the capacity to understand another person's action through the body prior to, and as a condition for, cognition" (Atkins, 2008, p. 48). Gallagher and Payne (2014) argue that the contribution of embodiment to cognition, and therefore, clinical reasoning, is inescapable.

This discourse revolves around research on the role of emotions in development, psychopathology and psychotherapeutic processes, and the importance of body-felt affective processes in human experience (Gainotti, 2012; Schore, 2012). Damasio (2003) offered a helpful division between emotions as observable body states, and feelings as mental events noticed only by the one experiencing them. He argued that "emoting" begins with an emotionally competent stimulus (e.g., an attractive or scary person). The organism automatically appraises the stimulant as conducive or not to survival or wellbeing. As a result, a complex range of physiological reactions are mapped onto the brain such as a faster heartbeat, tension of facial muscles etc., from which a feeling arises. Feelings, he claimed, corroborate the state of life deep within and are a guide to decision-making.

In contrast, Stern (2010) proposed that vitality, first conceptualized in his work with mother-infant nonverbal communication (Stern, 1985), and grounded in the body, is the life force exhibited by all living organisms. His research demonstrates that it is possible to trace vitality to real physical and mental operations including movement, time, perception of force and the spatial aspects of the movement and its underlying intention. He shows us that the multimodality of sensorimotor experience is a cornerstone for the emergence of a vitality form. He explains that forms of vitality characterize personal feelings as well as dynamics of movement.

Thus, these forms are related to feelings of agency and self-efficacy and may be shaped and influenced by the early interactions between caregivers and infants. The origin of these vital feelings takes place within the infant's psychobiological rhythms of the body, which arise from relationships with others, particularly with the mother. The early mother-infant interaction can be considered a bio-behavioural system that is regulated in the brain through complex neurochemical systems and circuits involved in reward and motivation.

Maternal attunement is "a partial and 'purposely' selective kind of imitation" (Stern, 2010, p. 113) supporting a correspondence of the infant's vitality form. The difference between attunement (Kestenberg, 1995; Keysers, 2011) and imitation is that in the former mothers match and focus the dynamic features of their infant's inner state. Markova and Legerstee (2006) found that maternal attunement leads to more infant gazing, smiles and positive vocalizations towards the mother when compared with maternal imitation. In DMP it is the therapist's capacity for intentional attunement communicated to clients through her bodymind which supports the therapeutic alliance. By this emphasis on the primary role of movement in creating forms of vitality, it is clear that the physical aspects and mechanics of movement in time are the building blocks for the creation of a mind that is shaped to capture the dynamics of forces and sensations linked to movement, whether self-generated or produced by others.

The experience of vitality is expressed in movement by considering time, space, force and intention. Interpreting the intentionality of movement, rather than simply the individual movements themselves, is advantageous because it allows the observer to filter out all the irrelevant observed movements. While interacting with someone, the observer attends to a very limited set of stimuli and only those expressing intentionality are relevant (Stern, 2010).

Embodied Simulation

The concept of embodied simulation (ES) goes beyond the reading of bodies and minds; it involves the psychology of movement. Proposed by Gallese (2011), this concept is explored later as inherent to the practice of DMP. It is particularly relevant to the discipline of authentic movement and LMA because of the interrelationship between the mover/movement behaviour and the witness/Laban movement observer respectively. The concept applied here results in the witness/observer engaging with actions and emotions internally, rather than acted on, during their respective tasks. Thus, the processes underlying interpretations of movement actions in others in both authentic movement and LMA can be explained by ES.

Simulation theory states that one way to make sense of another's behaviours and beliefs is when an agent ascribes to them mental states by simulating them internally in his/her cognitive system (Gordon, 2009; Gallese & Goldman, 1998; Currie & Ravenscroft, 2002) in a form of re-cognition. Embodied simulation, according to Gallese and Sinigaglia (2011a), is a unitary description of the fundamental features of intersubjectivity. The authors demonstrate that people recycle mental states/processes represented in a bodily format, expressed as functionality, which they then attribute to others. We experience others as having experiences similar to ours.

Making sense of others' alive and dynamic bodies is rooted in the power of re-using our own motor, somatosensory and viscero-motor resources (Gallese & Ebisch, 2013) facilitated by mirror neurones (Berrol, 2006; Gallese & Sinigaglia, 2011b).

This is similar in the field of social cognition to mentalization – the process by which we are attentive to, and make sense of, (implicitly or explicitly) others and ourselves in terms of subjective states and mental processes (for example interpreting needs, goals, reasons, desires, feelings, beliefs, intentions). The related area of Theory of Mind, in which it is assumed that others have minds by analogy with one's own mind, also refers to the ability to attribute/infer these mental states to oneself and others and to understand perspectives that are different from our own. This attunement, or "tuning into" others, a capacity which develops in the first five years of life, is intuitive, allowing us to predict and interpret another's actions by evaluating their intention/motive, thoughts, feelings or desires, and is linked to our capacity to empathize with others.

Embodied simulation has been debated in the study of intersubjectivity, whereby social cognition can be defined as understanding another's sensations and emotions without any kind of folk psychology (Gallese, 2001, 2005) required. This position has been interpreted as a low-level form of mental simulation (Goldman, 2006) based on the "unmediated – below the threshold of consciousness – processes underlying mirror-neuronal activity" (Gallese & Lakoff, 2005, p. 5). This is in contrast to a high level one, associated with the attribution of complex mental states (for example, propositional attitudes), "accessible to consciousness" (Goldman, 2006, p. 147).

Mirror neurones discovered in the premotor cortex of rhesus monkeys were shown to be involved in action understanding (Rizzolatti et al., 1996). Single-electrode recordings revealed that these neurones fired both when a monkey performed an action and when the monkey viewed another agent carrying out the same task. Studies with human participants have shown that the brain regions containing mirror neurones are active when one person sees another person's goal-directed action, suggesting that mirror neurones may provide the basis for theory of mind and support the simulation theory of mind reading (Haroush & Williams, 2015).

Essentially, the point is that mirror neurones and associated neuroscience studies show that witnessing the actions of others rather than being simply a visual exercise, is one that co-involves our own actions and emotions. Consequently, our motor and affective systems, which are inevitably shaped by our history of personal actions and emotions, will always infiltrate our perception of the emotions and actions of others, and thus be intrinsically subjective. Similar processes take place when dance movement psychotherapists implement the group model termed Chacian circles (often with music) (Chaiklin, 1975), which utilizes a mirroring method. Participants in the circle are invited to copy the group therapist's movements and to synchronize with others' movement so that all move to the same rhythm at the same time and with similar movements (termed entrainment in music). In this approach the therapist leads the group by attuning to the group, picking up on and mirroring back to the group individual participant's divergent movements which reflect emotional aspects being expressed in the group movement. This method enhances and amplifies communication in different nonverbal ways. Mirroring by the Chacian group therapist is a body-felt response to the group's non-verbal expression, a way of incorporating movements spontaneously performed by participants. The therapist is bodily engaged in the active, expressive movement dialogue and expression; she is relating non-verbally to participants and nurturing a sense of belonging by incorporating members' movements (whether they are conscious of this or not) to form a cohesive group process. Research has demonstrated that this synchronous group process of dancing together to music can reduce pain and increase social bonding (Stone et al., 2015). The therapist's reflection-in-action (Schon, 1983) of physically mirroring movements in Chacian circles makes it different from the authentic movement and movement observation examples. In these the witness and observer respectively are not engaged physically (reflecting-on-action) and are instead receptive to the movement yet outside the action. However, the same processes of ES may also be at work in Chacian circles.

When applying the ES conceptual framework to the reception of movement, as in witnessing experiences, it is suggested that there could be a representational equivalence between the perception of a given movement behaviour and its neural simulation. In potentially shaping the degree of the agent's practical knowledge of movement, ES offers an explanation of the way a witness meaningfully understands the movement she sees. Moreover, ES refers to a basic form of (action) understanding, which regulates pre-conceptual responses to the movement stimulus according to the witness's motor expertise, providing her with a different, intrinsically motoric, modality of movement understanding. This would suggest that the witness, in the presence of a mover, accesses her own imagination, sensations, interpretations, intentions and emotional feedback in an "as if" (Damasio, 2003) scenario, i.e., as if she were actually performing the movements herself.

At the beginning of the causal process, the brain's emotion is triggered by detecting a simulation mechanism, which is done by the individual's belief or imagination creating the movement (in the example of authentic movement, this would be the mover). Then the intermodal connection between emotion and bodily movements is utilized in the "witness", leading to the mirroring of these movements from a first-person perspective and eliciting a simulation of emotions in the witness. It is action-empathy and is interpersonal since the witness has no access to the mover's mind.

When taking the practice of authentic movement as illustrative, it is proposed that the notion of ES may be conceptualized, therefore, as the method by which a witness might make sense of the movement expressed by the mover. The mover, expresser or actor is the one who spontaneously moves with eyes closed in response to an impulse whilst in the presence of a witness. This witness remains still yet attentive to the mover, and to their own experience in the presence of their mover, whether imaginatively, through body sensations, emotionally, kinaesthetically, cognitively etc. Such meaning-making ability allows the witness to infer, for example, the intentions behind the movement material being witnessed in the dynamic movement interaction. In the case of the witness being in the role of the therapist, with an in-depth knowledge of the psychopathology and history of the client/mover, it would be treating the movement as a form of interpersonal (involving the transferential relationship) interpretation. Connections made by the therapist with the client's personal history, life events and current conflicts might also contribute to the therapist's interpretation.

Neuroscientific research indicates that neural mechanisms mediate between personal, experiential knowledge held about our lived body and the implicit knowing held about others. Our body-held experiential knowledge, or body memory (Fuchs, 2003), facilitates an intentional attunement with others, co-creating a mutual intersubjectivity. Through this "we-centric" environment we characterize and bring experiential understanding to the actions, emotions and sensations of others. This body-felt, experiential understanding is achieved by modelling another's behaviour as intentional experience on the basis that there is a correspondence between what the other does, sensates, imagines and feels, and what we do, sensate, imagine and feel.

Consequently, it can be said that the therapist (or the person in the role of witness) is connecting with their client/mover through ES with the mirror neurone system a likely neural correlate of this process. The mirror mechanism, given the present state of knowledge, maps the sensory representation of the action, emotion or sensation of another onto the perceiver's own motor, viscera-motor or somatosensory representation of that action, emotion or sensation. This mapping enables one to perceive the action, emotion or sensation of another as if she were performing that action or experiencing that emotion or sensation herself (Gallese & Sinigaglia, 2011b, p. 2).

In authentic movement groupwork, when a witness sees a mover creating movement, making/receiving physical contact with/from another or to herself (tactile empathy activated through her somatosensory cortex), or hears the sounds of the mover (auditory empathy) she resonates with these, while in stillness herself, interpreting the movement/touch/sound through ES. Later, if requested by her mover on her return from the moving experience, she can speak about her experience of these moments of resonance with her mover. The witness speaks about her experience in the present tense, thereby enlivening those same pathways, to give clear, empathic and potentially profound witnessing. Optimally, the mover will feel clearly seen by the witness who verbalizes her experience of their meeting in the mover's movement, touch or sound-making.

The importance of the relative immobility of the witness has been demonstrated to be crucial to this process. Gallese (2017) indicates that it is this relative inactivity (calling it the "neotenic look" as found in infancy) which enables the emotional responses to the action to be felt in more depth (for example, when watching a film that touches us emotionally).

Our being still enables us to fully deploy our simulative resources at the service of the immersive relationship with the fictional world, thus generating an even greater feeling of body. Being forced to inaction, we are more open to feelings and emotions. The "specific and particularly moving experience generated when immersed in fictional worlds is thus likely also driven by this sense of safe intimacy with a world we not only imagine, but also literally embody" (Gallese, 2017, p. 325).

If the witness is craning to see a mover, fidgeting or turning to other distractions, she is violating the requirement for her to absorb fully the impact of the mover's action on her body-mind. Stillness in this context can be understood as a form of meditation in which the whole body-mind is open and receptive to whatever comes its way from the mover and the environment in which she moves. The witness aims to attend to (or regard) the mover, while, at the same time, noticing the inner experiences in her lived body in the mover's presence.

We share various states with others including emotions, actions and sensations, and these bind us in shared identity providing a sense of belonging and community.

Intersubjectivity enables us to conceptualize that we recognize others as similar to ourselves in making communication and ascribing possible intentionality. Through the practice of such disciplines as authentic movement, deep empathy and compassion can be experienced. Through ES, our most fundamental beingness can be experienced again and again as we are seen, and we see others clearly.

An Example From Authentic Movement

I am a witness to a mover. I see this mover begin by walking from one pillar to another as though checking the boundaries around the space (my interpretation). I see her enter the middle of the space and spread into it, using all there is available. She expands her body on the floor and now raises up and travels around and around in circles. I feel dizzy; she stops. I do not feel dizzy anymore. I get a sense of restlessness in my mover, no place feels quite right to settle in (my interpretation). I see her flick away, with her fingers, bits she finds on the floor, the unwanted debris from life (my interpretation). I see her open her arms as she runs around the space, I see play, laughter, and smiles across her face, and I hear her voice. I feel joy, expansion, release of baggage, I feel light and airy in my body. I have space all around me to be who I am without judgement. Am I seen? I am a plane turning its wings skyward, side to side, held by the air (my interpretation), the energy diminishes, her arms come down and I hear her breath. There is more to come (my interpretation), but time is up.

Laban Movement Analysis

Laban Movement Analysis (LMA) (Laban, 1980) is a tool that dance movement psychotherapists sometimes use to assess clients' movement profiles. It is sometimes called Laban/Bartenieff Movement Analysis (Fernandes, 2014). The attribution of meaning to movement has been claimed by many including Laban and

Lawrence (1974), and others employing the theory: Dell (1977), Ramsden (2004), Lamb and Watson (1979), Moore (1988), Moore and Kaoru (1988), Newlove and Dalby (2005), Bloom (2005), and Davies (2005). Numerous body-language authors and researchers in the field of nonverbal communication and psychology have advanced similar claims. In the holistic/complementary health fields there are claims that diagnosis/meaning-making of issues with internal organs etc. can be conducted and healed through the stimulation of areas in other body parts, for example, in reflexology the hands or feet.

Laban Movement Analysis in particular has led the DMP field with reference to the assessment and diagnosis of, for example, personality, as in North (1972), and various mental disorders, such as schizophrenia (Higgins, 2004), irritable bowel disease and eating disorders (Lausberg et al., 1996). Such authors illustrate how the Laban system can be utilized as an assessment methodology for session planning with a range of populations. This chapter disputes the so-called objectivity of this observation, description and meaning-making of movement behaviour.

When movement analysts observe and ascribe meaning to movement by using LMA categories, they are doing more than applying a cognitive understanding of those categories. Fitting what they observe into the categories (Kestenberg-Amighi et al., 1999) is achieved in part through the analyst's ES, which involves neither mental nor cognitive states. The acts mirrored in ES are goal-directed acts within the motor repertoire of the perceiving subject, or the movement observer in this example. The resemblance on which ES relies here is intrapersonal, as the perceiving subject does not have direct access to the other's mental states. Only the outward behaviour is observed, and from that exterior perspective, analysts assign their own meaning and categorize the movement. This action-simulation mechanism, embodied in mirror neurones, is consistent with the idea that a subject can re-enact her own motor experience through an automatic, involuntary process in order to give sense with her own body to a movement seen. Dance movement psychotherapists and certified Laban movement analysts train their bodies in LMA's various effort combinations and shape elements, in order more readily to recognize these patterns of postures and gestures in mover behaviour (Bartenieff & Lewis, 1980/2002). It could be inferred that the development of the capacity to dance in the performer's motor system leads to a vocabulary of motor actions that can be employed to simulate the actions, emotions and the intentions evoked by movement patterns expressed by another. It is this which enables an intentional meaning to be ascribed to a movement expression observed.

Most dance movement psychotherapists are bodily intelligent, having trained for many years in one or more forms of dance and/or movement practice, in Laban movement, including all the elements of Body, Effort, Shape and Space, and in movement observation and analysis. It follows that as therapists employing LMA they would be able to see and interpret a wide range of movement repertoire.

On the other hand, aspects of movement can also be interpreted by people without similar training, and by those who do not have in their motor repertoire any particular sequence of acts. These untutored observers become "thought dancers" in that they do not know, in their bones as it were, how to dance/move the particular movements they are observing. Despite the lack of specific training, they will have experienced a range of feeling-states and associated movement patterns throughout life. Hence, anyone can become a witness or interpret another's movement patterns at a particular level, and may, for example, feel empathic towards a mover and "read", or ascribe meaning to body movement.

Empathy involves the recognition of another's emotions by noticing their expressive behaviour (Prinz, 2004). The observer's recognition of this movement behaviour triggers emotion, thereby prompting simulation mechanisms regarding the intention, belief or imagination of the agency (the expresser) generating the movement. The intermodal connection between feeling and bodily movements is promoted resulting in the internal mirroring of these expressive movements from a first-person perspective, which elicits in the observer a simulation of emotions being felt by the expresser. This can unify the observer's sense-making abilities, where memory, imagination and sensation can be integrated in a motor-grounded framework. However, this view relies on an autonomous domain to simulate emotions, which, according to Gallese (2005, 2011), is not necessary, and is prone to circularity in the context of embodied approaches to sense-making where imagination is conceived of as an example of ES.

The body is the vehicle for emotional expression, and the feedback from the body when interacting with the environment affords bodily resonance (sensations, posture, gesture or a "readiness" for movement) (Husserl, 1952; Merleau-Ponty, 1962) and leads to emotional perception. Thus, interaffectivity, or embodied interaffectivity (Fuchs & Koch, 2014), and intercorporeality are intertwined in and through our bodies. That is, I am affected by your emotional expression since I experience my response to it through my body's sensation and kinaesthesia. Furthermore, at the same time I am also affecting your bodily resonance, creating a mutuality of inter-subjective affectivity. Emotions are brought about by this inter-conversation within the embodied appraisal (Prinz, 2004) and cognitive appreciation of the situation, which may subsequently be modified by any relevant body memory, as examined by Fuchs (2012). Consequently, any interpretation will be a subjective, embodied response rather than an objective stance towards the one observed. Movement observation and analysis, similar to any observation and subsequent interpretation of behaviour/actions, is a subjective process.

Summary

An observer of another's movement, such as a certified Laban movement analyst, will bring to the observation process all factors discussed earlier, which, in turn, affect the analyst's observation (depending on the resonance through ES), and subsequently their interpretation of the observed movement patterns. It can therefore be established that when we consider the concept of ES in a movement observation context or in the discipline of authentic movement practice, it appears to serve as a fitting model for identifying the multifaceted affinity between an agent (whether observer or witness) and the mover. In the examples of authentic movement and Laban movement observation/analysis, it can be concluded that the witness and the movement observer respectively bring to that experience (and interpretation) their own neuronal pathways imbued with personal history including emotional and motoric experiences. Thus, these are entirely subjective processes rather than visual exercises in the objective sense. The processes underpinning such pivotal approaches as Chacian circles, authentic movement and movement observation can benefit from the research into ES, and interpersonal neurobiology more broadly, including the concepts of attunement, embodied interaffectivity and intersubjectivity.

Note

1 In the UK the professional association (ADMP UK) has adopted the term dance movement psychotherapy (DMP) and is an organizational member of the United Kingdom Council for Psychotherapy (UKCP), and therefore this is the term employed throughout this chapter since it was written in the UK by a UK practitioner.

References

Adler, J. (2002). *Offering from the conscious body: The discipline of authentic movement.* Inner Traditions.

Atkins, K. (2008). *Narrative identity and moral identity. A practical perspective.* Routledge.

Bartenieff, I., & Lewis, D. (1980/2002). *Body movement. Coping with the environment.* Routledge.

Beebe, B., & Lachmann, F. M. (2014). *The origins of attachment. Infant research and adult treatment.* Routledge.

Berrol, C. F. (1992). The neurophysiologic basis of the mind-body connection in dance movement therapy. *American Journal of Dance Therapy, 14*(1), 19–29.

Berrol, C. F. (2006). Neuroscience meets dance/movement therapy: Mirror neurons, the therapeutic process and empathy. *The Arts in Psychotherapy, 33,* 302–315.

Bloom, K. (2005). *The embodied self: Movement and psychoanalysis.* Karnac.

Chaiklin, H. (1975). *Marian Chace: Her papers.* American Dance Therapy Association.

Colombetti, G. (2013). *The feeling body.* MIT Press.

Csordas, T. (1999). Feeling through the body. In G. Weiss & H. Haber (Eds.), *Perspectives on embodiment.* Routledge.

Currie, G., & Ravenscroft, I. (2002). *Recreative minds: Imagination in philosophy and psychology.* Oxford University Press.

Damasio, A. (2003). *Looking for Spinoza: Joy, sorrow, and the feeling brain.* A Harvest Book, Harcourt Inc.

Davies, E. (2005). *Beyond dance: Laban's legacy of movement analysis.* Routledge.

Dell, C. (1977). *Primer for movement description using effort and shape.* Princeton Book Company.

Dennett, D. (1987). *The intentional stance.* MIT Press.

Engel, A. K., Maye, A., Kurthen, M., & König, P. (2013). Where's the action? The pragmatic turn in cognitive science. *Trends in Cognitive Science, 17*(5), 202–209.

Fernandes, C. (2014). *The moving researcher: Laban/Bartenieff movement analysis in performing arts education and creative arts therapies.* Jessica Kingsley Publishers.

Ferrari, P. F., Gallese, V., Rizzolatti, G., & Fogassi, L. (2003). Mirror neurons responding to the observation of ingestive and communicative mouth actions in the monkey ventral premotor cortex. *European Journal of Neuroscience, 17,* 1703–1714.

Fogassi, L., Ferrari, P. F., Gesierich, B., Rozzi, S., Chersi, F., & Rizzolatti, G. (2005). Parietal lobe: From action organization to intention understanding. *Science, 308*, 662–667.

Fuchs, T. (2003). *The memory of the body*. Retrieved December 7, 2015, from https://www.klinikum.uniheidelberg.de/fileadmin/zpm/psychatrie/ppp2004/manuskript/fuchs.pdf

Fuchs, T. (2012). The phenomenology of body memory. In S. Koch, T. Fuchs, M. Summa, & C. Muller (Eds.), *Body memory, metaphor and movement* (pp. 84–89). John Benjamins Publishing Company.

Fuchs, T., & Koch, S. (2014). Embodied affectivity: On moving and being moved. *Frontiers in Psychology, 5*(508), 1–12. https://doi.org/10.3389/fpsyg.2014.00508

Gainotti, G. (2012). Unconscious processing of emotions and the right hemisphere. *Neuropsychologia, 50*(2), 205–218.

Gallagher, S. (2005). *How the body shapes the mind*. Oxford University Press.

Gallagher, S. (2015). The new hybrids: Continuing debates on social perception. *Consciousness and Cognition, 36*, 452–465.

Gallagher, S., Hutto, D. D., Slaby, J., & Cole, J. (2013). The brain as part of an enactive system. *Behavioral and Brain Sciences, 36*(4), 421–422.

Gallagher, S., & Payne, H. (2014). The role of embodiment and intersubjectivity in clinical reasoning. *Body, Movement and Dance in Psychotherapy, 5*(1), 68–78. https://doi.org/10.1080/17432979.2014.980320

Gallese, V. (2001). The "Shared Manifold" hypothesis: From mirror neurons to empathy. *Journal of Consciousness Studies, 8*(5–7), 33–50.

Gallese, V. (2005). Embodied simulation: From neurons to phenomenal experience. *Phenomenology and the Cognitive Sciences, 4*, 23–48.

Gallese, V. (2011). Embodied simulation theory: Imagination and narrative: A commentary on Siri Hustvedt. *Neuropsychoanalysis, 13*(2), 196–200.

Gallese, V. (2014). Bodily selves in relation: Embodied simulation as second-person perspective on intersubjectivity. *Philosophical Transactions of the Royal Society* B, *369*(1644), 20130177.

Gallese, V. (2017). Neoteny and social cognition: A neuroscientific perspective on embodiment. In C. Durt, T. Fuchs, & C. Tewes (Eds.), *Embodiment, enaction and culture* (pp. 309–332). MIT Press.

Gallese, V., & Ebisch, S. (2013). Embodied simulation and touch: The sense of touch in social cognition. *Phenomenology and Mind, 4*, 269–291.

Gallese, V., Fadiga, L., Fogassi, L., & Rizzolatti, G. (1996). Action recognition in the premotor cortex. *Brain, 119*, 593–609.

Gallese, V., & Goldman, A. I. (1998). Mirror neurons and the simulation theory of mind-reading. *Trends in Cognitive Neuroscience, 2*(12), 493–501.

Gallese, V., & Lakoff, G. (2005). The brain's concepts: The role of the sensory-motor system in conceptual knowledge. *Cognitive Neuropsychology, 22*(4), 455–479. https://doi.org/10.1080/02643290442000310

Gallese, V., & Sinigaglia, C. (2011a). How the body in action shapes the self. *Journal of Consciousness Studies, 18*(7–8), 117–143.

Gallese, V., & Sinigaglia, C. (2011b). What is so special about embodied simulation? *Trends in Cognitive Neuroscience, 15*(11), 512–519.

Goldman, A. I. (2006). *Simulating minds: The philosophy, psychology, and neuroscience of mindreading*. Oxford University Press.

Gordon, R. M. (2009). Folk psychology as mental simulation. In M. Davies & T. Stone (Eds.), *Folk psychology: The theory of mind debate* (pp. 53–67). Blackwell Publishers.

Haroush, K., & Williams, Z. (2015). Neuronal prediction of opponent's behavior during cooperative social interchange in primates. *Cell, 160*(6), 1233–1245.

Higgins, L. (2004). Movement assessment in schizophrenia. In H. Payne (Ed.), *Handbook of inquiry in the arts therapies: One river many currents* (pp. 138–163). Jessica Kingsley Publishers.

Homann, K. B. (2010). Embodied concepts of neurobiology in dance/movement therapy practice. *American Journal of Dance Therapy, 32*(2), 80–99.

Husserl, E. (1952). *Ideas pertaining to a pure phenomenology and a phenomenological philosophy* (Ideas II). Martinus Nijhoff.

Hutto, D. D. (2003). Folk psychological narratives and the case of autism. *Philosophical Papers, 32*(3), 345–361.

Hutto, D. D., & Myin, E. (2013). *Radicalizing enactivism: Basic minds without content*. The MIT Press.

Kelso, S. (1995). *Dynamic patterns*. The MIT Press.

Kestenberg, J. S. (1995). *Sexuality, body movement, and the rhythms of development*. Jason Aronson.

Kestenberg-Amighi, J., Loman, S., Lewis, P., & Sossin, K. M. (1999). *The meaning of movement: Developmental and clinical perspectives of the Kestenberg Movement Profile*. Gordon and Breach.

Keysers, C. (2011). *The empathic brain*. Social Brain Press.

Kirchhoff, M. (2018). The body in action: Predictive processing and the embodiment thesis. In A. Newen, L. De Bruin, & S. Gallagher (Eds.), *Oxford handbook of 4E cognition*. Oxford University Press.

Laban, R. (1980). *The mastery of movement* (4th ed.). L. Ullmann (Ed.). Mac Donald and Evans.

Laban, R., & Lawrence, F. C. (1974). *Effort*. MacDonald and Evans.

Lamb, W., & Watson, E. (1979). *Body code: The meaning in movement*. Routledge and Kegan Paul.

Lausberg, H., von Wietersheim, J., & Feiereis, H. (1996). Movement behavior of patients with eating disorders and inflammatory bowel disease: A controlled study. *Psychotherapy and Psychosomatics, 65*, 272–276.

Lyons-Ruth, K. (1998). Implicit relational knowing: Its role in development and psychoanalytic treatment. *Infant Mental Health Journal, 19*(3), 282–289.

Markova, G., & Legerstee, M. (2006). Contingency, imitation and affect sharing: Foundations of infants' social awareness. *Developmental Psychology, 42*, 132–141.

Merleau-Ponty, M. (1962). *Phenomenology of perception*. Routledge.

Merleau-Ponty, M. (1968). *The visible and the invisible. Followed by working notes* (A. Lingis, Trans.). Northwestern University Press.

Moore, C. L. (1988). *Executives in action: A guide to balanced decision-making in management*. Pitman.

Moore, C. L., & Kaoru, Y. (1988). *Beyond words*. Gordon and Breach.

Newlove, J., & Dalby, J. (2005). *Laban for all*. Nick Hern Books.

North, M. (1972). *Personality assessment through movement*. MacDonald and Evans.

Prinz, J. J. (2004). Which emotions are basic? In D. Evans & P. Cruse (Eds.), *Emotion, evolution, and rationality* (pp. 1–19). Oxford University Press.

Ramsden, P. (2004). The action profile system of movement assessment for personal development. In H. Payne (Ed.), *Dance movement therapy: Theory and practice* (pp. 218–241). Routledge.

Rizzolatti, G., & Craighero, L. (2004). The mirror neuron system. *Annual Review of Neuroscience, 27*, 169–192.

Rizzolatti, G., Fadiga, L., Gallese, V., & Fogassi, L. (1996). Premotor cortex and the recognition of motor actions. *Cognitive Brain Research, 3*(2), 131–141. https://doi.org/10.1016/0926-6410(95)00038-0

Rustin, J. (2013). *Infant research and neuroscience at work in psychotherapy: Expanding the clinical repertoire*. W.W. Norton.

Scholl, B. J., & Leslie, A. M. (1999). Modularity, development and "theory of mind". *Mind & Language, 14*(1), 131–153.

Schon, D. (1983). *The reflective practitioner: How professionals think in action*. Temple Smith.

Schore, A. N. (2003). *Affect dysregulation and disorders of the self*. W.W. Norton.

Schore, A. N. (2011). The right brain implicit self lies at the core of psychoanalytic psychotherapy. *Psychoanalytic Dialogues, 21*, 75–100.

Schore, A. N. (2012). *The science of the art of psychotherapy*. W.W. Norton.

Siegel, D. J. (2012). *Pocket guide to interpersonal neurobiology: An integrative handbook of the mind*. W.W. Norton.

Stern, D. (2004). *The present moment in psychotherapy and everyday life*. W.W. Norton.

Stern, D. N. (1985). *The interpersonal world of the infant*. Basic Books.

Stern, D. N. (2010). *Forms of vitality. Exploring dynamic experience in psychology and the arts*. Oxford University Press.

Stich, S., & Nichols, S. (1992). Folk psychology: Simulation or tacit theory. *Mind & Language, 7*(1), 35–71.

Stone, J., Wojcik, W., & Dunbar, R. (2015). Synchrony and exertion during dance independently raise pain threshold and encourage social bonding. *Biology Letter, 11*, 20150767. https://doi.org/10.1098/rsbl.2015.0767

Thelen, E., & Smith, L. (1994). *A dynamic systems approach to the development of cognition and action*. MIT Press.

Thompson, E. (2007). *Mind in life: Biology, phenomenology and the science of mind*. MIT Press.

Travarthen, C. (1977). Descriptive analyses of infant communicative behaviour. In H. R. Shaffer (Ed.), *Studies in mother-infant interaction* (pp. 227–270). Academic Press.

Travarthen, C., & Aitken, K. J. (2001). Infant intersubjectivity: Research, theory, and clinical applications: Annual research review. *Child Psychology and Psychiatry, 42*, 3–48.

van der Kolk, B. (2014). *The body keeps the score*. Viking Press.

Varela, F., Thompson, E., & Rosch, E. (1991). *The embodied mind*. MIT Press.

Photograph 7.1 Ferns

To Look at Any Thing

To look at any thing,
If you would know that thing,
You must look at it long:
To look at this green and say,
"I have seen spring in these
Woods," will not do – you must
Be the thing you see:
You must be the dark snakes of
Stems and ferny plumes of leaves,
You must enter in
To the small silences between
The leaves,
You must take your time
And touch the very peace
They issue from.

Moffitt, J. (2003). To look at any thing.
In S. M. Intrator & M. Scribner (Eds.),
*Teaching with fire: Poetry that sustains
the courage to teach.* Jossey-Bass.

Chapter 7

Nature Connectedness and Authentic Movement

Abstract

This chapter follows a path linking the discipline of authentic movement with nature connectedness. This deep empathic practice seeks to change empathy from the interpersonal solely to an interspecies dialogue, cultivating a shift from human-focussed to an earthly perspective of the world. It offers reflections and examples from practice of an adapted model of the discipline of authentic movement which employs the roles of witness and mover outdoors to cultivate opportunities to experience participatory knowing from, and with, the more-than-human world. There are enormous challenges to be met by the human species in the face of the climate catastrophe. This proposed creative, enactive, embodied, embedded model is another way to promote nature connectedness to develop an ecological self which recognizes an ethical responsibility for the planet and its interdependence with humans.

Introduction

Heaven's Wife

We are called by drums
to move outside
to hear tambourines sing
of colours within
for the pulse of our planet
has rhythms that cry
out to our hearts
in this moving time
where evening fires
warm without
as the airs of flesh

of gathering moments
we sing for the days
that lay ahead
for the airs of flesh
unite us now;
and some of us sit
to consume the views
to take in the humour
of every mood
while some of us dance
in the evening light

(Originally published in the *International Journal of Body, Movement and Dance in Psychotherapy*, 18(4), 275–289. https://doi.org/10.1080/17432979.2023.2205921)

DOI: 10.4324/9781003479413-8

unite us now;
we play with the pounding
echoes that shift
and skip to the pace
of quivering heat
as crackling flames
join in the beat
for we meet
at a time
when our notes
sing sweet
as the airs of flesh
unite us now;
so, we sing for the horses
at ease in the meadow
we sing for the trees
dressed in their best
we sing for the sun
to accompany her journey
we sing for the joy

to revel in the motion
of heaven's wife
as we greet
this mother earth
for the airs of flesh
unite us now;
and the body of ground
beneath our feet
connects our breathing
with every beat
as voices merge
with blending themes
to join the streams
that
flow in the past
flow in the present
flow in the future's waiting
where
the airs of flesh
unite us now (AM Circle outdoors,
    Bracegirdle, 2021).

The chapter provides an overview of the discipline of authentic movement (Adler, 2002) as integrated with, and applied to, deep ecology to support connectedness with nature leading towards the development of an ecological self. In doing so, it can create a way of growing individual's ethical responsibility for the climate catastrophe by healing the dissociation between humans and the "more-than-human world" (Abram, 1996).

My practice of the discipline of authentic movement (a method employed in dance movement psychotherapy) is informed both by my teacher Janet Adler, whose approach cultivates the spiritual self, as well as my background in, for example, Buddhism, integrative psychotherapy and group analysis. I was privileged to grow up on a farm in the English countryside, and I trained in, and pursued, a range of outdoor activities throughout my life. I have been fortunate to have always maintained a strong connection with sentient beings and the more-than-human world. The practice encompasses an embodied, enactive, relational, creative arts model within an eco-psychotherapy perspective (Chalquist, 2009) i.e., recognizing the connectivity between the individual bodymind and the wider body of the Earth.

The proposed model described here (examples taken from training group-work with members' full acknowledgement) aims to bring authentic movement circle members into closer relationship with the natural environment. The chapter proposes how authentic movement can raise a greater awareness of the more-than-human-world and its interconnectivity with humans.

The Discipline of Authentic Movement

The mystical/spiritual orientation of the practice was developed by Adler (1995) and Stromsted (2009) who have written on the transpersonal, divine or archetypal wisdom beyond words in which numinous encounters in altered states of consciousness shift awareness to something beyond, and more than the self. Movers may disidentify from the personal to experience states of "being moved" (Whitehouse, 1999a, p. 47), impulses to move arising from cultural or the collective unconscious (Chodorow, 1999; Stromsted, 2009, 2019). Payne (2006) elaborates on how authentic movement connects with "trancing" citing Chodorow (1997, 2003) in which the self-hypnotic trance state offers a third person perspective providing access to, and activating, the personal somatic unconscious through implicit dreamlike memories. Life forms can be seen arising from the collective unconscious such as aspects of nature being metamorphosed as in the shape shifting of the Shaman. It is often the speaking witness who offers the necessary symbols to the mover as a context for the individual or collective unconscious embodied (Payne, 2003, 2006). Whitehouse writes:

> Each contact was an existential moment . . . consisting of I and Thou and a third element – that which is between us, that which is not mine, though I am in it, and not yours, though you are in it. . . . When this third element is present, the movement takes on simplicity and inevitability.
>
> (Whitehouse, 1999b, p. 62)

Transpersonal states have been described as emerging from, and within, the relational connections between mover and witness as well as between movers where separation between self and other dissolves (Adler, 1999; Bull, 2007; Chodorow, 1999). This phenomenological understanding offers a philosophical perspective of the potential transpersonal characteristic of moving and witnessing and has been linked to eco-psychology (Fisher, 2006). Merleau-Ponty (2002) proposes this as another way of understanding the body in which psychological processes are created from bodily states. On this view the brain is acknowledged to be within the body rather than directing it in the context of where action is created (Michalak et al., 2009). Bodily systems provide information for perceiving, recognizing and interpreting an emotion, and bodily states affect the processing of emotional information as can be seen when different postures release distinct emotional experiences (Shafir, 2015).

The ground form consists of a dyad – a mover who makes eye contact with a witness then enters a clear space to wait for an impulse to move (or not) with eyes closed for a pre-determined duration held by the witness. The witness sits still and tracks their internal experiences such as kinaesthetic impulses (which are not enacted), feelings, images, thought/stories and sensations whilst tracking the mover's overt actions/sounds etc. The impact these have on their internal world will be shared with the mover later if the mover speaks of those movements/sounds. Following the mover's return to the speaking witness she reports her experience ensuring the significant movement-moments are communicated with any accompanying thoughts, feelings, images or sensation. She can then request witnessing. The witness recalls those movements mentioned and her experience in their presence. If she did not see them, she cannot offer witnessing. She owns her projections and interpretations. She is a benign presence for her mover. There follows a shared dialogue in which the mover accepts, or not, the witnessing leading to a unitive or differentiated experience. There may be a transition time following the mover's return in which mark-making, writing or clay sculpting can take place as a bridge between moving and speaking for both mover and witness.

The creative arts therapies (of which dance movement psychotherapy is one) have been actively involved in supporting the evolving change in the collective (Atkins & Snyder, 2018), for example, adapting clinical practice to include nurturing the relationship and engaging creatively with the natural environment (Kopytin, 2021; Nash, 2020). Artistic engagement and reflective self-attention with nature has been suggested as key to building a new relationship with nature (Richardson & Sheffield, 2015).

By cultivating interdependence through participatory somatic awareness of embedment, of being in and living through, embodied reciprocity with the animal and plant kingdoms, there is an argument for employing the embodied, mindful, inner witnessing of authentic movement to support and enhance nature connectedness and the development of a mindful, spiritual, ecological self. It is proposed that experiential, creative and embodied practices within an ecological framework have a role in the development of an ecological self which can bring about increased ethical responsibility.

Nature Connectedness

According to deep ecology (Naess, 1973), the self should be understood as deeply connected to nature, as a part of it as opposed to separate from it. Deep ecologists often call that conception of human nature the "ecological self" (Devall & Sessions, 1985; Matthews, 2021; Sessions, 1995), and it represents humans acting and being in harmony with nature, not in opposition to it (Vining et al., 2008). Healing the Earth as opposed to destroying it by a collective unconsciousness (Aizenstat, 1995). The climate catastrophe highlights the need to take responsibility for the interdependence between human beings and nature if we are to save humanity from extinction.

The challenge of the climate catastrophe is often presented as an issue for scientists and policymakers making it easy for the human collective to remain disconnected. Human suffering can be viewed as intertwined with the suffering of the larger Earth community, and/or as alienation from the more-than-human world (Abram, 1996). There is a collective guilt, grief and/or denial for our actions/inaction causing an environmental despair (Macy, 1995) and referred to as eco-sorrow by Orbach (2019). It is suggested here that if humans do not respect and protect biodiversity and wild animals, they may cease to exist. UK activist and conservationist Jane Goodall (2021) states that a biocentric perspective is to live in greater harmony with the natural world and that every individual can make a positive change through consumer action, lifestyle change and activism. Ecology needs to come before economy – there cannot be a healthy economy without a healthy ecology, suggests Goodall (2021). This requires collaboration and sharing of resources and wealth across the globe to address the inequalities and threats to our home, this planet.

Lumber et al. (2018) call for further empirical studies after finding that nature connectedness may result from specific interactions with nature within several pathways. These include engaging the senses and noting nature through artistry both of which, they claim, have implications for the creation and maintenance of nature connectedness and interventions to increase that connectedness for individuals with a weak connection. Mackay and Schmitt (2019) in a meta-analysis suggest that nature connection is a promising avenue for promoting pro-environmental behaviour.

Referring to the practice of psychotherapy Harris (2018) acknowledges the central role of the therapeutic relationship and found working outdoors marked the entry into a liminal or transitional space that facilitated psychological healing. He suggests there are implications for the psychodynamic model of transference (unconscious affect from one is transferred to another) based on dualistic ontology. He reframes transference as a local environment "becoming 'a world which speaks' to the client" acknowledging that "client and place are 'intermingled' such that they 'constitute a new whole' (Merleau-Ponty, 2002, p. 13)" (as cited in Harris, 2018, p. 44). Healing this disconnection involves remembering, re-connecting and re-associating through re-placing our human selves within the larger place of the more-than-human world. Eco-psychotherapy (Rust, 2020) practices offer clients opportunities to explore relationships with nature (Burns, 2012) and to heal the mind (Rozak et al., 1995).

Rather than the web of life being taken as a set of objective entities and processes, Merleau-Ponty (2002) believed it is the biosphere as lived from within (the lived body). Humans inhabit the body of the Earth just as they dwell in their bodies. He proposed that the more this intertwined relationship between human and the natural world becomes a two-way dialogue the more recognition there will be there is some of us in nature and some of nature in us. He invites us to listen to what speaks to us from nature. People can develop an identity of an embodied, ecological self by fostering this listening by being present to the here and now experience. As a result, compassion, consciousness (state of awareness), cognizance (taking notice of) and conscience (a moral sense of right and wrong) can combine to lead to ethical responsibility. Authentic movement offers opportunities for developing presence, by re-associating with the more-than-human world.

Expanding the sense of self while becoming aware of this connection and interdependence between self and nature and experiencing the impact on the body from the more-than-human world, may generate greater knowledge in how to live in, and relate to, the Earth which sustains all sentient beings. It may lead to more humans becoming ethically responsible contributing to slowing down climate change through ecologically ethical decision-making and possibly helping to prevent another pandemic. Hasbach (2015) notes the challenge of climate change requires a fundamental reorientation of our relationship with the Earth and those who share it. This change requires an alteration in consciousness, from viewing the world as an object ripe for exploitation and a resource to be plundered to knowing and living a deep interconnection with all that is. This awareness might enable greater respect for the animal/plant worlds, cultivating eco-systems rather than destroying them, reducing climate change and possibly opportunities for future pandemics to flourish. In nourishing and protecting the natural environment there is nourishment and protection of humans.

Jordan (2014) proposed the natural world can become a co-therapist offering an invitation to animation and connection with the more-than-human world, i.e., an increased intersubjectivity. There is an earnestness to enhance our embodied awareness of living within a complex ecosystem. Eco-psychotherapists regard human suffering as intertwined with the suffering of the larger Earth community as opposed to a mutual dis-ease rooted in people's "dissociative alienation" (Metzner, 1995, p. 64) from the Earth and all thereon. However, by cultivating awareness of this interdependence and our "ecological selves" (Naess, 1995, p. 226; Totton, 2003) perhaps improved relationship can take place for both humans and the Earth.

Working outdoors can also be a remedy for the restrictions and fatigue-making of online worlds and offers opportunities for, and just being with, wide, open attention, with less direction and dependence on verbalizing (Marshall, 2020). There are additional experiences outdoors to feel alive in our bodies, for example, the sensation of cold, frosty air on skin, hot sun on backs, wind buffeting hair etc. and to relate to, and witness, nature, whereby a greater participatory knowing and intersubjectivity can enhance our embodied awareness of living within a complex ecosystem.

Authentic Movement in the Outdoors

Contact, emotion, compassion, meaning and beauty have been found to be pathways to nature connection (Lumber et al., 2017). Authentic movement for working in the outdoors and nature has the potential to foster an ecological self through: a) cultivating connection and contact though noticing, b) providing reflective self-attention and compassion (including self-compassion), c) acknowledging repressed emotions with compassion, d) making meaning from the experiences of moving and witnessing in nature, e) promoting a sense of aesthetics, beauty and wellbeing and the auto-regulation of emotions any of which can lead to transpersonal experiences, and f) connecting to one's own body in nature to create more connectivity.

When referring to authentic movement embodiment is defined as the active, engaged process of sensory awareness of being in, and living through, the subjective body interacting with having a body (Husserl, 1989). Embodiment can also involve cultivating somatic awareness of being in, and living through, embodied reciprocity with the more-than-human world (Abram, 1996). Participating in embodied relationships with nature (Burns, 2012) in the roles of both mover and witness can evoke a felt sense of one's ecological self and spirituality. Humans know their bodies only in relation to other bodies and that these "others" include cawing crows, drifting clouds, reaching poplar trees, soaring kites, running hares and breaking waves.

The aim here is to cultivate, through the practice of presence, an awareness of embodiment and embeddedness to foster transformation to ecological consciousness (O'Sullivan & Taylor, 2004; Mest, 2008). Through empathic experiences during authentic movement emerges an embodied, ecological self, involving relational skills that nourish reciprocal connections with parts and wholes of ecological systems. This can be viewed as participatory knowing which requires receptivity, creativity, being authentically present in the moment, embodied, somatically engaged, and physically and energetically open to change i.e., knowledge is alive/enactive (Ferrer, 2002) and is interspecies (shared amongst all sentient beings). Participatory knowing, or consciousness, involves active engagement in reciprocal, co-creative happenings of making contact (Abram, 2010) and occurs in dialogue, i.e., an event in which one participates rather than within the confines of the intra-subjective world solely. The embodied experience of participatory knowing can be understood as kinaesthetic empathy, a felt sense of reciprocity and somatic resonance vibrating between bodies.

Sensory perception, as employed in both mover and witness, is dynamic, an exchange between sensing and the sensed, both engaged, responsive, alive and animate. Sensing bodies are "open circuits" (Abram, 1996, p. 62) that complete in other beings as the act of ecological perception occurs (Sewall, 1995). As Goldhahn (2003) notes, observing nature and employing elements of authentic movement can offer opportunities to engage in this sort of sensory perception within an embodied relationship with other movers and witnesses, expanding capacities for empathy with environments/organisms, creative intuition and awareness of projections. The notion of co-embodiment is relevant here. Our body is openly intersubjective; our aliveness both connects us to each other and to other beings. The self-other differentiation is thus a function of a complementarity between independence and interdependence from others, rather than of individual organismic embodiment. On the enactive view, subjectivity is a function of the autonomous self and vice versa, the sense of openness towards others could be seen as an expression of the primarily social and co-embodied ontology of the human self (Kyselo, 2023). This author goes on to postulate we can understand how the living body can bring about the lived body and sense of self by considering the self in terms of enactive autonomous self-organization (Thompson, 2005).

Although authentic movement is traditionally practised between humans, authentic movement practice and training in the rural setting affords members to engage co-embodiment with the sentient world and nature (outdoors with trees, vegetation, animals etc.) both as movers and as witnesses. In this adapted form of authentic movement the human witness and/or the selected "other" – be it sentient being or an element of nature – complete each other in the exchange between mover and witness.

Indoors, in the studio movers also engage in numerous imaginative, embodied relationships with nature, for example, embodying "as if" animals, beings in water, digging into and being buried in the earth and so on. "Owning up to being an animal, a creature of the earth . . . this huge windswept body of water and stone. This vexed being in whose flesh we're entangled. Becoming earth. Becoming animal. Becoming in this manner, fully human" (Abram, 2010, p. 3). Here a mover writes of her experience in the presence of witnesses:

Changing

Curving round
on the floor
crossing legs
feeling bound
around the room
listening
concentrating
breathing
changing
suckers for fingers
suction to the floor
pull round
this cold body
this slithering reptile
marking territory.
　(authentic movement
circle indoors, Christina
Bracegirdle, circa: 2015)

One way to practise opening the door into nature as a witness is detailed in the following as a first-person example:

As a witness I allow myself with eyes open to be drawn to the other in Nature, for example, a tree, flower/plant or animal and for a pre-arranged duration pay kind, non-judgemental attention to the "other" and be present to my own experience whilst in its presence. I notice what happens in my body, any movement impulse, sound, sensation, thoughts/story, images, associations, memories, feelings. At the end of the time duration, I can make gesture(s)/postures, write, make marks, produce a collage or sculpt in clay my embodied experience. Then, I return to the group to share some experiences as a witness, if requested by my mover and they resonate with theirs, verbally in the present tense and/or by showing the artefact.

To illustrate the practice of witnessing nature herewith an example from outdoors:

A Flower in a Pot

This flower is towards the end of life,
I become aware of my own aging process.
    It has been rained on – the petals remind me of tear puddles
I notice the warm sun on my neck and feel grateful for being here
    I see the flower vibrate and am reminded of the vibrations across all things
My body begins to sway in time with the movement of my flower
    I notice a sparkle deep down near the red centre of my flower
and feel a sense of excitement mount in my body
    It is as though this is a treasure I have found, one to be honoured.

(extract from personal development journal
outdoors, Helen Payne, 2021)

In Jungian analysis the patient, with closed eyes, is invited to enter a fantasy and observe the evolving scene. It can materialize to afford the patient to engage in spontaneous dialogue with the imagined entities. The patient enters this imaginal world with personal responses "as if" a reality. Similarly, a method to open the door into nature might be to facilitate movers to be afforded the possibility of having an imaginary, spontaneous dialogue but within the reality of the more-than-human world when they move in the presence of this silent witness. In this way nature can become a silent witness by the mover selecting a sentient being, or a plant (as in the preceding poem), tree etc. with which they resonate, and moving in its presence for a pre-determined time frame, with eyes closed/half closed (i.e., an internal focus).

The mover's inner witness becomes alive to the sensations in the context in which their body moves. Participation is evident by, for example, the grass on which bare feet tread affording a different way of moving. In sensing the wind, rain, sun through their body they are moved to respond or not. The natural environment as a silent witness can provoke body-felt responses in movement which can make sense to movers and/or witnesses at the same time as bringing them into relational experiences with the more-than-human world. With reference to this, when practising outdoors the discipline goes something like:

An invitation is offered to become a mover, to move spontaneously from an internal or external impulse with eyes closed or half closed in the presence of human witnesses and the silent witness of nature. The mover follows the scenarios brought about by the moving body and the environ responding in a dialogue with the movement (and sometimes with sound too). A human outer witness in silence accompanies the mover with their benign, non-judgemental attention, using kinaesthetic empathy and presence. Before beginning there is eye contact between mover/s and witnesses. The witness regards their mover with eyes open, attending to their embodied response in the mover's presence, as the mover moves in their presence and that of another sentient being or aspect of nature inside or outdoors – a silent witness. Following transition, the mover speaks in the present tense, first recalling any significant movement actions and accompanying thoughts, feelings, images, sensations etc. The mover can ask her speaking witness for witnessing which she gives in self-referential present tense language.

In this format, the mover speaks about their experience of moving in the presence of nature and their witness to the witness/group in the present tense. She may imagine (project onto) the more-than-human silent witness (possibly previously selected) thoughts, feelings, images, sensations this element of nature may have evoked during her movement experience. A group member in an authentic movement open circle outdoors writes:

The Tree

I move
shaping your growing
with this body's limbs
aware
of your still heart
watching
from where movement
cannot be seen
as you observe
this figure
stretching to the sky
reaching for heights
unknown to me;
I feel
the tangling expansion
of your branches
curling these arms
into moving echoes
of your form;
I sense
your search for light
for even through

I envy
your longevity
for you will be here
when I am gone
as you continue
to give back
so much more
than you take;
through decades of life
and still today
I love
shelter under
lean against
and admire
many of your race
while you continually witness
our need to care
for if all your kind
are wiped away
dug up
decimated
we will lose our lives
for the many gifts you give
like the precious present

the sleeping dark of winter
you never bow down
but deepen your roots
into the warmth
and containment of the earth;

of cool clean air
give us
and this planet
life.
(AM circle outdoors, Christina Bracegirdle, 2021)

A Breathing Circle in a Field

Me witnessing:

M is leaving the circle.
YC is lying on the Earth crying
M is eating something or drinking

Me as a mover:

I enjoy the open space!
I am cutting something, a work takes place, an agricultural work which gives me pleasure produced by the body's functioning.
The smell of the wind,
The horizon to look far away.
Fulfilment.

The contact with a plant makes me think what P said to J, and I start moving, as I am the plant moved by the wind. From this swing movement I am swinging my baby as my hands become a crib, but the wind takes my baby away leaving me alone, however conscious, mindful able to witness the loss.

In the circle we receive witnessing:

M says that she sees me caring [for] something priceless and she is afraid.
M: the wind inside her hair
Y: The Earth can carry everything even my burden
M: Feelings of loneliness
Me: Nothing belongs to us. But what if for avoiding the unexpected pain of loss, I make the loss happen in order to have control?
H said about a conscious, mindful, ritualistic sacrifice!
My drawing: "M" a piece of matter in the water (authentic movement open circle outdoors, Georgia Bara, 2018).

Summary

The proposal here is that by creating an environment in which there are pathways to connectedness authentic movement circle members can come into closer connection with nature. This may help to bring about increased cognizance of the urgent need to act more responsibly and mindfully in the contexts of the climate catastrophe benefiting people's wellbeing in the process. Employing authentic movement to engage both the mover and witness to sensitize them to their ecological selves can be a valuable process to creating ecological empathy through relational, spiritual and eco-embodied experience. By working with individuals in groups in this way whether as psychotherapy (Payne, 2003, 2017), teaching or with creative collaborations with artists/scientists, each one of us can provide opportunities for humans to become increasingly whole and attuned to the more-than-human world, raising consciousness and healing for both the self and the planet. A future study could involve an exploration of authentic movement and the collective unconscious.

Acknowledgements

Appreciations to Dr. Christina Bracegirdle for permission to include her poems from authentic movement open circles at The Empty Studio 2013–2021 and to Georgia Bara, an ex-trainee in authentic movement from 2014–2018 and current doctoral candidate, for permission to include an extract from her personal journal.

References

Abram, D. (1996). *The spell of the sensuous: Perception and language in a more-than-human world.* Vintage Books.

Abram, D. (2010). *Becoming animal: An earthly cosmology.* Pantheon Books.

Adler, J. (1995). *Arching backward: The mystical initiation of a contemporary woman.* Inner Traditions.

Adler, J. (1999). Body and soul. In P. Pallaro (Ed.), *Authentic movement: Essays by Mary Starks Whitehouse, Janet Adler and Joan Chodorow* (pp. 160–189). Jessica Kingsley Publishers.

Adler, J. (2002). *Offering from the conscious body: The discipline of authentic movement.* Inner Traditions.

Aizenstat, S. (1995). Jungian psychology and the world unconscious. In T. Rozak, M. E. Gomes, & A. D. Kanner (Eds.), *Ecopsychology: Restoring the earth, healing the mind* (pp. 92–100). Sierra Club Books.

Atkins, S., & Snyder, M. (2018). *Nature-based expressive arts therapy: Integrating the expressive arts and ecotherapy.* Jessica Kingsley Publishers.

Bara, G. (2018). Personal communication of reflections on authentic movement circles outdoors.

Bracegirdle, C. (2015). Personal communication of poems written from 2014 onwards when participating in authentic movement circles outdoors and in the Empty Studio, UK.

Bracegirdle, C. (2021). Personal communication of poems written at an AM Open Circle outdoors, at The Empty Studio, UK.

Bull, C. A. (2007). The discovery of deep ecology through the body. In P. Pallaro (Ed.), *Authentic movement: Moving the body, moving the self, being moved, volume two* (pp. 361–363). Jessica Kingsley Publishers.

Burns, C. A. (2012). Embodiment and embedment: Integrating dance/movement therapy, body psychotherapy and ecopsychology. *Body, Movement and Dance in Psychotherapy, 7*(1), 39–54.

Chalquist, C. (2009). A look at ecotherapy research evidence. *Ecopsychology, 1*(2), 64–74.

.Chodorow, J. (1997). *Jung on active imagination.* Princeton University Press.

Chodorow, J. (1999). To move and be moved. In P. Pallaro (Ed.), *Authentic movement: Essays by Mary Starks Whitehouse, Janet Adler and Joan Chodorow* (pp. 267–278). Jessica Kingsley.

Chodorow, J. (2003). *The body as symbol: Dance/movement in analysis.* http://www.cgjungpage.org/index.php?option=com_content&task=view&id=88&Itemid=40.

Devall, W., & Sessions, G. (1985). *Deep ecology: Living as if nature mattered.* Gibbs M. Smith, Inc.

Ferrer, J. N. (2002). *Revisioning transpersonal theory: A participatory vision of human spirituality.* State University of New York Press.

Fisher, A. (2006). To praise again: Phenomenology and the project of ecopsychology. *Psyche and Nature: A Journal of Archetype and Culture, 76*(2), 153–174.

Goldhahn, E. (2003). Authentic movement and science. *A Moving Journal,* (Fall), 12–15.

Goodall, J. (2021). Retrieved May 12, 2021, from https://www.janegoodall.org.uk/news-and-events/115-jane-goodall-hopecast

Harris, A. (2018). What impact – If any – Does working outdoors have on the therapeutic relationship? *European Journal of Ecopsychology, 6,* 23–46.

Hasbach, P. H. (2015). Therapy in the face of climate change. *Ecopsychology, 7*(4), 205–210.

Husserl, E. (1989). *Ideas pertaining to a pure phenomenology and to a phenomenological philosophy,* second book. Studies in the phenomenology of constitution. In collected works of Edmund Husserl (Vol. 3). Trans. Springer.

Jordan, M. (2014). *Nature and therapy: Understanding counselling and psychotherapy in outdoor spaces.* Abingdon Routledge.

Kopytin, A. (2021). Ecological/nature-assisted arts therapies and the paradigm change. *Journal of Creative Arts in Education and Therapy, 7*(1), 34–45. https://doi.org/10.15212/CAET/2021/7/2

Kyselo, M. (2023). What self in self-organization? Engaging Varela's epistemology for the co-embodied self. *Journal of Consciousness Studies, 30*(11–12), 80–103. https://doi.org/10.53765/20512201.30.11.080

Lumber, R., Richardson, M., & Sheffield, D. (2017). Beyond knowing nature: Contact, emotion, compassion, meaning, and beauty are pathways to nature connection. *PLoS One, 12*(5).

Lumber, R., Richardson, M., & Sheffield, D. (2018). The pathways to nature connectedness: A focus group exploration. *European Journal of Ecopsychology, 6,* 47–68.

Mackay, C. M. L., & Schmitt, M. T. (2019). Do people who feel connected to nature do more to protect it? A meta-analysis. *Journal of Environmental Psychology, 65,* 101323. https://doi.org/10.1016/j.jenvp.2019.101323

Macy, J. (1995). Working through environmental despair. In T. Rozak, M. Gomes, & A. D. Kanner (Eds.), *Ecopsychology: Restoring the earth, healing the mind* (pp. 240–259). Sierra Club Books.

Marshall, H. (2020). An elemental relationship: Nature-based trauma therapy. In A. Chesner & S. Lykou (Eds.), *Trauma in the creative and embodied therapies: When words are not enough* (pp. 128–140). Routledge.

Matthews, F. (2021). *The ecological self.* Routledge.

Merleau-Ponty, M. (2002). *Phenomenology of perception* (2nd ed., C. Smith, Trans.). Routledge. (Original work published 1945). https://doi.org/10.4324/9780203994610

Mest, R. A. (2008). Ecopsychology: The transformative power of home. *The Humanistic Psychologist, 36,* 52–71.

Metzner, R. (1995). The psychopathology of the human-nature relationship. In T. Rozak, M. E. Gomes, & A. D. Kanner (Eds.), *Ecopsychology: Restoring the earth, healing the mind* (pp. 55–67). Sierra Club Books.

Michalak, J., Troje, N. F., Fischer, J., Vollmar, P., Heidenreich, T., & Schulte, D. (2009). Embodiment of sadness and depression – Gait patterns associated with dysphoric mood. *Psychosomatic Medicine, 71,* 580–587. https://doi.org/10.1097/PSY.0b013e3181a2515c

Naess, A. (1973). The shallow and the deep, long-range ecology movement. A summary, *Inquiry, 16*(1–4), 95–100. https://doi.org/10.1080/00201747308601682

Naess, A. (1995). Self-realization: An ecological approach to being in the world. In G. Sessions (Ed.), *Deep ecology for the twenty-first century* (pp. 225–239). Shambala Publications, Inc.

Nash, G. (2020). Taking art therapy outdoors: A circle of trees. In I. Siddons Heginworth & G. Nash (Eds.), *Environmental arts therapy: Wild frontiers of the heart* (pp. 137–150). Routledge.

Orbach, S. (2019). Climate sorrow. In Extinction Rebellion (Ed.), *This is not a drill: An Extinction Rebellion Handbook* (pp. 65–69). Penguin Random House.

O'Sullivan, E. V., & Taylor, M. M. (Eds.). (2004). *Learning toward an ecological consciousness: Selected transformative practices.* Palgrave Macmillan.

Payne, H. (2003). Authentic movement and groupwork. *Moving On-Journal, 2*(2), 15–17. Dance Therapy Association of Australia.

Payne, H. (2006). The body as container and expresser: Authentic Movement groups in the development of wellbeing in our bodymindspirit. In J. Corrigall, H. Payne, & H. Wilkinson (Eds.), *About a body: Working with the embodied mind in psychotherapy* (pp. 162–181). Routledge.

Payne, H. (2017). The psycho-neurology of embodiment with examples from authentic movement and Laban movement analysis. *American Journal of Dance Therapy, 39*(2), 163–178. https://doi.org/10.1007/s10465-017-9256-2

Payne, H. (2021). Extract from personal journal.

Richardson, M., & Sheffield, D. (2015). Reflective self-attention: A more stable predictor of connection to nature than mindful attention. *Ecopsychology, 7*(30), 166–175.

Rozak, T., Gome M. E., & Kanner, A. D. (Eds.). (1995). *Ecopsychology: Restoring the earth, healing the mind* (pp. 201–215). Sierra Club Books.

Rust, M. J. (2020). *Towards an eco-psychotherapy.* Confer books.

Sessions, G. (Ed.). (1995). *Deep ecology for the twenty-first century.* Shambala Publications, Inc.

Sewall, L. (1995). The skill of ecological perception. In T. Rozak, M. E. Gomes, & A. D. Kanner (Eds.), *Ecopsychology: Restoring the earth, healing the mind* (pp. 201–215). San Francisco, CA: Sierra Club Bks.

Shafir, T. (2015). Body-based strategies for emotion regulation. In M. L. Bryant (Ed.), *Handbook on emotion regulation: Processes, cognitive effects and social consequences* (pp. 231–249). Nova Science Publishers.

Stromsted, T. (2009). Authentic movement: A dance with the divine. *Body, Movement and Dance in Psychotherapy, 4*(3), 201–213.

Stromsted, T. (2019). Witnessing practice: In the eyes of the beholder. In H. Payne, S. Koch, J. Tantia, with T. Fuchs (Eds.), *The Routledge international handbook: Embodied perspectives in psychotherapy: Approaches from dance movement and body psychotherapies* (pp. 95–103). Routledge.

Thompson, E. (2005). Sensorimotor subjectivity and the enactive approach to experience. *Phenomenology and the Cognitive Sciences, 4*(4), 407–427.

Totton, N. (2003). The ecological self: Introducing ecopsychology. *Counselling and Psychotherapy Journal, 14,* 14–17.

Vining, J., Merrick, M. S., & Price, E. A. (2008). The distinction between humans and nature: Human perceptions of connectedness to nature and elements of the natural and unnatural. *Human Ecology Review*, *15*(1), 1–11. http://www.jstor.org/stable/24707479

Whitehouse, M. S. (1999a). The Tao of the body. In P. Pallaro, (Ed.), *Authentic Movement: Essays by Mary Starks Whitehouse, Janet Adler and Joan Chodorow* (pp. 41–50). Jessica Kingsley Publishers.

Whitehouse, M. S. (1999b). Reflections on a metamorphosis. In P. Pallero (Ed.), *Authentic movement: Essays by Mary Starkes Whitehouse, Janet Adler and Joan Chodorow*. Jessica Kingsley Publishers.

Photograph 8.1 A group of movers in contact

Credit: Photography by Lucie Payne

Chapter 8

Relational Integrative Psychotherapy and Authentic Movement

Abstract

This research-informed chapter discusses authentic movement relative to concepts drawn from the theory and practice of relational integrative psychotherapy (combining the transpersonal, person-centred and psychodynamic models). There is an elaboration of the discipline itself with a focus on the mover and witness roles which are then transformed into client and therapist. The discipline is analysed as a form of relational integrative psychotherapy for individual clients. Examples are provided to illustrate the concepts discussed. The importance of the therapeutic alliance, i.e., the relationship between client and that of the therapist is emphasized. Integrative psychotherapy and authentic movement are two powerful and distinct therapeutic approaches that, when woven together in practice, provide a firm platform for supporting the assimilation of trauma for healing and growth.

Introduction

An overview of the discipline of authentic movement as developed by Adler (2002; Morrissey & Sager, 2022), is conceptualized here as applied to the practice of relational integrative psychotherapy. My practice in authentic movement is informed not only by my teacher Janet Adler, whose approach aims to cultivate the mystical or spirituality (Adler, 1995) but also by my background, in, for example, Buddhism (in meditation what is moving in the mind or body is also simultaneously witnessed by the one engaged in the practice), person-centred psychotherapy, integrative psychotherapy and group analysis. These elements encompass an embodied, enactive, relational, creative arts psychotherapy practice in which existential questions commonly arise.

Merleau-Ponty (2002), who established phenomenology, proposes another way of understanding the body in which psychological processes are based on bodily states. The brain does not direct the body but is within it in the context of where action is developed (Michalak et al., 2009). Perceiving, recognizing and interpreting an emotion requires information from bodily systems. Thus, bodily states affect how emotional information is processed. For example, different postures release different

(Originally published in 2024, *American J Dance Therapy* 46, 34–51 (2024). https://doi.org/10.1007/s10465-023-09394-5 amended and updated)

DOI: 10.4324/9781003479413-9

emotional experiences as Shafir (2015) has demonstrated. Thus, when employing embodied practices as psychotherapy, authentic movement in this case, bodily action supplies information enabling perception of emotion and offers opportunities to process and integrate emotions stimulated by the movement experience.

Relational integrative psychotherapy stems from the combination of many different strands of psychotherapy (Gilbert & Orlans, 2011) recognizing that different psychotherapy models may complement one another in general or for a particular client. No single therapy model fits every individual or issue. Instead, integrative psychotherapy tailors the treatment to the unique needs of the client, drawing upon elements from different therapeutic approaches such as transpersonal, psychodynamic, cognitive-behavioural, humanistic and experiential therapies. Rather than requiring the client to fit into a particular approach and/or following a manual for practice it aims to be comprehensive, providing the flexibility to address the complexity of the human organism, their psychological, emotional and relational experiences.

The proposed approach to psychotherapy described here aims to contribute to the discourse of ways in which psychotherapy concepts and practice inform authentic movement, when practised as psychotherapy. Examples are taken from my training group with members' full acknowledgement and factional vignettes from my individual private practice. The chapter draws on authentic movement as a practice when woven within a framework of relational integrative psychotherapy (including transpersonal, psychodynamic and person-centred theories). The theory of relational integrative psychotherapy offers a lens through which authentic movement can be viewed.

American dance therapist Mary Starks Whitehouse, who originated authentic movement, was influenced by modern (contemporary) dance, Eastern philosophy/practices and Jungian thought, specifically active imagination in the latter. She, and two of her students Adler (2002) and Chodorow (1991), were interested in the ways expressive movement could integrate mind, body and spirit. These two students grew their practice in two distinct ways. Active imagination was developed further by Jungian analyst and dance movement therapist Joan Chodorow as a form of inner work as a way of evoking dream states whilst awake. In meditation the intention is for images entering consciousness to flow in and out. However, the Jungian notion of active imagination in the transpersonal psychotherapy model is an energetic, dynamic state in which emergent fantasies from the unconscious are focussed upon and followed in action. The imaginer may explore images, sensations, feelings or narratives, for example. According to Jung imaginings provide access to aspects of the psyche which have been split off and disconnected which can lead to integration.

Adler, on the other hand, developed authentic movement practice along a spiritual or mystical pathway. Emphasizing the mover's "longing to be seen" by the witness, and the witness's longing to see their mover, she proposed a developmental framework whereby the mover practises moving with her outer witness until their inner witness is sufficiently developed to become an outer witness. Contrary to this formulation, Barkai (2022) found in a survey that the majority of participants who had experienced authentic movement courses indicated that being a witness as well as moving in front of witnesses was a highly significant experience for them.

Transpersonal

Both Adler and Chodorow appear to fit neatly into the transpersonal. For example, when authentic movement is viewed as an opening to mystical practice (Adler, 1995; Morrissey & Sager, 2022) transpersonal ideas/perspectives come to mind. These are formulations within a particular approach or philosophical worldview rather than a generally established, recognized phenomena or scientific term. The transpersonal, divine or archetypal wisdom (Stromsted, 2009) has supported for example, visual artists, musicians, choreographers, sculptors and poets. Transpersonal experiences can be defined as those in which the sense of identity or self extends beyond (trans) the individual to encompass wider aspects of humankind, life, psyche or cosmos. They can be described as beyond words – numinous encounters in altered states of consciousness – shifting awareness to something beyond, more than the self.

In authentic movement, movers may disidentify from the personal and experience states of "I am being moved" as noted by Whitehouse (1999b, p. 47) by impulses from the cultural and/or collective unconscious (Chodorow, 1999; Stromsted, 2009, 2019). Whitehouse (1999c) reports "each contact was an existential moment . . . consisting of I and Thou and a third element – that which is between us, that which is not mine, though I am in it, and not yours, though you are in it" (p. 62). These transpersonal states have also been described as emerging from, and within, the relational connections between mover and witness as well as between movers (in groupwork) – any separation between self and other dissolves (Adler, 1999a; Chodorow, 1999; Bull, 2007). Within existential and hermeneutic philosophy, the focus is on making sense of the meaning structures of the lived experience of the client. Solowoniuk and Nixon (2009) make links between the transpersonal and phenomenology whereby the individual accepts a non-dual reality, unconditionally accepting many phenomenological states, conditions, experiences and modes of Being and non-Being. Transpersonal phenomenology is supported by undiluted awareness independent of an interrelationship between perceiver and object. Valle (1998) suggests this is a noumenal space from which both intentionality and phenomenology come into our awareness. Transpersonal phenomenology is an approach that invites the witnessing of one's lifeworld in a radically different fashion, going beyond the embodied ego to reveal a re-remembering of, for example, a primordial existence. This phenomenological understanding offers a philosophical perspective of the possible transpersonal nature of moving and witnessing.

A Relational Approach

This section examines the relationship between mover and witness roles. In the context of psychotherapy, the client takes the role of the mover and the therapist the role of witness (Payne, 2006). Subsequently, there is a verbal sharing of the mover's experience followed by an offering from the witness/therapist if the mover/client wishes to be witnessed. The language employed for this verbal exchange is self-referential and in the present tense. The practice of this discipline produces a reparative environment.

In the mover-witness relationship the experience of the other develops within deep embodied, kinaesthetic empathy (the capacity to participate in somebody's movement, or their sensory experience of movement). A relational dance arises between witness and mover which bodily resonates in the present moment (awareness and mindfulness of what is happening at this very moment). The witness intends clear presence "as a living being" (Gendlin, 1990, p. 205) in the here and now, offering a genuine relationship, mindful of all that is happening in what can be seen. Geller (2013) from person-centred therapy described the notion of presence as a way of being and as a "possible underlying condition for the relationship conditions" (p. 211). Kinaesthetic empathic attunement emanating from the witness to the client in movement and the languaging facilitates the client's meaning-making as they learn to understand themselves and their experiences. An unconditional positive regard (Rogers, 1957) attitude in the witness allows acceptance toward both their own experiences as a witness-therapist and those of the mover-client, which sustain therapeutic presence. Relational skills nourish reciprocal connections with parts, and wholes, of ecological systems.

The practice of authentic movement can be in a group or individual formats, as one-to-one or group psychotherapy using active imagination as in Jungian analysis (Fleischer, 2020, 2023), or as free association in psychoanalysis (Penfield, 2006) to support artists in their creative process (Bacon, 2010; Goldhahn, 2022), scientists (Goldhahn, 2003), in nature connectedness (see Chapter 7), and as a form of meditation (Marcow Speiser & Franklin, 2007) or for wellbeing. The basic sequence of events in the model for relational integrative psychotherapy is provided in Figure 8.1.

The Mover

The role of mover will be reiterated here as the context is as psychotherapy. Prior to making eye contact between the client and therapist (mover and witness) the mover is invited to decide on the duration which can be as little as four minutes up to at most 20 minutes in a 50-minute session. It is not advisable to begin a new move beyond the final ten minutes of a session to ensure sufficient time for the languaging of the experience and closure. The mover/client then makes eye contact with the witness/therapist if they wish, and, on the therapist's verbal signal, or the sounding of a singing bowl, closes their eyes and waits for the movement impulse to guide their movements. If none arise, that too is acceptable, as there is no right or wrong. The movement space will need to be private and unencumbered by obstacles for safety. When practising online, cushions surrounding a two-meter square area with the camera adjusted to enable the whole body to be seen is recommended.

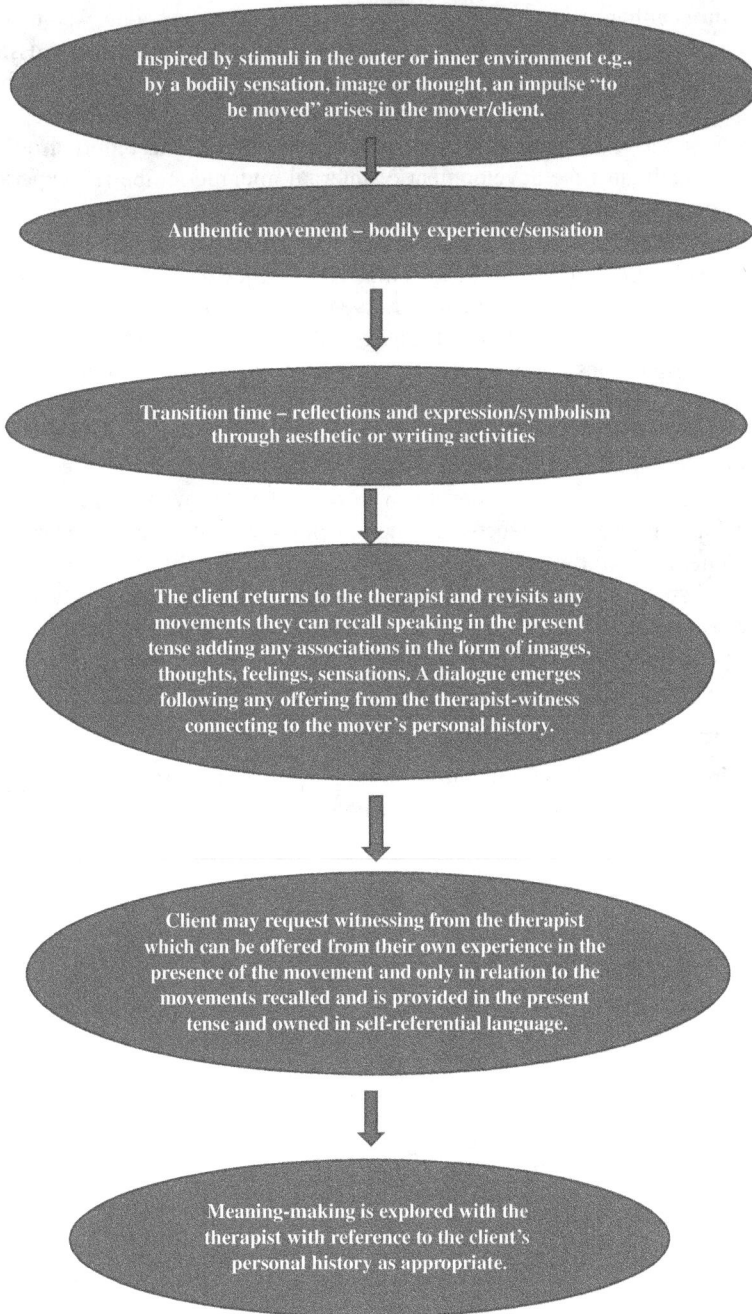

Figure 8.1 Sequence of the authentic movement model in relational integrative psychotherapy

The mover then follows with their mind's eye their emerging, spontaneous movements and with their inner witness (or observing self) notices any associations, sensations, images, feelings or thoughts which arise. They may also make sounds freely. Over time the inner/internal witness in the mover develops sufficiently for the more significant moments to be noticed and reported on. The awareness facilitates the development of internal integration, the felt experience of inner connectivity and skills for authentically expressing internal phenomena (Hackney, 2002).

The development of an unobtrusive, kind and non-judgemental internal witness enables movers to non-judgementally observe their thoughts, kinaesthetic impulses, feelings, movements, sensations and images as they regress into more receptive states of consciousness. When grounded in the body, this increased awareness to sensation etc., can lead to a greater capacity to consciously choose how to respond to inner experiences i.e., to notice without identifying with, or unconsciously reacting to, immediate experiences (Wallin, 2007). For the mover, connecting with bodily felt experiences in relationship with the other (the witness/therapist) may involve fluctuating attention between internal experience and the awareness of the outer witness and/or the outer environment. For example, there may be attention to external stimuli (Aposhyan, 1999) such as bird song, other movers' sounds (if groupwork) etc. to which the mover may respond. Here some writing following a mover's transition after a group experience which involved sound:

"Losing ourselves in a group move, through sounds and responding to those sounds/active imagination within the whole group.

The Siren

Sharing rhythms
through legs and feet
we chat
in the metre
of the beat
two together
laughing
playing
till the Siren
seduces us
with such an air
to touch
to listen
as fingertips speak

to echo the tones
that move our bones
as a circle forms
through unseen arms
hesitantly shifting solidity
into the fluid
of the raging sea
as we pitch and roar
our transforming call
into the harmony
that assimilates
us all
until . . .
we are . . .
completely . . .
spent . . .
ebbing
on the shore".

(Extract from personal journal, Christina Bracegirdle, open training circle, 2015)

On hearing the sound (often a singing bowl) made by the witness/therapist signalling the time is up the mover/client slowly emerges from the movement to make eye contact again with their witness/therapist if they wish. The movement expressed may lead to creative narratives, and, during an intermediary phase between moving and speaking called "transition", writing, clay sculpting, visual art forms or a poetic response may be engaged with by both witnesses and movers (see Bracegirdle, 2023b on the concept of transition in authentic movement). For example, the poetic use of language can hold and reflect paradox, uncertainty and ambiguity, consolidating a creative presence through the playful association of words. Literal words may misrepresent, underplay, hide rather than reveal and frequently offer only approximations to the recalled experience whereas poetry, being multi-sensorial, may amplify the embodied experience.

If there is to be no transition time, the mover can return immediately to share any recalled significant actions/sounds and accompanying feelings, images, thoughts or sensations with the witness/therapist. The verbal dialogue with an outer witness/therapist following the movement experience helps movers to link evolving images with their associated affects which can facilitate the process of symbol formation and understanding and differentiating their body-felt experiences (Lucchi, 2018). Subsequently, following the mover's spoken recall they can, if they wish, invite the outer witness/therapist to share their experience in the presence of the movements/

postures/sounds mentioned, also in the present tense, called witnessing or an offering. Links may be made with the personal autobiography of the client during the subsequent dialogue together. Self-awareness is thus cultivated for the client mover through this interpersonal, subjective relationship born out of the embodied consciousness of the nonverbal experience and the verbal exchange. Now there is an exploration of the role of the witness/therapist.

The Witness

Psychotherapists with an awareness of the importance of the body and expressive movement support clients in raising awareness of their bodies, through cultivating a "tuning into" their own felt sense of internal body sensations (interoception) and their developed skill for kinaesthetically sensing movement (Gendlin, 1981; Ogden, 1997; Whitehouse, 1999a). The witness/therapist deeply listens and attends to their interior environments in the body and/or sensations on the skin, their thoughts, any impulse to move themselves (although they do not act on this), images and feelings impacted by the mover's action/posture/sounds etc. This is a form of somatic resonance in that the inner mover is kindled. The witness may at time, feel the desire to move in relation to the mover, for example, reaching out to them or sitting close by, or even touching. However, these impulses are all contained. The witness may notice elements which arise from time to time in the external environment. This is the inner witness experience in the outer witness, which can kindly and mindfully observe the self (Aposhyan, 1999; Avstreih, 2008). Through this form of self-witnessing (otherwise termed the observing self/ego) emotions can be felt, impulses tracked, sensations, thoughts, images and needs noticed.

The outer witness in authentic movement – the psychotherapist – holds the psychic space for the mover and notices what is happening in their inner world in the presence of the mover's expressive movement. This reliable, predictable outer witness, or "withness" as referred to by Anderson (2007), always remains seated in the same place, holding the movement time as agreed with the mover beforehand. In the verbal sharing the outer witness/therapist waits until the mover has expressed, in the present tense, all that they experienced, noting the physical actions/sounds/ postures reported. It is important to practise using the present tense to remain close to the experience despite it being in the past.

The speaking outer witness/therapist responds to the actions/sounds/postures of which the mover has spoken as this is what has been seen. Responses experienced in the outer witness may include, for example, any images, desires to move, sensations, feelings, thoughts/stories etc. Projections are owned, and the therapist refrains from an interpretation of the mover's actions, sharing only her own experience of what is directly relevant to the mover's shared significant moments. If the mover has not reported any actions (postures, gestures etc.) even though the witness may have seen, and been present to, those actions, they cannot make an offering in the speaking of their witnessing, since the two (the mover and witness) can only meet each other in the physical movement action or sound.

To illustrate the experience of an outer, speaking witness here is a poem shared with their mover.

Waking

A baby sighs
turns
wriggles around
stretches
legs up
arms up
pushing
rolls over
a moment's quiet
waiting . . .
waiting . . .
silently transforming
and when she rises
slowly
purposefully
on all fours
to claw the ground
to look around
a bear is seen
slowly
oh so gradually
waking from hibernation (Bracegirdle, training circle, circa 2016).

The responsibilities of the outer witness are tracking their movers' experiences, facilitating witness/mover dialogue (Lucchi, 2018), and, at the same time, tracking their own experience in the presence of the mover's movement. This relationship between mover client and the benign outer witness therapist is important to the development of embodied consciousness in the mover. The mover and witness explore somatic experiences as emergent phenomena within the relational contexts of, if in a group setting, movers and witnesses (Adler, 1999a) or, if individual practice, the mover and witness.

Mirror neurone research in relation to the witness in authentic movement (see Chapter 6) and to kinaesthetic empathy which involves "the embodying of a client's feeling states and movement qualities by the therapist" (Pallaro, 2007b, p. 182) has been described as affect attunement, resonance, synchronicity and/ or intersubjectivity between therapist and client (Pallaro, 2007b; Siegel, 2007; Wallin, 2007). From this embodied attunement experience in the therapist, they can verbalize their inner response in the presence of the mover's movement to provide validation to the mover's experience (a unitive experience). When the client's internal experience and external expression through the movement and the subsequent verbal therapist responses resonate with the mover it may be viscerally experienced in the body of the client and/or therapist through the senses and affective domains. Nevertheless, it is recognized that not all that is shared by the therapist may be congruent/a unitive experience with the client's experience, resulting in a differentiation of experiences. The client can choose not to accept these elements as "in tune" with their experience. This could become part of the process.

Through the lens of relational integrative psychotherapy, Gilbert and Orlans (2011) propose integrative psychotherapy as a "unifying approach that brings together physiological, affective, cognitive, contextual and behavioural systems, creating a multi-dimensional relational framework that can be created anew for each individual case" (2011, p. i). There are four characteristics: 1) the therapist sees individuals and groups holistically as integrated wholes with interrelated experiences of body, mind, physiology and psychology, affective and cognitive, physically and spiritually; 2) there is an integration of theories and concepts and/or techniques from different psychological and psychotherapeutic approaches; 3) the therapist's personal and professional integration maintains an authentic, responsive and creative contact with self and others; and 4) there is an integration of research and practice so research informs practice and the reflective evaluation of practice informs research.

From a relational perspective, the therapeutic process occurs both in terms of the intrapsychic object relations and within the intersubjective dimensions (Benjamin, 1999). In terms of the intersubjective, the psychotherapist's subjective experiences are viewed as inextricably linked to the implicit and explicit client experiences – a reciprocal exchange of energy, sensation, affect and imaginative responses occurring in the embodied mind of the therapist and, when spoken, contributing to the client's personal meaning-making.

The combination of relational integrative psychotherapy and authentic movement can be a powerful combination of the benefits of both. They can complement each other in the following ways, for example:

1. Authentic movement allows access to embodied experiences and their expression through movement which provides valuable insights into unconscious processes to facilitate self-discovery. Integrative psychotherapy can then help to make sense of these experiences within the broader context of clients' lives, relationships and emotional patterns.
2. Authentic movement can address trauma as the body holds the imprints of traumatic experiences. Through the movement process access to, and release of, these stored sensations and emotions is more possible due to the somatic marker hypothesis (Damasio, 1996) left by the physiological responses to trauma. This is especially so if the trauma was pre-verbal. Integrative psychotherapy can provide additional support by helping clients to process and integrate the insights and emotions arising during the movement practice.

3. Authentic movement can serve as a robust method for self-expression, enabling clients to communicate inner experiences and emotions beyond words or that that might be too difficult to language. Integrative psychotherapy can then facilitate the assimilation of these expressions into the therapeutic process, helping clients explore underlying meanings, beliefs and narratives.
4. By combining authentic movement with the inclusive and adjustable characteristics of integrative psychotherapy an even more holistic approach evolves. It addresses cognitive, emotional, somatic and relational dimensions of the client's experience providing a flexible and rounded approach to psychotherapy. The combination of these two approaches should be carried out by qualified professionals trained in both integrative psychotherapy and authentic movement. These can provide the guidance, support and expertise to ensure the safety and effectiveness of the psychotherapeutic process.

When interweaving authentic movement into a psychotherapy practice the process is a journey from the bodily experience to transition time when the client comes out from the dream state/kinetic meditation of authentic movement to write, make marks on paper or sculpt clay. Thereafter, it moves into the languaging of the embodied experience whereby the client reports on the moving experience and any significant moments related to those reported actions, followed by the receiving of any offering the witness/therapist can make. In gestalt therapy terms, the transition time in which clients may create visual imagery, poems, sculpture or narratives could be viewed as the formation of a figure by establishing the ground in body sensation (Perls et al., 1994).

In authentic movement practised as a form of individual psychotherapy, clients are invited to enter their "suffering" without judgement. As client and therapist dwell in, and behold it, they both disappear into the phenomena manifested through the movement, thereby relinquishing control of interpretation to gain awareness of what is simply present in the "here and now". Meaning-making is where the person-to-person relationship is foreground, where "inner and outer experiences are intimately interrelated and co-existent" (Gilbert & Orlans, 2011, p. 69). Here might be a place to work with childhood relationships and/or trauma which can emerge during the movement and speaking elements (and can be framed as both the transference/counter-transference relationship). The therapist's somatic counter-transference experiences might inform interpretations about the therapeutic relationship being enacted. Here, after the movement and dialoguing, interpretations by the therapist of the (somatic) transference (Pallaro, 2007[b]) or in relation to psychological history/trauma may be helpful. For example, this short composite vignette from my private practice may illustrate this point:

The therapist notes they want to turn away from (but not enacting this action) when seeing a moving client turning their back on the therapist and covering their eyes, as if hiding from being seen. When the mover (who is always invited to speak first) reports about their experience, they mention covering their face with their hands and explain about feeling uncertain and self-conscious, wanting to hide away from the therapist's gaze. On hearing the therapist's experience of the impact on them of that movement scenario the client/mover speaks of feeling validated and affirmed in their own experience.

The therapist, in speaking to their client about their experience of wanting to turn away, offers and owns their interpretation that the mover does not appear to want to be seen by the therapist. This offers the opportunity to explore the I-Thou relationship (the person-to-person relationship), as described by Buber (1958), which emphasizes a core meeting between persons. The client in the preceding vignette had difficulties in socializing, her anxiety about someone seeing through her had been overwhelming at times resulting in her leaving her employment and spending more and more time isolating herself at home. It transpired she feared being seen as vulnerable and ineffective whereby all her fragilities would be seen by others so avoided social contact. It stemmed from being shamed in public at school where she was the only girl amidst boys in that school. This acknowledgment within the therapeutic alliance was a step towards transformation of her fears towards reclaiming her self-worth, putting down the shame from the past. In this vignette the way the client stimulated the therapist in terms of movement impulses, thought, feelings, sensations, images and/or kinaesthetically can be conceived of as counter-transferential material in the therapist. This awareness led to a languaging with the client to uncover a traumatic experience which was holding her back from social engagement.

It is important to highlight that the use of self-referencing language (Adler, 1999b), especially in the offerings from the therapist, minimizes defensiveness in the client and facilitates open dialogue (Lucchi, 1998). Self-referencing languaging uses "I", "me" or "my" leading to an owning of the experience by the therapist rather than projecting interpretations onto the mover with terms such as "you" or "your" thus reducing interpreting their movement, and making judgements. It helps to delineate the boundaries between self, other, inner and outer experiences. The client and therapist are their own experts on their experience in this model.

The therapist sits still and silent remaining in the same place as when the client began moving after eye contact has been made between them. This stationary seating position fosters a reliability and predictability for the client which is essential for a therapeutic bond to develop. Furthermore, the eye-to-eye contact traditionally practised between therapist and client before the client closes their eyes can be viewed as reflective of early attachment or object relations in psychodynamic psychotherapy.

Freud's use of free association in words, where the patient lies on a couch with the analyst behind them, out of sight, to reflect verbally, frequently with closed eyes (Penfield, 2006; Searle & Streng, 2001), is mirrored in authentic movement where, with closed eyes, free, spontaneous movement is expressed and tracked by the client who is also unable to see the therapist. At the mirror stage of early development, the infant sees themselves reflected in the gaze of others enabling them to develop an image of their own body as a whole entity rather than a fragmented mass of sensations (Winnicott, 1971; Krishner, 2012). Similarly, the client knows they are witnessed by the therapist's gaze at the outset of and during their movement, seeing themself being seen as a whole person in the nonverbal experience, whether or not they are conscious of the therapist at the time. The client can also make eye contact with the therapist afterwards if they wish. In this way the client knows their experience was shared with this benign other. Eye contact is an empathic gesture enabling the mover to know their experiences will be shared within the contained space of a non-judgemental other.

Research suggests that authentic movement practice provokes an awareness of emotions that are being inhibited. The positive affective trait shapes the effect of authentic movement on an emotional state, increasing the trait which is opposite to their own affective trait (Garcia-Diaz, 2018). This means the client may contact repressed emotional content and face emotions previously avoided, for example, decreased happiness and increased anger. In contrast to the desire to be seen there is also the desire to hide. The following is a factional account (i.e., re-configured material from other client work and elements made up) of an early session with a client from private practice illustrating how the unnamed fear of being seen can show up even in a short movement piece. Adler (2002, p. 6) gives a passing reference to the fear of being seen.

Composite Vignette

Therapist tracking: My client shuffles her feet, rising on a one ball she stretches her toes. I imagine a warming up of the feet as a preparation. She then proceeds to hide her face in her hands as she stands in front of me. I am shut out; I must not look. I feel the impulse to turn my gaze away from her but do not act upon it, of course. Noticing this impulse provides me with information that I am intruding on my client's privacy. For me her desire not to be seen is profound. Now my mover sits down and curls up as if a foetus, her back towards me. She is very small, and I imagine she must protect herself from something (my interpretation), from me perhaps. I begin to wonder who I might be symbolizing for her. I feel tension in my body. She rolls onto her side legs stretch out and takes up a sleeping posture. It is time to rest (my interpretation), I breath out and find myself relaxing my back into the chair. Then she sits up quickly. It is a surprise to me. I am left feeling short-changed in my relaxation. She holds her hands to her face again. Her head is bowed; in this moment I feel shame. What has been done that is so shameful?

The client's report: The mover returns to share she is uncertain what she should do, she wants to be a good client and fears the therapist's judgement.

She may "do it wrong" she feels. She recalls holding her hands to her face and turning away in a curled-up position – as though a foetus – to protect herself from being seen by the witness. She recalls lying in a sleeping posture, hands under her head as a pillow. She moves her legs to find the right position. She says she needs to get her legs just right to sleep. She feels rested and relaxed now, but very soon she sits up. She recalls asking herself if perhaps she should not do this; she is supposed to move, although she says she knows it is not essential, i.e., that no movement is possible too. Yet she felt ashamed of not doing it right, of not pleasing her therapist.

The therapist's offering: I see you hold your hands to your face. I feel I am intruding on your private space with my gaze. I find it hard to hold it as I feel so shut out. The impulse is to avert my gaze (kinaesthetic impulse not acted upon). I am not to see you. I see you sit down and curl up as if a foetus, your back towards me. You are very small. I imagine you need to protect yourself (my interpretation) from something, from me perhaps. . . . I feel tension in my body. Your legs stretch out, and I see you take up a sleeping posture. It is time to rest (my interpretation); I breath out and find myself relaxing my back into the chair. Then you sit up quickly surprising me. I am left feeling short-changed in my relaxation, and in this moment I feel shame. What has been done that is so shameful?

In the dialogue which followed the therapist's offering, the client explained her parents, although loving, always told her as a child that she was doing things wrong, she felt undermined by them. She had always tried to please them but felt they were never satiated. This feeling of never being good enough had been projected onto me, the therapist, whom she felt she had to please by moving, although her instinct was to rest. She felt the shame of getting it wrong as if she were in relationship with her parents again in her relationship to me. She thought I might judge her for "getting it wrong".

This revelation enabled the client to consider why she has such low self-esteem now and how she projects her feelings of being judged as inadequate onto figures she sees as authority. Although the importance of a non-judgemental ethos in the therapeutic alliance is crucial, in the transference lack of trust in a benign other can still emerge, safety remains compromised, and this is the content which needs to be integrated. As time goes forward her consistent experience of the non-judgemental, holding therapeutic alliance, the movement practice and the offerings from the therapist provided her with a sense of trust, safety and agency, cultivating a sense of empowerment and a corrective emotional experience (Alexander & French, 1946; Summers, 1994; Winnicott, 1971). She found what she needed. Previously, she had feared and avoided others, but now she can be approached (and approach others) more confidently as she learns to develop a wider range of expectations and responses. It can be speculated that her childhood needs were inadequately met, or not met at all from an object relations perspective; the underlying assumption of transference is that these unmet needs re-emerge in the therapeutic relationship.

The connection between body and the imagination in employing authentic movement as psychotherapy is created by the expressive movement element (and through writing or artwork if employed in the transition stage, see Bracegirdle, 2023b). Furthermore, the client sees their internal world in the artefacts made during transition and in any languaging from the witness if it is a unitive experience, rather than a differentiating one. Thereafter, via this visibility, the client may verbalize their inner experience which previously was unable to be spoken. Stating that which, thus far, had been invisible, naming it, making it visible. Attunement and affirmation of the client are "significant for communicating the three core conditions" in person-centred psychotherapy according to O'Brian and Houston (2007, p. 38). All three are found in the therapist's presence to their client.

Contrary to the belief that it is the desire to be seen which is paramount for the client, what can also surface is the desire not to be seen. In my experience some clients may not wish to be seen by the therapist, at least initially. There is a strong desire to be hidden rather than seen. As part of this desire clients may not wish to make eye contact with the therapist before going into their movement, which must be accepted by the therapist. When reflected upon later this unspoken, pre-verbal pattern may be understood. As in the aforementioned vignette, the client's personal psychological history may become especially important as they make links, together with their therapist, to the movement experience made conscious through verbal discourse to co-create meaning. Seeing old patterns re-emerge and transform moment-by-moment helps clients to open spaces for different choices to be made.

Languaging the witnessing also connects to humanistic psychotherapy, for example, the therapist only speaking about the movements the client has reported and using their words as in person-centred psychotherapy (Rogers, 1977). The therapist, in a non-judgemental ethos, provides affective engagement, good listening skills and interest. By clarifying and summarizing both what has been told and the associated feelings, the therapist helps the client to feel accepted, seen (even if their wish is not to be seen – they feel seen in their hiding) and heard.

The therapist has no agenda, only offering witnessing solely on the movements/ actions and/or sounds the mover has reported. The therapist contains elements unreported by the mover even though they may have much significance to the therapist and although they may want to share them (and the mover may wish to hear them) they are not revealed. The therapists' attributes of providing sufficient congruence (genuineness i.e., being true to oneself) require a "life-lasting ongoing process, the importance of constant care, the role of relationships, and being in contact" (Kaimaxi & Lakioti, 2021, p. 232), as well as unconditional positive regard (care and acceptance) (Ort et al., 2022) and accurate empathy. These represent the three core conditions for change and the potential for clients becoming fully functioning persons as found in Rogers (1951).

Congruence

This final section explores the connection between congruence as found in Carl Rogers's (1961) person-centred psychotherapy, as one of the three necessary conditions for change, and authenticity in authentic movement. Congruence may be defined as the capacity to access internal processes at any given moment. It has an inner and outer aspect. The inner concerns the receptivity of the person to her own feelings and experiencing (the consistency to which it refers is the unity of the experience and awareness). The outer aspect concerns the communication of perceptions and attitudes to another, transparency or apparency, implying congruence is a way of being inside, not doing.

In discussing congruence, it might be useful to illustrate when incongruence can occur. This is when the person is unaware of their feelings and so vehemently denies them, for example "I am NOT ANGRY!" as well as when they are completely aware of what it is they are experiencing and yet say something completely contrary, for example, "the meal was delicious", when it made them feel quite ill! The incongruence here is between awareness and communication rather than experience, awareness and communication as in the first example.

Rogers's theoretical statements show congruence involves experiencing and awareness in relation to self-concept (the experience is accurately symbolized by the self-concept, a matching between experience and awareness with self-perception). Here the person is seen as an embodied being with the self-concept understood as those attributes or areas of experiencing a person can speak of, and concerned with, "I am . . ." (angry sometimes, nurturing, strong etc.). Therefore, in this approach when a person says they feel sad, happy, strong or angry (and they really are) there will be a congruence observed between their feelings and their resulting words and actions. But, if the person does not define themselves as, for example "sad", yet describes a situation in which a feeling of sadness is evoked they will not be able to put that feeling into words accurately. Instead, they will express the feeling in an altered, sometimes unfortunate way. Where this mismatching of feeling and capacity for awareness and symbolization of these feelings occurs, there is a state of incongruence (or inauthenticity) for example, in either mover or witness. The person may have learned as a child to define themselves conditionally according to parental values, for example, where love was offered conditionally (conditions of worth and external locus of control). Incongruence therefore arises out of gaps in the self-concept caused by exposure to conditions of worth or an over-dependence on external evaluations/beliefs/attitudes. Alternatively, when relying on an internal locus of control the organismic valuing process results in a fully functioning person, that is, they have the capacity to accept and use feelings from within to guide action.

Congruence is a multi-faceted process similar to Rogers's concept of the organismic integration of the fully functioning person in which the connection throughout our being is open in a cordial rhythm. Consequentially, congruence is linked to a deeper, broader, integral self that holds previously fragmented parts to create a more coherent whole. Congruence could be said to be only possible when this integral self is forming, to facilitate the connection and communication between different configurations of the self. Without self-acceptance, self-awareness and authenticity this integral self cannot occur. Naturally, personal development is essential to honing these capacities in the witness-therapist.

Rogers emphasized a third aspect of congruence (the other two phenomena are experience and awareness), that of communication. The transfer of congruence, for example from the witness-therapist to the mover-client within expression and behaviour, is vital to the change process. Infants are normally totally congruent with their communication and experience; they are their experience whether fearful, joyful, hungry or angry. They simply "do" themselves.

Congruence could be related to the concept of presence whereby the witness-therapist is working towards being fully present both to herself and the mover-client in the moment, engaged in a mutual flow of immersion in the process. Furthermore, the mover-client is intending to be fully present to their experience in the moment. Both congruence and its derivative presence underlie the approach of both authentic movement and person-centred psychotherapy; instances of authentic engagement between mover-client and witness-therapist are seen when the most meaningful and significant learning takes place. Congruence cannot be fully achieved, and certainly not all the time, as it is an ongoing practice. Yet in authentic movement as psychotherapy the more the mover-client and witness-therapist can listen with an inward ear, accepting what is going on inside, the more they can be present to the complexity of feelings, thoughts etc., in the moment, without fear, and the higher the degree of congruence.

Congruence is the product of the witness-therapist's inner state and has an active quality and apparency (Tudor & Worrall, 1994) as received by the mover. The witness-therapist may reveal to the mover truths about what is going on for them in the presence of the mover's expression but also may not. The witness-therapist needs to remain, as far as possible, open to feelings, memories, images, sensations and thoughts, to live them, be them, but also crucially to communicate them to the mover-client if appropriate (Tudor & Worrall, 1994), that is, if they resonate with the movement spoken by the mover-client. The witness-therapist is aware of these feelings, thoughts etc., but allows the situation to determine whether they are revealed or not to the mover, and if so how.

By paying attention to their own inner experience whilst tracking the mover-client's movement and/or sound the witness-therapist enables a reduction in conditions of worth (that is to seek approval or avoid disappointment from others). This can lead to more alignment between the "real self" (organismic) and the self-perception. Importance is placed on being "real". The greater the communication of congruence by the witness-therapist the clearer that communication to the mover-client, that is, the less likely it is to have an ambiguous meaning. The witness-therapist is unified in gestures, speech and tone of voice as these arise from her unity, resulting in more clarity communicated from the mover-client.

The more congruent the witness-therapist is in the topic about which they are communicating the less they need to defend against, and the more open they can be to really listen to the mover-client. Rogers discovered facades need to be defended and this can get in the way of listening to the mover-client and the self. If a mover-client feels understood in so far as they have been able to express themself, it can result in them feeling warmth and positive regard from the witness-therapist. The mover-client then appears to experience fewer barriers to their communication and hence tends to become more congruent themself, more themself. Defensiveness decreases bit by bit. This leads the mover-client towards being more receptive to further communications from the witness-therapist (the desire to be seen).

Incongruence (seen to be detrimental to the psychotherapeutic process) is more directly perceived than congruence itself. Incongruence may result in loss of trust in the witness-therapist and a lack of safety reducing the effectiveness of the process. "The more genuine and congruent the counsellor the more probability there is that change in the personality in the client will occur" (Rogers, 1961, p. 62). In authentic movement a greater authenticity may be experienced by both mover and witness when there is congruence between them.

It is explicit in the person-centred theory that, even though the aim is not necessarily to increase the client's congruence this is the outcome of successful psychotherapy. In authentic movement one of the processes crucial to successful witnessing is the witness's congruence as experienced by the mover; there is the specific language used by the witness to support their communication of congruence.

In authentic movement the witness does not communicate to the mover their authenticity itself but their personal experiencing, which is the outcome of congruence rather than congruence itself. The expressive body (for example, gesture) and verbalization speak about the self in authentic movement. It might be useful to note that this indwelling or embodiment of experiencing by the witness is part of their response to the mover, and its helpfulness is a shared concept with the psychodynamic approach termed countertransference. Wilkins (1997) discusses the similarities and differences between these two notions.

In authentic movement there is a bi-directionality, just as in mother-infant relationships, with reciprocal interaction in the verbal sharing dialogue. There may be opportunities to speak of what is happening in the relationship in the here and now as in psychodynamic psychotherapy. The humanistic model emphasizes the real aspects of the relationship, however, for both humanistic and psychodynamic models, it is the relationship which is central albeit with differing roles and therapy elements. For example, in the humanistic model therapist self-disclosure might be acceptable if it serves a therapeutic need. The therapist may disclose to the client the impact on them of the movement seen such as sensations, images, feelings, thoughts and kinaesthetic impulses, although omitting their own personal history material/memories. Links may be made to previous client material communicating these in honest (congruent) reporting of the therapist's experience in the presence of the client movement. Here is a poem written during transition by a mover on being seen in the witness-mover relationship:

Follow to Follow

Fingers reach
stretch back
curve round
past the sigh of another
found
then
follow to follow
a shadow around
feel the hand lead
down
down
down
past the sun
into earth
into shadow
with sun on my back
moving inside
in the shadow within
into the dark
the black of night
where this self can't see
but knows
I'm seen.

(Extract from personal journal, Christina Bracegirdle, open training circle, 2015)

Summary

This chapter has provided the reader with some connections between concepts and processes found in relational integrative psychotherapy with those from the Discipline of Authentic Movement and illustrated with examples when it is practised as a form of psychotherapy. The relationship between therapist and client is key as has been shown in research into both humanistic and psychodynamic psychotherapy (Clarkson, 1995).

References

Adler, J. (1995). *Arching backward: The mystical initiation of a contemporary woman.* Inner Traditions.
Adler, J. (1999a). Body and soul. In P. Pallaro (Ed.), *Authentic movement: Essays by Mary Starks Whitehouse, Janet Adler and Joan Chodorow* (pp. 160–189). Jessica Kingsley.
Adler, J. (1999b). Who is the witness? A description of authentic movement. In P. Pallaro (Ed.), *Authentic movement: Essays by Mary Starks Whitehouse, Janet Adler and Joan Chodorow* (pp. 141–159). Jessica Kingsley.

Adler, J. (2002). *Offering from the conscious body: The discipline of authentic movement.* Inner Traditions.

Alexander, F., & French, T. M. (1946). *Psychoanalytic therapy: Principles and application.* Ronald Press.

Anderson, H. (2007). The heart and spirit of collaborative therapy: The philosophical stance – "A way of being" in relationship and conversation. In H. Anderson & G. D. Gerhart (Eds.), *Collaborative therapy: Relationships and conversations that make a difference.* Routledge.

Aposhyan, S. (1999). *Natural intelligence: Body-mind integration and human development.* Now Press.

Avstreih, Z. (2008). The body in psychotherapy: Dancing with the paradox. In F. J. Kaklauskas, S. Nimanheminda, L. Hoffman, & M. S. Jack (Eds.), *Brilliant sanity: Buddhist approaches to psychotherapy* (pp. 213–221). University of the Rockies.

Bacon, J. (2010). Sitting practice: Reflections on a woman's creative process. *Gender Forum, Women and Performance, 31.*

Barkai, Y. (2022). On the authentic movement model: A space for creation – A place to be. *American Journal of Dance Therapy, 44,* 4–20.

Benjamin, J. (1999). Recognition and destruction: An outline of inter-subjectivity. In S. Mitchell & L. Aron (Eds), *Relational psychoanalysis: The relation of a tradition.* Routledge.

Bracegirdle, C. (2015). *Authentic movement open circle indoors.* The Empty Studio, UK.

Bracegirdle, C. (2016). *Authentic movement training open circle.* The Empty Studio, UK.

Bracegirdle, C. (2023a). Personal communication of poems written from 2014 onwards when participating in authentic movement training circles online, outdoors and in The Empty Studio.

Bracegirdle, C. (2023b). A movers practice of transition in authentic movement: An embodied non-dual lived experience. *Body, Movement and Dance in Psychotherapy, 19*(4), 381–396. https://doi.org/10.1080/17432979.2023.2254834

Buber, M. (1958). *I and Thou* (2nd ed., R. G. Smith, Trans.). T & T Clark.

Bull, C. A. (2007). The discovery of deep ecology through the body. In P. Pallaro (Ed.), *Authentic movement: Moving the body, moving the self, being moved, volume two* (pp. 361–363). Jessica Kingsley Publishers.

Chodorow, J. (1991). *Dance therapy in depth: The moving imagination.* Routledge.

Chodorow, J. (1999). To move and be moved. In P. Pallaro (Ed.), *Authentic movement: Essays by Mary Starks Whitehouse, Janet Adler and Joan Chodorow* (pp. 267–278). Jessica Kingsley.

Clarkson, P. (1995). *The therapeutic relationship.* Whurr.

Damasio, A. R. (1996). The somatic marker hypothesis and the possible functions of the prefrontal cortex. *Philosophical Transactions of the Royal Society B: Biological Sciences, 351*(1346), 1413–1420.

Fleischer, K. (2020). The symbol in the body: The un-doing of a dissociation through embodied active imagination in Jungian analysis. *Journal of Analytical Psychology, 65*(3), 558–583.

Fleischer, K. (2023). Collective trauma, implicit memories, the body, and active imagination in Jungian analysis. *Journal of Analytical Psychology, 68*(2), 1–21.

Garcia-Diaz, S. (2018). The effect of the practice of authentic movement on the emotional state. *Arts in Psychotherapy, 58,* 17–26.

Geller, S. M. (2013). Therapeutic presence: An essential way of being. In M. Cooper, P. F. Schmid, M. O'Hara, & A. C. Bohart (Eds.), *Handbook of person-centred psychotherapy and counselling* (2nd ed., pp. 209–222). Palgrave.

Gendlin, E. T. (1981). *Focusing.* Bantam Books.

Gendlin, E. T. (1990). The small steps of the therapy process: How they come and how to help them come. In G. Lietaer, J. Rombauts, & R. Van Balen (Eds.), *Client-centered and experiential psychotherapy in the nineties* (pp. 205–224). Leuven University Press.

Gilbert, M., & Orlans, V. (2011). *Integrative therapy: 100 key points and techniques*. Routledge.
Goldhahn, E. (2003). Authentic movement and science. *A Moving Journal*, (Fall), 12–15.
Goldhahn, E. (2022). *Reflections on authentic movement: Theory, practice and arts-led research*. Routledge.
Hackney, P. (2002). *Making connections: Total body integration through Bartenieff fundamentals*. Routledge.
Kaimaxi, D., & Lakioti, A. (2021). The development of congruence: A thematic analysis of person-centered counselors' perspectives. *Person-Centered & Experiential Psychotherapies, 20*(3), 232–249.
Krishner, A. (2012). An integrative review of sensory marketing: Engaging the senses to affect perception, judgment and behavior. *Consumer Psychology, 22*(3), 332–351.
Lucchi, B. A. (1998). *Authentic movement as a training modality for private practice clinicians* (Unpublished doctoral dissertation). California Graduate Institute, Los Angeles.
Lucchi, B. A. (2018). Authentic movement as a training modality for private practice clinicians. *American Journal of Dance Therapy, 40*, 300–317, 305.
Marcow Speiser, V., & Franklin, M. (2007). Authentic movement as a meditative practice. *Pedagogy, Pluralism and Practice, 12*, 1–11.
Merleau-Ponty. (2002). *Phenomenology of perception* (2nd ed., C. Smith, Trans.). Routledge. (Original work published 1945).
Michalak, J., Troje, N. F., Fischer, J., Vollmar, P., Heidenreich, T., & Schulte, D. (2009). Embodiment of sadness and depression – Gait patterns associated with dysphoric mood. *Psychosomatic Medicine, 71*, 580–587. https://doi.org/10.1097/PSY.0b013e3181a2515c
Morrissey, B., & Sager, P. (Eds.). (2022). *Intimacy in emptiness: An evolution of embodied consciousness. Collected writings of Janet Adler*. Inner Traditions Press.
O'Brian, M., & Houston, G. (2007). *Integrative therapy*. Sage.
Ogden, P. (1997). Hakomi integrative somatics: Hands-on psychotherapy. In C. Caldwell (Ed.), *Getting in touch: The guide to new body-centered therapies* (pp. 153–178). Insert Publishers.
Ort, D., Moore, C., & Farber, B. A. (2022). Therapists' perspectives on positive regard. *Person-Centered & Experiential Psychotherapies, 22*(2), 139–153. https://doi.org/10.1080/14779757.2022.2104751
Pallaro, P. (Ed.). (2007a). *Authentic movement: Moving the body, moving the self, being moved: A collection of essays* (Vol. 2). Jessica Kingsley.
Pallaro, P. (2007b). Somatic countertransference: The therapist in relationship. In P. Pallaro (Ed.), *Authentic movement: Moving the body, moving the self, being moved: A collection of essays* (Vol. 2, pp. 176–193). Jessica Kingsley.
Payne, H. (2006). The body as container and expresser: Authentic movement groups in the development of wellbeing in our bodymindspirit. In J. Corrigall, H. Payne, & H. Wilkinson (Eds.), *About a body: Working with the embodied mind in psychotherapy* (pp. 162–181). Routledge.
Penfield, K. (2006). Another royal road: Freudian thought applied to authentic movement. In H. Payne (Ed.), *Dance movement therapy: Theory, research, and practice* (pp. 132–149). Routledge.
Perls, F., Hefferline, R. F., & Goodman, P. (1994). *Gestalt therapy excitement and growth in the human personality*. Souvenir Press.
Rogers, C. R. (1951). *Client-centered therapy; Its current practice, implications, and theory*. Houghton Mifflin.
Rogers, C. (1961). *Client-centered therapy*. Houghton-Mifflin.
Rogers, C. R. (1957). The necessary and sufficient conditions of therapeutic personality change. *Consulting Psychology, 21*(2), 95–103.
Rogers, C. (1977). *A therapist's view of psychotherapy: On becoming a person*. Constable.
Searle, Y., & Streng, I. (Eds.). (2001). *Where analysis meets the arts: The integration of the arts therapies with psychoanalytic theory*. Karnac Books Ltd.

Shafir, T. (2015). Body-based strategies for emotion regulation. In M. L. Bryant (Ed.), *Handbook on emotion regulation: Processes, cognitive effects and social consequences* (pp. 231–249). Nova Science Publishers.

Siegel, D. J. (2007). *The mindful brain: Reflection and attunement in the cultivation of well-being*. W. W. Norton and Company.

Solowoniuk, J., & Nixon, G. (2009). Introducing transpersonal phenomenology: The direct experience of a sudden awakening. *Paradoxica: Nondual Psychology, 1*.

Stromsted, T. (2009). Authentic movement: A dance with the divine. *Body, Movement and Dance in Psychotherapy, 4*(3), 201–213.

Stromsted, T. (2019). Witnessing practice: In the eyes of the beholder. In H. Payne, S. Koch, J. Tantia, with T. Fuchs (Eds.), *The Routledge international handbook: Embodied perspectives in psychotherapy: Approaches from dance movement and body psychotherapies* (pp. 95–103). Routledge.

Summers, F. (1994). *Object relations theories and psychopathology: A comprehensive text*. Analytic Press.

Tudor, K., & Worrall, M. (1994). Congruence reconsidered. *British Journal of Guidance and Counselling, 22*(2), 197–205.

Valle, R. S. (1998). Transpersonal awareness: Implications for phenomenological research. In R. S. Valle (Ed.), *Phenomenological inquiry in psychology: Existential and transpersonal dimensions* (pp. 270–280). Plenum Press.

Wallin, D. J. (2007). *Attachment in psychotherapy*. Guilford Press.

Whitehouse, M. S. (1999a). C. G. Jung and dance therapy: Two major principles. In P. Pallaro (Ed.), *Authentic movement: Essays by Mary Starks Whitehouse, Janet Adler and Joan Chodorow* (pp. 73–101). Jessica Kingsley.

Whitehouse, M. S. (1999b). The Tao of the body. In P. Pallaro (Ed.), *Authentic movement: Essays by Mary Starks Whitehouse, Janet Adler and Joan Chodorow* (pp. 41–50). Jessica Kingsley.

Whitehouse, M. S. (1999c). Reflections on a metamorphosis. In P. Pallaro (Ed.), *Authentic movement: Essays by Mary Starks Whitehouse, Janet Adler and Joan Chodorow* (pp. 58–62). Jessica Kingsley.

Wilkins, P. (1997, February). Congruence and countertransference; similarities and differences. *Counselling*, 36–41.

Winnicott, D. (1971). *Playing and reality*. Penguin.

Photograph 9.1 Two witnesses, one witness replaces the singing bowl after the movers have left the space

Credit: Photography by Lucie Payne

I attune to my truth through the access in the body
I join with healing companions, to share in the ups and downs of my inner journey who
support my becoming lighter
Spending time with my authentic self, my truth, is transformative
It speaks to me and serves lessons
It invites me to embody my learning carrying it with me
Accepting myself, loving myself, and meeting each part of me
with kindness and compassion
This can sustain when storms come, as they do, when I am overwhelmed and drenched
There is the intention – to be an asset to healing each one of us
and the world, both,
where there is in so much need in the web of humanity
and its interconnectivity with the earth.

Helen Payne

Chapter 9

Adapted Authentic Movement as a Gateway to Supporting People Living With Medically Unexplained Symptoms/Body Distress Disorder to Self-Manage

Abstract

This chapter provides an insight into how authentic movement has been modified to provide a model for working with people experiencing undiagnosed chronic distressing symptoms for which tests and scans return normal. There is often co-morbid anxiety and/or depression with these undiagnosable conditions (for example, with labels such as chronic fatigue, chronic pain, fibromyalgia, respiratory problems, digestive issues etc.). The term for such chronic bodily symptoms was medically unexplained symptoms which has now been outmoded to be included under the umbrella term body distress disorder in DSM5. Following a brief literature review of medically unexplained symptoms a novel intervention is introduced called The BodyMind Approach (TBMA) based on an adaption of authentic movement drawing on other arts and somatic practices. There is an explanation of the rationale for such a holistic, perceptual, experiential learning model which uses the bodily sensory experience as the vehicle towards exploratory expressive movement leading to self-understanding, the self-management of symptoms and an improved quality of life. Self-management has been used in several aspects of health care and in TBMA is employed for people living with chronic symptoms for which all tests and scan etc., return normal.

Introduction

The adaption of authentic movement (AM) to access meaning-making through engaging with sensation in undiagnosed chronic somatic symptoms is presented here. The chapter explains how employing the experience of the chronic, distressing bodily symptom as a gateway to understanding the self and gain a handle on managing the symptom and the accompanying emotional distress can improve quality of life despite the presence of the symptom.

The term medically unexplained symptoms (MUS) replaced the term psychosomatic conditions and is now subsumed under the term 'body distress disorder' in the DSM5 (American Psychiatric Association, 2013). These chronic symptoms are very distressing and debilitating conditions with all tests and scans returning without a diagnosis. Amongst the most frequently reported persistent somatic complaints in primary care are back pain, headache, abdominal symptoms and fatigue accounting for up to 50% of all consultations (Löwe et al., 2022). Around one third cannot be attributed to a recognized disease, although their prevalence

DOI: 10.4324/9781003479413-10

in chronic diseases is also high. For example, 70% of patients with chronic kidney disease have persistent fatigue (Fletcher et al., 2022); 63% with coronary heart disease have persistent pain in the arms, legs or joints (Kohlmann et al., 2013); and 31% with ulcerative colitis in remission have persistent gastrointestinal symptoms (Halpin & Ford, 2012). The persistent symptoms are often not specific to the organ systems in the primary condition (Hansen et al., 2022; Conway et al., 2011).

Labels such as chronic pain, fatigue, fibromyalgia (in the USA this is a diagnosis), irritable bowel syndrome, headache and back pain are included in these conditions. It may be that medicine has just not found an organic cause yet. Many chronic illnesses were not recognized until technology and/or advances in science enabled some conditions to receive a medical diagnosis. However, in the meantime the lack of an organic, pathological medical explanation leaves patients experiencing a "no man's land" of not knowing what is happening in their body and without supportive treatment.

Frequently, depression and anxiety accompany the bodily distress, and sometimes suicide attempts (Löwe et al., 2008; Torres et al., 2021). The capacity to work, functioning day-to-day and quality of life are limited. Over 20% of new primary care appointments are for such symptoms (Haller et al., 2015). Pain medication and clinics can treat the physicality of the symptoms, although there is little evidence that they help long term. Mental health services are provided; however, patients often resist any referral to them due to their physical explanatory model of their symptoms even though there is no medical evidence to support this. Many patients believe their anxiety and/or depression are caused by their physical condition attributing distress to a purely physical explanation often due to stigma and/or cultural beliefs around mental health or their personal understanding of illness. Additionally, there is only minor evidence cognitive approaches are helpful and none across all unexplained conditions (Leaviss et al., 2020).

Persistent physical symptoms remain the major unmet need in the management of many chronic conditions (McGing et al., 2021; Pope, 2020). Löwe et al. (2024, p. 1) call for a better understanding of the many factors involved in the persistence of somatic symptoms which could lead to "more specific, personalised, and mechanism-based treatment, and a reduction in the stigma patients commonly face". The design of The BodyMind Approach (TBMA) addresses both the personalized, mechanism-based approach and the stigma experienced by patients.

The following is an overview of how some embodied approaches have understood medically undiagnosed bodily symptoms.

Historical Background to Undiagnosed Somatic Conditions

With reference to psychoanalysis Breuer and Freud (1895), while treating Anna O for what was then labelled as "hysteria", understood these physical manifestations (such as paralysis) were a form of communication which may have valuable personal meaning. Breuer (1955) stated Anna O understood and resolved her symptoms by recalling a memory of the situation where they first occurred. Breuer and Freud demonstrated that these physical symptoms were expressions of nonconscious processes which could be understood by recalling memories of the origin of the symptoms (as in body memory) as well as through free association and dreamwork.

Of relevance to dance movement therapy Marion North (1972), a student of Von Laban (1973), demonstrated through her research that personality was expressed through nonverbal movement expression. Wilheim Reich (2013) posited that the way the body moves expresses personality. He influenced many body psychotherapies such as Bioenergetics (Lowen, 1994); Integrative Body Psychotherapy (Rosenberg, 1985); Biosynthesis (Boadella, 1987); as well as the trauma-informed approaches such as Sensorimotor Psychotherapy (Ogden, 2014), Rothschild's (2000) psychophysiological model and Levine's (1997) Somatic Experiencing method.

Body psychotherapies reject the mind-body duality. Rather they share the notion there is bidirectionality between body and mind, and that feelings are embodied i.e., the body holds and expresses emotions. Unfortunately, to date, there is little evidence to support these interventions hence they are not yet a replacement for those which have a research basis. Ideas such as polyvagal theory, incorporated into the latter two models, have yet to be proven. In contrast, the rigorous research by Van der Kolk (2014) provides evidence for trauma treatment, moving away from the talking and drug therapies towards an alternative model healing mind, brain and body.

Focussing (Gendlin, 1978, 1982, 1996) employs the body as a pathway to experiencing the inner voice which may indicate a direction for change. Gendlin recognized the value of bodily symptoms as the language of unspoken, pre-conscious processes and that they may unlock meaningful experiences. According to Gendlin, by attending to the physical sensory experience (the felt sense) the personal, bodily meaning releases held energy. What is at the edge of awareness may come into awareness through an empathic conversation between the bodily felt sense of the symptom and the conceptual aspects of self. Accessing the felt sense can be cultivated through, for example, progressive relaxation and guided imagery to facilitate nonverbal bodily awareness. Distressing, chronic physical symptoms need to be heard and understood in a relational context. The bodily felt experience of the symptoms may reveal meaning to support a feeling of greater control.

Embodiment research reminds us that body memory with its phenomenology of the lived-body (Merleau-Ponty, 1962) and its dynamic aspects (Fuchs, 2000, 2012) has six forms: procedural, situational, intercorporeal, incorporative, pain and traumatic (Fuchs, 2011). Intercorporeal, pain and traumatic memory are most relevant to distressing, chronic, bodily symptoms. It holds a synopsis of the history of interactions with others and unconsciously affects further encounters. Bodies interact and understand each other in these embodied interactions. Merleau-Ponty

(1962, 1989) named this influence of pre-reflective bodily understanding as inter-corporeality. Painful experiences leading to fear and avoidance of fear-related situations can be recorded into the body memory (possibly, but not only, leading to symptoms for which tests and scans come back negative yet cause great distress). To demonstrate support for this notion, Fillingim et al. (1999) found up to 50% of all patients diagnosed with somatoform pain disorders suffered severe pain or violence in childhood.

People may learn avoidance strategies to dissociate from, forget, protect or isolate themselves from traumatic memory since trauma (or more accurately the responses to it) may not have been successfully integrated into a meaningful context. The trauma may have been developmental and pre-verbal and/or have faded from conscious recall although it remains present in the lived body memory. When a situation evokes the trauma again, the body recollects it as if it were occurring in the present moment and the physiological fight, flight, freeze, fold, faint responses occur (for example increased heart rate, dry mouth, sweating or shut down etc.). It is important to note the precursor of persistent somatic symptoms for which all tests and scans return normal is not necessarily trauma; there are normally multiple factors involved. There follows an introduction to TBMA for working with people experiencing these chronic conditions.

The BodyMind Approach

TBMA is designed for people with somatic symptoms for which all investigations return with normal findings. It is a biopsychosocial intervention focussing on the self-management of symptoms. It is practised with small groups face-to-face over 12 weekly × two hourly sessions. The group format enables patients to feel less isolated and more supported. For example, others in the group will have experienced similar dismissals of their symptoms from health professionals.

The research evidence on TBMA showed outcomes were sustained over three and six months. Findings included decreased symptom distress (or complete disappearance of symptoms), depression and anxiety and increased activity levels, wellbeing and overall functioning. Additionally, patients did not return to primary care for these symptoms post intervention or at follow-up (three and six months). Some patients reported increased social activity and disappearance of symptoms, although this was never the goal (Payne & Stott, 2010; Payne & Brooks, 2016, 2018, 2019, 2020). (For a full review of TBMA, please see Payne & Brooks, 2025.) One of the major outcomes from the research is acceptance of the symptoms which is believed to be key to self-management.

Patients with MUS have difficulties accepting their somatic symptoms for two reasons. Firstly, the health professionals constantly say there is nothing wrong with them (all tests and scans coming back as normal). This is little comfort when the bodily and emotional experience (co-morbid depression and/or anxiety) is that of distress. Secondly, the experience of the symptoms for the patient is that they are physical, and it is this which makes it so difficult to cultivate acceptance that there is nothing wrong. There is a mismatch between the lack of an organic diagnosis and experience.

In authentic movement the body does not lie; the movement conveys what is experienced both physically and emotionally. TBMA although informed by authentic movement, the practice has been adapted to the population and context. The authenticity in the movement helps the individual to consider the meaning of the symptom from the embodied experience, and in a different way gain new insight about the meaning of the symptom within their situation and perhaps aid acceptance. It can be assumed, this acceptance helps reduce the aforementioned conflict and promote the willingness or motivation to self-manage, i.e., take control and reduce visits to healthcare professionals.

Another important element in the biopsychosocial model of TBMA is that of the social relationships within the group and between the facilitator and the group. The isolation individuals with these symptoms experience is addressed by the group process and by the relational movement practices. Many will have felt out of control because no one could find out what is wrong, and they suffer alone; friends and family having heard it all before lose interest, and their support is lost.

Groups are heterogeneous with reference to symptoms, however patients have often had very similar experiences within the health care system, for example not being believed, called malingerers etc. The TBMA groups therefore provide for support and a universality of experience and purpose. In TBMA adapted authentic movement (aAM) considers the importance of the relationship between mover and witness, participant and facilitator, as well as the relationship between the participant and their symptom/s.

Focussing on an embodied sensation such as the breath or movement to begin with helps individuals to experience a non-distressing aspect of their body. This gives confidence for further exploration of the site of bodily distress at a later stage. These practices support their capacity to inhibit other bodily sensations while focussing on one which is non-distressing (unless there is a respiratory symptom).

Interoception

Interoception is the feeing we have of inner bodily sensations such as the heartbeat, muscle tension, digestive processes, position and movement, all engaging the sensory self. All emotions start in the body. The seeing of the lion is the stimulus which leads to, for example, heart rate increasing, perspiration and so on which leads to the feeling of fear (fear being interpreted by the brain from the body signals) and running away. It is a bottom-up survival mechanism. Body sensation is crucial for emotion. Muscle tension (Khalsa et al., 2018), for example, can be felt as we move. In authentic movement the visceral movement of the mover is attended to mindfully through proprioception and the kinaesthetic sense. The witness seeing the action experiences it pre-consciously in their own body through the mirror neurones. This action (as seen by the witness and undertaken by the mover) can evoke memories, images, other sensations, feelings and thoughts etc. Both mover and witness may or may not share similar experiences in the subsequent verbal dialogue between them, however at the very least the witness should be able to report they have seen the action/movement. Even though the witness experience (for example, the impact of the action on them) may be different from that reported by the mover, the witness offering may give the mover food for thought.

There is a bidirectional process between the body and the brain, signals sent both ways with the driver being the interaction between the two and how that is interpreted by the brain. The insula is the primary interoceptive area in the brain, as most signals from the body are integrated there to support emotional regulation. The interpretation of our interoceptive signals takes place within the context of the current life situation and/or history. This context determines the attentional biases, such as hyper and hypo vigilance towards the body, and thus affects the accuracy in the perception of the symptom (Khalsa et al., 2017). Cognitive biases such as catastrophizing may also be involved. However, what appears to be apparent catastrophizing may actually be logical due to the hypervigilance from past traumatic event/s. Distorted physiological sensitivity results in perceiving normal changes in, for example, the heartbeat, interpreted as a panic attack.

Following this argument further it is hypothesized here that patients with chronic somatic symptoms which have no diagnosis could have a reduced capacity to perceive accurate interoception messages. It is impossible to be accurate because there is no inhibition of sensation which detracts from accurate interoception. Avoiding the sensations by distraction has the opposite effect long term. Learning to inhibit other sensations whilst attending to, for example, the breath or movement in aAM (normally with eyes closed/half closed depending on the degree of anxiety present) helps to become present to the sensation and the self. It is important to point out that all practices in aAM will be with the symptom in mind.

Since aAM and other somatic practices in TBMA emphasize the body first and foremost the term "bodymindfulness" has been coined. An example is the practice of mindful movement such as slow walking, noticing each step and how the foot is placed on the floor induces increased body awareness from within. Or, focussing on slowing down the breath, for example, noticing it come in through the nose, go down the back of the throat and into the lungs which, together with the abdomen, expand before pausing then exhaling, again through the nose, thereby attending to the contraction and shrinking of the torso etc., to cultivate interoceptive exposure. Furthermore, authentic movement could be conceived of as mindful movement or kinetic meditation.

There has been research into the role of interoception and somatic symptoms, in particular chronic pain, for example the systematic review by Horsburgh et al. (2024). It recommended behaviour change interventions such as interoceptive exposure, mindfulness and slow breathing. Schaefer et al. (2014) showed in patients with chronic pain there was an inhibition of distractions when focussing on the heartbeat. This resulted in less pain after such training as well as a reduction in negative emotions, whilst Gnall et al. (2024) in a meta-analysis suggest mind-body therapies work well to reduce chronic pain. Since participants and their symptoms feel accepted in the group, they feel safe enough to enter into these explorations. This is particularly important if they undertake practices with closed eyes.

To conclude, interoception is a key factor in undiagnosed somatic conditions and accompanying poor mental health with a significant role in chronic pain (many MUS patients experience this condition). Altered body awareness may underlie the persistent discomfort. More studies on the interrelationship between neuroscience, psychology and clinical practice to manage distressing somatic conditions and mental health correlates are needed.

Attending to body sensations without judgement, but with kind inner witnessing/observation from within may be crucial to increasing interoception accuracy for MUS patients.

Adapted Authentic Movement

Authentic movement, as offered in TBMA, has been specifically adapted and designed to enable meaning-making to emerge from the movement experience emerging from the patient's experience of any bodily sensation connected to the symptom (adapted authentic movement/aAM). The insights gained support the self-management strategies which patients may then follow to live a more fruitful life despite their symptoms.

The rationale for using elements of authentic movement with this patient population is twofold. Firstly, it helps increase body awareness whereby the embodied practice of attending to the inner witness (the observing self), who notices the body and its sensations (through interoception), is separated out from the one who experiences the body as a dynamic, enactive entity. An external witness is provided too, i.e., the one who takes the role of witness external to the mover in their dynamic, moving body. This role may be occupied by the facilitator as in the early stages of the TBMA programme, although later it may be a peer. This outer witness seeing the mover enables the nurturing of the mover's inner witness to become stronger in being more aware of their bodily signals. The more we are clearly seen by another the more we can clearly see ourselves. When the patient is seen in their body and its expression, new parts of the self are brought into consciousness. When the patient moves from their sensory experience, as presented by their symptom, they begin to see how the symptom can be a symbol for aspects of themselves previously unknown and unseen. They see how their symptom is part of them, not uninvolved in their emotional life.

Patients are invited to bear their symptom in mind when engaging in movement, allowing sensation experienced in the body to bubble up and be surfaced through expressive movement. The benign, compassionate witness sees the movers outwardly expressed unchoreographed action, and its impact on her bodymind whether that be feelings, sensation, memories, kinaesthetic impulses (which are never acted out), images or thoughts etc.

If a transition is used following the movement piece, arts materials and/or journalling are made available to both witness and mover. These help to hold the embodied experience before languaging in the present tense (to keep the experience current i.e., it revives the embodied experience) may bring forward a greater insight since the movement and symptom have been the focus. In the languaging there is a repetition through the reporting back of movements recalled in the present tense to the witness, and then hearing the offering from the witness in the present tense (although strange) builds a confirmation of the wisdom of the body and a different sort of knowing. The repetition confirms being seen, by both the mover to herself and by the witness too, a validation for the mover i.e., to be seen. What has until now been undiscovered may become recognized. For example, one participant reported experiencing herself as if a lion, clawing at the air as a symbol of the symptom, and this led her to realize the strength of her anger. The witness also reports seeing the clawing lion and describes in detail the movements and the image she experienced. The faithful making of the action and the recounting of it can either bring a confirmation from the witness to the mover or a difference in insight, which the mover can take or leave. This connection between the mover and the witness confirms the intelligence of the physical subjective body.

The expressed movement (or sound) arising in the mover emerges from a place where the sensation is located and so is truly connected to the self. The expression is authentic and consequently is clear to the witness. This embodied unity, or congruence, brings about clarity of presence in the witness and in the mover's expression.

Presence entails a here and now indivisible relationship to the self, another and the transpersonal, and is the source from which grows all that it means to be human. The practice of authentic movement enables access to the present moment, to our authenticity and to enhanced presence to self and others. Through this experience of presence, mindfulness is experienced as "bodymindfulness" and an acceptance of all the parts of the self as embodied. Any changes in perception of the symptoms are thus deeply connected to the patient's bones, muscles, neuronal networks, lymphatic system, fascia etc., to bring forth lasting change.

Another important aspect of TBMA is how it indirectly addresses adult attachment (for further details see Payne & Brooks, 2020). The patient's attachment patterns present in relation to their symptom and in relation to the health professionals from whom they have sought help. The patterns may become apparent through their relationship with the facilitator and/or witness. For example, the inner negative, critical judge which often makes itself known to this population may be projected onto the witness by the mover, creating fear in the mover. It may also happen the other way around whereby the witness projects their critical judge onto the mover. However, after experiencing little or no judgement over time as modelled by the facilitator the critical judge melts into the experience of a benign and kind, supportive outer, and inner, witness in the mover and witness. This helps make changes in perception towards their initial presenting symptom and their body. Patients begin to re-associate with their body and re-claim parts they had previously split off as "bad" and needing to be "got rid of" (understandable as symptoms can be so very debilitating). Alternatively, they begin to own aspects of themselves that they may have converted into a physical manifestation of their inner suffering which becomes the symptom/s.

This population, who frequently visit their GP, are not from backgrounds where body practices or movement features in their lives. Therefore, adaption of authentic movement to their lived experience is required both in terminology and practice.

There are numerous barriers to expression through movement, especially in the general population. Self-consciousness and feeling exposed is one such obstacle. In TBMA these fears are overcome by enabling patients to feel safe in their expression through small gestural movement especially at the beginning of the programme. This safety is provided by the facilitator, experienced in holding groups of adults and aware of the need for a safe environment both physically and psychologically. Furthermore, and in particular, patients are invited to use their hands (termed "making an action or gesture") solely, in expressing their lived experience of the inner bodily sensation of their symptom/s. Hands are used in our communication etc., all the time. People are used to expressing themselves with their hands, even with emojis! Therefore, hands are safer to employ for the layperson as a pathway to expression from the body than whole-body movement normally found in authentic movement, at least at the outset until confidence increases. Restricting a patient's expression in action to their hands makes it possible for them to feel secure, even with eyes closed, in the presence of their witness, firstly with the facilitator, then later with a peer.

The timeframe for the gestures is short, for example only two or three minutes. There may be a transition time of five minutes to record any element which was significant by writing in their personal journal. Additionally, mark-making is suggested as an option and felt tips and paper provided if required.

Rather than closing eyes as in the traditional model of authentic movement, if too anxiety-provoking it is suggested that patients gaze downwards, or half close their eyes to cultivate an inner focus of attention. If a patient is still too anxious to even gaze downwards, it is suggested they look at their abdomen to see it moving up and down with the in and outward breath. Then, with an inward focus, encouraging them to feel the rise and fall of the abdomen's movement from the inside. Additionally, patients in TBMA groups are normally seated in a circle of chairs which, although limiting mobility, gives a feeling of safety. All members can be seen by each other and the facilitator. Practices are normally undertaken in chairs at least at the beginning of the programme.

The aAM allows for safety, reducing self-consciousness and vulnerability yet facilitating the beginning of distancing between the inner lived sensation of the symptom and themselves, making for a relationship with the symptom (Selu, 2020). The outward expression of the hand gestures (just one hand to start with perhaps) representing the feeling of the sensation can create a symbol which can be useful when making meaning of the symptom. For example, to start with simply expressing in gesture/s what the symptom feels like from the inside or later in the programme asking the symptom about its nature or its purpose in their life and expressing that through hand gestures.

The witness for the hand actions is initially solely the group facilitator, who makes eye contact with each participant prior to the gesture/s being made. The facilitator is benign, sees, non-judgementally and without projection or interpretation, the gestures. In the offering phase the witness recalls her own experience in the presence of the gestures. When there is resonance, it is termed a unitive experience whereas when they differ it becomes a differentiated experience. Any personal material such as memories evoked would not be shared with the patient-mover, however. This is because the witness is there in the service of the patient, and their personal content may not be helpful to their mover.

When someone listens to and aligns with the bodily experiences of another this process has been described as resonance (Gendlin, 1978), empathy (Rogers, 1957) or attunement (Cooper, 2001). The non-interpretive, non-judgemental offering from a witness can contribute to increased understanding of the symptom in relation to the patient's everyday life/context and the interaction with their inner psychological world. This increased understanding can provide for a feeling of being more in control, which may cultivate less anxiety/depression and the capacity to get on with their lives, despite the symptoms. The understanding is noted in the patient's personal journal and later, in discussion with the facilitator, integrated into an action plan for embodying new self-management habits over the subsequent six months once the group has ended.

When participants have been scaffolded into the role of witness, they are able to see clearly and make offerings based on the facilitator's modelling of the role and languaging. Reading another's feelings through nonverbal communication is essential to normal communication. Empathy towards another's expressions of injury/illness/physical pain and/or feeling sympathy or compassion is natural, at times strongly identifying with another's physical suffering (Davis, 2018). Research on nonverbal communication has shown that for perceiving positive emotional effects in communication, people rely 7% on the words spoken, 38% on vocal elements and intonation, and 55% on facial cues (Mehrabian, 1971). Nevertheless, this formula has been criticized due to small size samples of women only, focussing on emotion and feeling topics solely, an artificial laboratory setting, only considering facial expressions, with no follow-up studies or actual conversations taking place (Dickinson, 2024). Despite this, although hand gestures are used for the intended action, facial signals and any vocalization will be received by the witness as well, which can embellish their empathetic/compassionate responses by, and impact of the action on, the witness.

Exploring bodily symptoms through creative, aAM together with self-reflective mark-making and writing during a short transitional period, then reporting the moving experience followed by witness offerings and dialoguing all enable the body to speak its mind.

Vignettes

Preamble

These three vignettes are examples of a later phase of the TBMA programme in which participants are paired up into a dyad in the role of witness and mover with the mover having the option to move anywhere in the space using whole body movement if desired for ten minutes. Timekeeping is by the facilitator. The setting is a community hall near to the GP surgery. The hall floor has been swept and chairs and tables put along one side of the room against the wall. All other objects have been removed to make the space as clear as possible.

The mover speaking: I am wandering around the room on all fours. I touch with my hands something metallic and cold (a leg of a table). I grab it and hold onto it while my legs are restless in motion, moving the rest of my body slowly and relying on the holding and trusting. It is as though I am in the water and when my hands find that metallic, cold thing I feel safer. I find an anchor that saved me.

The witness's offering: In the presence of these movements, I feel alert and slightly preoccupied. I imagine the sea as there are a lot of different emotions passing through my mind. As my mover grabs the metallic thing, I see the whole of her body's tension lessen.

The mover speaking in the dialogue ensuing: I am in a "tsunami" of difficult sensations and emotions and now feel seen as you recount your resonance with my experience. With reference to my symptom, I have learned I have been unanchored and emotions overwhelmed me. There is now an understanding of the need to find a way to anchor myself, to feel safer and less tense.

Commentary: This insight and goal will then be recorded in the mover's personal journal and entered into an action plan to embed a new habit for managing their symptoms going forward.

Preamble

This person has a symptom of a burning sensation felt in the whole body. There is no diagnosis except possibly fibromyalgia. Medication is not helping.

This practice is offered towards the end of the 12 sessions. The participants have been working in dyads for two sessions in both mover and witness roles. In this dyad, there is five minutes of whole-body movement with no transition. The focus is then on one movement that the mover recalls.

After the mover finishes their movement, they sit with the witness and talk in the present tense recalling their movement, their accompanying images, sensations, thoughts as well as their feelings, if there are any of these.

The mover speaking: I am standing still, feeling a burning sensation pervading my whole body. It is familiar. I focus on my breathing, my chest is lifting and dropping. My arms move symmetrically up, my hands are tense, I'm stretching all my body, I want to reach up to the sky. I'm stretching and I struggle, my hands want to reach something, there is no ladder, no hook to grab. I keep stretching up, my whole-body aching. The movement makes my mind say something: "I can, and I will". Although it feels insurmountable, I'm on this journey now.

I move my legs on the spot as if walking while I keep stretching my whole body upwards. I find a branch, it feels good, it is a support. Ah, that is my hand touching the other arm, I feel it with my hand. Yes, my arm, feels so strong so powerful. I keep moving on the spot, I can keep my balance by moving my legs while I stretch up, holding onto the branch, which is my arm. I can continue, but the bell rings, it tells me that I need to finish. My journey has just started but I have just been up there, I know now that I have the power to reach up and go to places with no pain, even for a few minutes. My support is in me!

The witness's offering: The other in the role of witness speaks of their experience while regarding the movement that the mover has recalled. The witness has been attending to their own feelings, sensation, thoughts, images and body reactions and is reminded to give no judgements or interpretations. Their images are shared, and as often as they resonate with the mover's words, helping the mover to add more to what they found.

In the presence of these movements of which you speak, I see someone struggling to go to the other side of the mountain, the peak is high, the route is vertical (my interpretation). I feel tension in my body and a strong feeling of wanting to give some of my strength as I see a lot of energy is being used for the ascending (my interpretation). I want to lift that body up and want to shout encouraging words (kinaesthetic impulse not acted upon). The effort to keep silent makes my shoulder lift very slightly as I see that body projected up high, I am lost in the movement repetition of stretching, in that I can feel my body relaxing, I trust that the motion will serve the purpose.

Commentary: The mover finds the witness's image of the mountain peak and the vertical route very touching, as they fit with her own imagery. She feels seen and feels how empowering it is to have experienced the movement without pain. Her action plan will refer to this image to support her working towards feeling supported in her everyday life.

Preamble

This participant suffers from frozen arms and hands, the pain slowly insinuated in the arms, then reached into the hands. There was no medical diagnosis. They were unable to hold a pen or a cup; it severely affected the quality of their life. After the first session, they announced that they were not returning: as a scientist, they did not believe the group would be of any help in reducing their symptoms. They were asked to keep going as they had nothing to lose. This opened the doorway for the participant to have a very significant experience in the seventh session when in a group whole body move, the whole group were invited to move with only the facilitator as witness.

The participants returned to the circle in silence. They are given time for a transition. They are invited to write or draw in their journal. After that this participant speaks first.

The mover speaking: I feel an impulse to stand up from the circle. I walk tentatively as my eyes are closed. My arms are beside my body, I wander slowly. Soon I am stopped by someone. Their hands are placed on my arms, gently searching for one of my elbows then the other. They are standing in front of me, holding my elbows, their arms touching softly on my arms. I stand still, I let my arms be held by their hands, my hands and arms rest on their lower arms. They are moving my arms, still held at the elbows, my upper body swings, one shoulder moves forward then the other and again, I feel their warm lower arms and hands: the heat transferring to my arms and hands. I am holding the other elbows, I feel the movement, slowly I find myself liking to be moved. I relax. I feel waves of heat travelling through my body. I feel sensation in my hands. We remain standing whilst I am moved and perceive the other moving. I lose sense of time.

The facilitator witness speaking: I see hands holding another body's arms and feel first cold shivers through my back. Then as I glance again, the arms seem attracted by an opposite force and seem glued together like magnets. I am reassured by the moving silent dialogue of arms holding. I feel hopeful as I see the arms that are held, holding as well.

Facilitator commentary: In the next session this participant announced to the group that they fully believed in the effectiveness of authentic movement. They told the group of their experience going home after the session that evening. They had an explosion of emotion, tears came down to their face, they found themself sobbing, they were tears of sadness, pain and anger, they said. They shared that in their tears and sadness there was a painful memory of early loss, at the time they were told not to show emotions. They reported their symptoms had receded. They were able to hold a cup and do many more functions as the "ice" in their lower arms and hands slowly melted. They understood the emotional connection with the symptoms.

Summary

This chapter has introduced medically unexplained symptoms, the history of embodied approaches and those for persistent physical symptoms (previously termed psychosomatic conditions), whether or not due to trauma. It highlighted how the self is first and foremost born out of body sensations, how sensation is crucial for emotion, how emotions start in the body, reflected in the body signals and interpreted by the brain. The importance of interoception to emotional regulation was emphasized. There was an exploration of how an adapted form of authentic movement (aAM), a key method in TBMA, can engage this hard-to-reach patient population who experience debilitating and distressing chronic bodily symptoms for which there are limited sustainable and effective interventions. Illustrated by vignettes of how participants responded to the model, the explanatory rationale for employing aAM has been provided for the reader. Three vignettes from practice provide illustrations of how aAM supported patients to learn more about themselves and their symptoms to take forward in their self-management.

References

Adler, J. (2002). *Offering from the conscious body: The discipline of authentic movement*. Inner Tradition.

American Psychiatric Association. (2013). *Diagnostic and statistical manual of mental disorders* (5th ed.). American Psychiatric Association.

Boadella, D. (1987). *An introduction to biosynthesis*. Routledge and Kegan Paul Ltd.

Breuer, J. (1955). Fräulein Anna O. In S. Freud & J. Strachey (Eds.), *The standard edition of the complete psychological works of Sigmund Freud* (Vol. II). Hogarth Press.

Breuer, J., & Freud, S. (1895). *Studies on hysteria* (Vol. 2, Standard ed.). Hogarth Press & The Institute of Psychoanalysis.

Conway, A. M., Nordon, I. M., Hinchliffe, R. J., Thompson, M. M., & Loftus, I. M. (2011). Patient-reported symptoms are independent of disease severity in patients with primary varicose veins. *Vascular, 19*, 262–268.

Cooper, M. (2001). Embodied empathy. In S. Haugh & T. Merry (Eds.), *Rogers' therapeutic conditions: Evolution, theory and practice. Vol. 2: Empathy* (pp. 218–229). PCCS Books.

Davis, M. H. (2018). *Empathy: A social psychological approach*. Routledge. (Original work published 1994).

Dickinson, K. (2024). *The 7–38–55 rule: Debunking the golden ratio of conversation*. The Learning Curve, May. https://bigthink.com/the-learning-curve/the-7-38-55-rule-debunking-the-golden-ratio-of-conversation/

Fletcher, B. R., Damery, S., Aiyegbusi, O. L., Anderson, N., Calvert, M., Cockwell, P., et al. (2022). Symptom burden and health-related quality of life in chronic kidney disease: A global systematic review and meta-analysis. *PLoS Med, 19*(4), e1003954. https://doi.org/10.1371/journal.pmed.1003954

Fillingim, R. B., Wilkinson, C. S., & Powell, T. (1999). Self-reported abuse history and pain complaints among young adults. *The Clinical Journal of Pain, 15*(2), 85–91. https://doi.org/10.1097/00002508-199906000-00004

Fuchs, T. (2000). Das Gedächtnis des Leibes [The memory of the body]. *Phänomenologische Forschungen, 5*, 71–89.

Fuchs, T. (2011). Body memory and the unconscious. In D. Lohmar & J. Brudzinska (Eds.), *Founding psychoanalysis. Phenomenological theory of subjectivity and the psychoanalytical experience* (pp. 69–82). Dordrecht: Kluwer.

Fuchs, T. (2012). The phenomenology of body memory. In S. C. Koch, T. Fuchs, M. Summa, & C. Müller (Eds.), Body *memory, metaphor and movement* (pp. 84–89). John Benjamins.

Gendlin, E. T. (1978). *Focusing*. Everest House.

Gendlin, E. T. (1982). *Focusing* (2nd ed.). Bantam Books.

Gendlin, E. T. (1996). *Focusing oriented therapy*. The Guilford Press.

Gnall, K. E., Sinnott, S. M., Laumann, L. E., Park, C. L., David, A., & Emrich, M. (2024). Changes in interoception in mind-body therapies for chronic pain: A systematic review and meta-analysis. *International Journal of Behavioral Medicine, 31*, 833–847. https://doi.org/10.1007/s12529-023-10249-z

Haller, H., Cramer, H., & Lauche, R. (2015). Somatoform disorders and medically unexplained symptoms in primary care: A systematic review and meta-analysis of prevalence. *Deutsches Ärzteblatt International, 112*, 279–287. https://doi.org/10.3238/arztebl.2015.0279

Halpin, S. J., & Ford, A. C. (2012). Prevalence of symptoms meeting criteria for irritable bowel syndrome in inflammatory bowel disease: Systematic review and meta-analysis. *The American Journal of Gastroenterology, 107*, 1474–1482.

Hansen, L., Chang, M. F., Hiatt, S., Dieckmann, N. F., Mitra, A., Lyons, K. S., & Lee, C. S. (2022). Symptom classes in decompensated liver disease. *Clinical Gastroenterology and Hepatology, 20*, 2551–2557.e1

Horsburgh, A., Summers, S. J., Lewis, A., Keegan, R. J., & Flood, A. (2024). The relationship between pain and interoception: A systematic review and meta-analysis. *The Journal of Pain, 25*, 104476. https://doi.org/10.1016/j.jpain.2024.01.341

Khalsa, S. S., Adolphs, R., Cameron, O. G., Critchley, H. D., Davenport, P. W., Feinstein, J. S., Feusner, J. D., Garfinkel, S. N., Lane, R. D., Mehling, W. E., & Zucker, N. (2018). Interoception and mental health: A roadmap. *Biological Psychiatry: Cognitive Neuroscience and Neuroimaging, 3*(6), 501–513. https://doi.org/10.1016/j.bpsc.2017.12.004

Khalsa, S. S., Portnoff, L. C., McCurdy-McKinnon, D., & Feusner, J. D. (2017). What happens after treatment? A systematic review of relapse, remission, and recovery in anorexia nervosa. *Journal of Eating Disorders, 5*, 20. https://doi.org/10.1186/s40337-017-0145-3

Kohlmann, S., Gierk, B., & Hümmelgen, M. (2013). Somatic symptoms in patients with coronary heart disease: Prevalence, risk factors, and quality of life. *JAMA Internal Medicine, 173*, 1469–1471.

Levine, P. (1997). *Waking the tiger: Healing trauma.* Simon and Schuster, UK.

Leaviss, J., Davis, S., Ren, S., Hamilton, J., Scope, A., Booth, A., Sutton, A., Parry, G., Buszewicz, M., Moss-Morris, R., & White, P. (2020). Behavioural modification interventions for medically unexplained symptoms in primary care: Systematic reviews and economic evaluation. *Health Technology Assessment, 24*(46), 1–490. https://doi.org/10.3310/hta24460

Löwe, B., Andresen, V., Andresen, V., Van den Bergh, O., Huber, T. B., von dem Knesebeck, O., Lohse, A. W., Nestoriuc, Y., Schneider, G., Schneider, S. W., Schramm, C., & Toussaint, A. (2022). Persistent somatic symptoms across diseases – From risk factors to modification: Scientific framework and overarching protocol of the interdisciplinary SOMACROSS research unit (RU 5211). *BMJ Open, 12*, e057596.

Löwe, B., Spitzer, R. L., Williams, J. B., Mussell, M., Schellberg, D., & Kroenke, K. (2008). Depression, anxiety and somatization in primary care: Syndrome overlap and functional impairment. *General Hospital Psychiatry, 30*, 191–199.

Löwe, B., Toussaint, A., Rosmalen, J. G., Huang, W. L., Burton, C., Weigel, A., Levenson, J. L., Henningsen, P. (2024). Persistent physical symptoms: Definition, genesis, and management. *The Lancet, 403*, 10444, 2649–2662. https://doi.org/10.1016/S0140-6736(24)00623-8

Lowen, A. (1994). *Bioenergetics: The revolutionary therapy that uses the language of the body to heal the problems of the mind.* Penguin books. ISBN: 0140194711.

McGing, J. J., Radford, S. J., Francis, S. T., Serres, S., Greenhaff, P. L., & Moran, G. W. (2021). Review article: The aetiology of fatigue in inflammatory bowel disease and potential therapeutic management strategies. *Alimentary Pharmacology & Therapeutics*, *54*(4), 368–387. https://doi.org/10.1111/apt.16465

Mehrabian, A. (1971). *Silent messages*. Wadsworth.

Merleau-Ponty, M. (1962). *Phenomenology of perception* (C. Smith, Trans.). Routledge and Kegan Paul.

Merleau-Ponty, M. (1989). *Phenomenology of perception* (C. Smith, Trans., with revisions by F. Williams & D. Gurrie). Routledge.

North, M. (1972). *Personality assessment through movement*. McDonald and Evans.

Ogden, P. (2014). *Sensorimotor psychotherapy – Interventions for trauma and attachment*. Norton Series on Interpersonal Neurobiology, Norton Books.

Payne, H., & Brooks, S. (2016). Clinical outcomes and cost benefits from The BodyMind Approach™ for patients with medically unexplained symptoms in primary health care in England: Practice-based evidence. *Arts in Psychotherapy*, *47*, 55–65.

Payne, H., & Brooks, S. (2018). Different strokes for different folks: The BodyMind approach as a learning tool for patients with medically unexplained symptoms to self-manage. *Frontiers in Psychology*. https://doi.org/10.3389/fpsyg.2018.02222

Payne, H., & Brooks, S. (2019, November 6). Medically unexplained symptoms and attachment theory: The BodyMind Approach®. *Frontiers in Psychology*, *10*, 1818. https://doi.org/10.3389/fpsyg.2019.01818

Payne, H., & Brooks, S. (2020, December 7). A qualitative study of the views of patients with medically unexplained symptoms on The BodyMind Approach®: Employing embodied methods and arts practices for self-management. *Frontiers in Psychology*, *11*, section Health Psychology.

Payne, H., & Brooks, S. (2025). *Management of distressing bodily symptoms in health: The BodyMind approach using a biopsychosocial model*. Routledge.

Payne, H., & Stott, D. (2010). Change in the moving bodymind: Quantitative results from a pilot study on the BodyMind Approach (BMA) as groupwork for patients with medically unexplained symptoms (MUS). *Counselling & Psychotherapy Research*, *10*(4), 295–307.

Pope, J. E. (2020). Management of fatigue in rheumatoid arthritis. *RMD Open*, *6*, e001084.

Reich, W. (2013). *Character analysis*. FSG, Macmillan.

Rogers, C. R. (1957). The necessary and sufficient conditions of therapeutic personality change. *Journal of Consulting Psychology*, *21*(2), 95–103. https://doi.org/10.1037/h0045357

Rosenberg, J. (1985). *Body, self and soul: Sustaining integration*. Humanics Ltd.

Rothschild, B. (2000). *The body remembers*. W.W. Norton.

Schaefer, J. T., & Magnuson, A. B. (2014). A review of interventions that promote eating by internal cues. *Journal of the Academy of Nutrition and Dietetics*, *114*(5), 734–760. https://doi.org/10.1016/j.jand.2013.12.024

Selu, E. (2020). Authentic movement as a movement meditation: Support for immune mediated inflammatory disease. *International Body Psychotherapy Journal*, *19*(1), 55–63.

Torres, M. E., Löwe, B., Schmitz, S., Pienta, J. N., Van Der Feltz-Cornelis, C., & Fiedorowicz, J. G. (2021). Suicide and suicidality in somatic symptom and related disorders: A systematic review. *Journal of Psychosomatic Research*, *140*, 110290.

van der Kolk, B. (2014). *The body keeps the score: Brain, mind, and body in the healing of trauma*. Viking.

Von Laban, R. (1973). *Modern educational dance*. MacDonald & Evans.

Photograph 10.1 Two witnesses contemplate the empty space
Credit: Photography by Lucie Payne

Chapter 10

Interoception and Student Anxiety

Adapted Authentic Movement as an Intervention

Abstract

This chapter identifies a theoretical argument drawn from neuroscience for the employ-ment of an embodied approach for supporting anxiety. It makes specific reference to stu-dent mental health, of which anxiety is the most common complaint. There is an overview of student mental health, particularly the increase for students in higher education when compared to their non-university peers, and some previous interventions to address these concerns. This is followed by a section on interoception and its entanglement in anxiety through the somatic error hypothesis. The importance of including self-reflection in embod-ied approaches together with a section on embodiment in the context of this model is then highlighted. After a brief introduction about The BodyMind Approach, which has as its core an adapted version of the discipline of authentic movement as the key methodology, a sec-tion on the relationship between interoception, the insula and anxiety is presented. Finally, the ways in which adapted authentic movement can be scaffolded up for participants with examples of practices are described. An embodied approach employing an adaption of the discipline of authentic movement may support more accurate perceptions of somatic signals and reduce student anxiety.

Introduction

The chapter explores the theoretical rationale for employing an embodied approach, namely aAM, to support students in higher education (HE) with mental health chal-lenges, most commonly anxiety. The relationship between authentic movement, interoception and anxiety is deeply interconnected through the body with mind relationship.

In the context of the increasing poor mental health amongst young people 16–24 years old (Ramón-Arbués et al., 2020), there is evidence that HE students (most of whom are in the 16–24-year age range) have poorer mental health than their non-university peers (Sanders, 2023). Outcomes include withdrawal from studies, reduced sociability, poor cognitive function, lack of enthusiasm/engage-ment, weak concentration or low academic achievement. We know mental health affects both learning and academic performance (Eisenberg et al., 2009; Agnafors et al., 2020), and mental health is a potential predicator of academic performance in HE (Zang et al., 2024).

DOI: 10.4324/9781003479413-11

The most common condition for students in HE is anxiety (Periera et al., 2019) which is known to be involved with interoception (Craig, 2002; Pollatos et al., 2007). A rationale can be argued for an embodied (body-based) intervention which targets interoception to reduce anxiety in students. For example, Freeston and Komes (2023) refer to the somatic error hypothesis, suggesting body-based interventions may increase relative predictability in the environment, whereby the resulting bodily signals are less likely to lead to large somatic discrepancies between the experienced and the expected. An embodied, experiential learning methodology such as the discipline of authentic movement (Adler, 2002, Morrissey & Sager, 2022) (hereafter termed authentic movement/AM) which is the main method in the biopsychosocial model called The BodyMind Approach (TBMA) which has had encouraging outcomes (Payne et al., 2020; Payne, 2017[a]; Payne & Brooks, 2019) may be more acceptable and accessible for students experiencing anxiety in HE.

Student Mental Health

Mental health refers to a wide spectrum of experience, is universal, not solely the absence of mental illness/distress but due to the inter/intrapersonal experiences and those related to the environment. The World Health Organization (2022) defines mental health as a state of mental wellbeing that enables people to cope with the stresses of life, realize their abilities, learn and work well. Poor mental health is associated with mental illness and distress (De Pury & Dicks, 2021) and impairs daily living, from minor occurrences of worry/stress to chronic, long-term conditions such as anxiety/depression (Mind, 2014).

The United Kingdom (UK) has an increasing prevalence of mental health issues, and the rate amongst the general population is increasing. There were 1.81 million referrals via the National Health Service (NHS) for talking therapies in 2021–2022, up 24.5% compared to the previous two years (NHS Digital, 2022). The impact of the pandemic, increased use of social media exposing people to information on mental health and, recently, the cost-of-living crisis all drive the increase. Mental health disorders are probable in 23.3% of 17–19-year-olds and 21.7% in ages 20–25 in England (NHS Digital, 2023) and peak from 16–24 years with 75% of problems established by age 25 (Kessler et al., 2005).

Many students do not disclose their mental health condition and/or fail to seek help until it becomes chronic (Equality Challenge Unit, 2014; Ramluggun et al., 2020). For some the lack of disclosure and help-seeking is due to stigma and/or cultural beliefs. Despite this, student wellbeing services are overwhelmed resulting in delays for all but the most serious situations (NatWest, 2020). Teaching staff pick up the slack without any training, time in their workload or expertise to effectively support students with their mental health (Hughes & Byrom, 2019).

One in five UK university students experience mental health concerns, a fivefold increase over the past decade (Thorley, 2017). A survey found 59% of respondents reported a mental health issue and of these, 29% reported a diagnosed mental health issue (Student Minds, 2022). Research commissioned by the Universities and Colleges Admissions Service/UCAS (2021) suggests risk factors make students particularly vulnerable to poor mental health, for example, age, transition into HE, stigma related to disclosure and the diversity of the student body. Payne (2022) delineates more detail on the additional risk factors applicable to students. In a review across 19 developed countries, it was reported anxiety, depression and suicidality were common (Bantjes et al., 2022). A US student survey showed that 80% were stressed daily and one third of first years reported a mental health condition (Mark in Style, 2021). Another found, in a sample of 1,074 college students, 23.6% reported anxiety, 18.4% depression and 34.5% stress (Ramón-Arbués et al., 2020). Auerbach et al. (2018) in a World Health Organization survey of 19 colleges across eight countries found 35% screened positive for at least one of the common lifetime disorders assessed, and 31% screened positive for at least one 12-month disorder. Overall, in the UK, poor mental health is worse in HE (Equality Challenge Unit, 2014), 57% of which are women aged 16–24 (HE Statistical Unit, 2020) who are three times more likely to have diagnosed/undiagnosed conditions, which increased by 38% in 1993–2015 (NHS Digital, 2016).

There has also been an increase in UK HE students disclosing a mental health condition at application stage. Of the 2020 applicants, 21,105 shared a mental health condition in their UCAS application, equating to nearly 1 in 25, a 450% increase since 2011 (UCAS, 2021). As an evaluation of the effect of mental health-related stigma in HE, UCAS estimates there were 40,000 students entering HE in 2020 with an existing mental health condition, over half choosing not to declare it. Research by UCAS (2021) also suggests that students believe disclosure will impact their chance of an offer. Students often do not seek help due to the stigma (Ramluggun et al., 2020) or only once severely unwell (Broglia et al., 2017). Unfortunately, poor mental health is the main reason students withdraw (Sanders, 2023). Many do not disclose (Equality Challenge Unit, 2014) so may be at more risk of deterioration. Nevertheless, student disclosure of mental health conditions to their university has increased sevenfold in last ten years (Lewis & Bolton, 2023). Students with a higher risk of poor mental health include females (YouGov., 2016); international (Atack, 2018) and marginalized groups, such as LGBTQ+ (YouGov., 2016); lower socioeconomic backgrounds, care leavers; disabled; and ethnic/religious minorities (Campbell et al., 2022). Despite government policy to improve health inequalities (Public Health England, 2018) these groups continue to experience health inequalities. For Black and Minority Ethnic groups facing barriers (for example, isolation, marginalization) there remains an impact on access to culturally appropriate services and health and educational outcomes (Busby, 2019).

Furthermore, only 27% of students thought their university provided adequate mental health support (Ramón-Arbués et al., 2020). The support-services in HE are strained by increases in students seeking help for anxiety/depression (NatWest, 2020) resulting in delays. The teaching staff shoulder the burden without the time, training or expertise (Hughes & Byrom, 2019; Payne, 2022) although there is guidance available for supporting teaching staff (Advance HE, 2025).

Student Anxiety

Anxiety often involves hyperarousal of the nervous system, leading to heightened physical sensations such as rapid heartbeat or shallow breathing and patterns of fear. Being overly sensitive to bodily sensations, or disconnected from them, can contribute to anxiety disorders. Anxiety is the most common mental health condition amongst young people (Bandelow & Michaelis, 2022) with negative impact on wellbeing (Kessler et al., 1994). This condition has worsened since the COVID-19 pandemic, with NHS referrals for anxiety in young people more than doubling (Public Health England, 2022).

The 2018 UK University Student Health Report (Periera et al., 2019) showed 55% of 37,500 students disclosed anxiety. This matches a meta-analysis that grouped 13 studies with a total of 18,220 students from nine European countries, showing a prevalence of 55% (Auerbach et al., 2018). Anxiety in students is the most common mental health condition by far, 49% in last two years (Higher Education Statistical Unit, 2020). In the ONS Census 2021–22, 39% of first year students reported anxiety, 25% higher than expected based on the average for ages 16–29 (ONS Census, 2021–22).

There are higher rates of anxiety in students because there are factors affecting students, for example, being away from home/family/friends, debt and lack of graduate jobs leading to pressure to obtain a first degree. Growing numbers from marginalized groups are more likely to experience anxiety due to additional factors (for example, first in family in HE, facing a new culture, financial issues etc.) (Harrison et al., 2021). They are less likely to engage with mental health resources to manage stress and/or anxiety (for cultural reasons, fear, assumptions, stigma or difficulty accessing the NHS due to unfamiliarity).

Interventions for Student Anxiety in Higher Education

As concerns for student mental health increase, universities are looking at preventative and universal interventions. There is evidence to support the impact of curriculum-embedded interventions for improving student stress or anxiety.

For example, stress management (Boath et al., 2017; Hahm et al., 2016; Shatkin et al., 2016) and mindfulness (Ramasubramanian, 2017; Ross & Carney, 2017) had a statistically significant positive effect on stress. Fernandez et al. (2016) undertook a review which found statistically significant improvements in anxiety following stress management (Bughi et al., 2006) and mindfulness (Hassed et al., 2009). It must be noted some mindfulness practices (such as body scan meditations) can cause agitation, anxiety, discomfort, confusion and resurfacing trauma/ unpleasant memories (Creswell, 2017). It can raise anxiety and lower self-efficacy (Clarke & Draper, 2020), and lead to participants being unable to manage their negative thoughts arising during meditation leading to the worsening of mental health (Lomas et al., 2014; Laurie & Blandford, 2016). Most mindfulness practices are simply attentional methods that likely do not trigger such reactions. Clinical skills programmes (for example, problem solving, communication, time management, interpersonal skills) (Bommer et al., 2017; Demirel et al., 2020; Halloran, 2017) have also shown significant positive effects on anxiety.

There is a need for robust evidence for interventions to inform policy and practice with the implications of poor mental health on education, learning, careers, wellbeing and the future lives of university students.

Interoception

Fogel (2009) conceptualized the term interoception as "the ability to feel one's own body states and emotions" (p. 39). It is the subjective perception of bodily states i.e., feeling sensations inside the body including the autonomic nervous system activity related to emotions which are recognized to play a role in mental health.

The bidirectional communication between body and brain "encompass(es) the complex interplay between the brain and other organs that is necessary to monitor and regulate internal states" (Chen et al., 2021, p. 4). Interoceptive awareness, bodymindfulness and mental wellbeing are therefore linked for emotional regulation. Interventions targeting one or more of these aspects can positively change the others (Fissler et al., 2016; Todd & Aspell, 2022). The suggested mechanism for this change is the associations between neural mechanisms sharing joint purposes of emotional and interoceptive functioning. Functional magnetic resonance imaging has examined neural responses to mindfulness meditation to show more interoceptive awareness brain activity in the anterior insula as well as other interoception associated brain areas (Farb et al., 2013). Von Economo Neurones, which function as a cerebral representation of the autonomic nervous system, are found only in the insula and the anterior cingulate cortex (Allman et al., 2011). Craig (2009) proposes the insula is implicated in a wide range of conditions and behaviours, for example, bowel distension, orgasm, cigarette craving, maternal love, decision making and sudden insight. He states, "[the insula's] function in the re-representation of interoception offers one possible basis for its involvement in all subjective feelings" (Craig, 2009). He goes on to say it also has a fundamental part to play in awareness, and thus it needs to be considered as a potential neural correlate of consciousness. This is why interoception is so crucial to the discipline of authentic movement. The relationships between interoception, the insula, anxiety and attachment patterns are all interwoven within the practice of authentic movement.

Interoception and Anxiety

Accurate interoceptive awareness can mediate the relationship between stress and emotion (Craig, 2002) and anxiety and the intensity of unpleasant feelings (Pollatos et al., 2007). A lack of interoception adversely affects mood disorders, addictions, post-traumatic stress disorder, anxiety and other mental health issues (Khalsa et al., 2018).

Interoception has been linked to anxiety in relation to body listening, emotional awareness, and self-regulation (Solano Durán et al., 2024). Anxiety involves both bodily reactions and subjective feelings. Furthermore, there is research on the efficacy for reducing anxiety via interoceptive training (Harrison et al., 2021; Quadt et al., 2021).

A primary dysfunction in perception and regulation of bodily states has been considered in emotional processing (Seth & Friston, 2016; Petzschner et al., 2021) and anxiety (Paulus & Stein, 2010; Herbert & Pollatos, 2012; Stephan et al., 2016). For example, learning to notice subtle tightening or retreating in the body is a response to a possible threatening situation (Craig, 2002; Dael et al., 2012).

The Somatic Error Hypothesis

It has been suggested that anxiety symptoms can arise from discrepancies between the individual's actual and expected bodily state i.e., greater body prediction error, or somatic error (Khalsa et al., 2018). That is, they fail to recognize their symptoms are natural when an unexpected stressful or traumatic event occurs. They do not expect, for example, their heart to race and breathing to become faster if stressed. So, when these physiological experiences occur automatically due to the body's reaction to an event, instead they believe they are seriously unwell, having a panic attack or even a heart attack or have a life-threatening condition. This makes for a downward spiral whereby the added stress of those beliefs increases the bodily autonomic survival mechanisms further still which eventually become chronic in which the stress hormones are constantly racing around the body maintaining a state of high alert.

Khalsa et al. (2018) call for mindfulness-based stress reduction, yoga and other meditation/movement-based treatments (Farb et al., 2015) which may improve metacognitive awareness of mind–body connections by systematically attending to sensations of breathing, cognitions and/or other modulated body states (for example, stretching/moving).

Based on computer learning and active inference approaches (i.e., if you search out things you expect, you will avoid surprises) (Friston et al., 2009), the somatic error hypothesis of anxiety states anxiety-related distress arises from the discrepancy between the actual and anticipated but habitually based, bodily state (Khalsa & Feinstein, 2018). Freeston and Komes (2023) refer to the somatic error theory in relation to the treatment of anxiety. They suggest using body-based interventions to increase relative predictability in the environment where the resulting bodily signals experienced are less likely to lead to large somatic discrepancies between the experienced and the expected. Those experiencing chronic anxiety-related distress seem to lose the ability to accurately sense what is happening in the body, which contributes to an increasing sense of dysregulation and threat even in the absence of such (Nord & Garfinkel, 2022; Sugawara et al., 2020).

Gibson (2019) links mindfulness, interoception and the body, acknowledging mindfulness and all other forms of meditation have been shown to modulate the insula, which is the primary hub for interoception. Mindfulness in motion is found in aAM as offered in TBMA. Bornemann et al. (2015) in a controlled study showed that the body scan and breath meditation improved aspects of interoceptive awareness, particularly in self-regulation. Both practices are found in TBMA. For example, conscious breathing with a focus on the sensation can help participants to learn accurate perception of these sensations and thus to regulate and manage emotions, reducing anxiety/stress and improving wellbeing.

Embodiment

Embodiment in this context refers to, and emphasizes, the subjective experience of the lived body. Embodiment denominates a field of research in which the reciprocal influence of the body as a living, animate, moving organism with cognition, sensation, emotion, perception and action is investigated in relation to the expressive and impressive functions at individual, interactional and extended levels (Koch & Fuchs, 2011). It holds that the attribution of meaning to movement is action-based and enactive involving the motor-knowing of the observer and performer.

Embodiment phenomena are related to bodily states such as postures, gestural movements, facial expressions etc., which play a central role in information processing (Barsalou et al., 2003). There is meaning-making of one's lived experience in the generation of symbolic representation that becomes available through the embodied experience found in the discipline of authentic movement (Adler, 2002).

Merleau-Ponty (1962) distinguishes between the objective body (the body as a physiological entity/having a body) and the phenomenal body, my (or your) body as I (or you) experience it (being a body). Thus, although there is an experience of our body as a physiological entity, the inclination is to experience it as a unified potential or capacity for doing things/responding to a need via movement. Embodiment could refer to the biological and physical presence of our bodies as necessary preconditions for subjectivity, emotion, language, thought and social interaction. Motor capacities (expressed as bodily confidence) do not require an understanding of the physiological processes involved in the execution of these actions. Embodiment in this context refers to the phenomenal body and the role it performs in object-directed experiences. Embodiment in this view is an existential condition in which the body is the subjective source of experience (Csordas, 1999). It arises from culture and the experience of being-in-the-world. Varela et al. (1991) speak about an "enactive" (Thompson, 2007; Thompson & Stapleton, 2009) approach to cognition which they claim is a dynamic interaction between an acting organism and its environment. This subjective experience of the body interacts with the environment and thus is affected by stress and anxiety which can cause physical symptoms, for example, fatigue, chronic pain, irritable bowel syndrome, respiratory problems and heart concerns. There are links between stress and wellbeing and levels of embodiment (body awareness) (Mehling et al., 2011; Tihanyi et al., 2016).

Self-Reflection

As well as embodiment, which is a new and emerging area of research interest in relation to treating mental health conditions, self-reflection is also receiving growing attention. Both are integral to the adapted form of authentic movement found in TBMA, which augments the hypothesis that TBMA may work for high levels of stress/anxiety.

Self-reflection (Philippi & Koenigs, 2014) turns attention inward to consider our imagination, thoughts, memories, feelings and actions. It is different from the maladaptive reflection of rumination/preoccupation with perceived threats to the self or fears etc. This is a type of repetitive, uncontrollable thinking that can be unhelpful involving focusing on disturbing experiences (such as expecting the worst, feelings of imperfection, or social exclusion) and can lead to depression. Self-reflection can increase insight and personal knowledge, and promote emotional regulation, recognition and understanding of thinking and feeling, all of which can lead to a higher level of self-awareness, helping mental health and wellbeing. The use of personal journalling, mark-making or clay sculpting in the transition after moving yet before speaking during TBMA sessions provides opportunities for participants to reflect on the embodied experiences recording nonverbally any meaning-making prior to verbal languaging.

The intensified levels of maladaptive self-reflection (rumination of negative thoughts) often present in anxiety and stress require a reduction which can be achieved through the emotional regulation found in interoception training. Although there are key theories to address rumination, commonly found as a stressor in anxiety, interoception is the focus in aAM (and TBMA more generally) rather than solely the reduction of rumination per se.

The BodyMind Approach

The BodyMind Approach (TBMA) is a perceptual learning method within a biopsychosocial model using aAM as its core content, framed as embodied experiential learning in a class. The approach stems from my background and training in the discipline of authentic movement practised with half closed/closed eyes making it ideal for sensing movement from within.

Authentic movement is one of the methods employed in dance movement psychotherapy (DMP) (Payne, 1992, 2006), but in TBMA it is integrated with other embodied and creative methods such as conscious breathing, progressive relaxation, mindful movement, journalling, expressive movement, mark-making etc. It has been re-designed as aAM specifically to support students with anxiety subsequent to its application to chronic bodily symptoms (Payne, 2017a, 2017b).

The term "bodymindfulness" employed in TBMA (Payne & Stott, 2010; Payne & Brooks, 2017, 2018, 2020, 2025) incorporates an awareness of physical sensations. It reflects mindful movement – the sensation of moving and being connected to it in the present moment. The term accepts the role of the body which the term mindfulness, although incorporating the body for example, the body scan or the breath, fails to truly acknowledge. Furthermore, it links the body and mind with fulness although paradoxically there is an emptiness of content when attending to the present moment.

Authentic movement is a relational practice (there is the one who makes the action – or not – and the one who is their witness). This practice helps individuals access unconscious material, deepen self-awareness and cultivate a sense of embodiment. Body, mind and spirit are viewed as interrelated, mutually influential: moving the body impacts how we feel emotionally and mentally, and vice versa. How we feel and think resides in the body and impacts how we move. The model used in TBMA emphasizes the importance of incorporating body and mind and being open to spirit (see Chapter 4) for managing anxiety (and any associated physical symptoms) acknowledging that emotional wellbeing is closely linked to physical health, and vice versa.

Research from dance movement psychotherapy, groupwork, safety, neuroscience (specifically interoception), adult attachment, mindfulness, adult learning theory and self-management are all drawn upon for TBMA practices. It stresses embodiment, the connection with the physical self, valued as supporting body with mind integration.

The creative process through expressive bodily movement and the arts is integral since it enables participants to find meaning and new solutions to problems. Dance movement therapy and artistic expression methods can help enhance interoceptive awareness, allowing individuals to reconnect with their bodies and achieve emotional regulation (Malchiodi, 2023; Gray, 2018).

The emphasis is on de-medicalizing/normalizing the experience of anxiety reducing the stigma still associated with mental health. Hence, the programme is framed as a class/workshop and a learning programme held in university classrooms.

By incorporating the principles of self-reflection and mindfulness a non-judgemental ethos is cultivated which facilitates the shift from the (usually negative rumination) evaluation of thoughts, feelings, sensations to a more curious and neutral mindset to break negative cycles.

The group facilitator trained in TBMA (and authentic movement) has skills to make it possible for students to safely participate using their bodies as expressive vehicles to make meaning of the sensation (Payne & Brooks, 2025). Using physical sensations as the internal focus and raising awareness of them while moving and in stillness encourages increased accurate interoception with the aim of reducing and integrating the stress response (supporting emotional regulation).

Since TBMA works primarily with the body as a source of learning/wisdom, participants are encouraged to acknowledge their body as an ally rather than the enemy, encouraged to come "home" to their body with acceptance and self-compassion. Perception of our body can significantly impact anxiety. A negative body image may lead to low self-esteem increasing anxiety while a positive body image, whereby the body is experienced as safe, contributes to a greater sense of wellbeing, reducing anxiety.

Imagery, symbolism and metaphor are important pathways to access unconscious/difficult feelings. Using creative methods allows participants to work through problematic issues indirectly. Beck (2025) claims employing more of the right brain can shift anxiety into creativity. Furthermore, people do not always have words to express what they feel. Sometimes it is easier to reach/communicate to others nonverbally through mark-making, posture or gesture.

Authentic Movement and Interoception

Authentic movement can enhance interoception through offering opportunities for participants to deeply attune to spontaneous bodily impulses and sensations, improving interoceptive awareness within a safe relational environment. This helps individuals distinguish between normal bodily fluctuations and anxiety-driven sensations, reducing misinterpretations that fuel panic or distress. Furthermore, the kind attention on the body sensations and spontaneous, expressive movement loosens embodied, chronic tension, discharging nervous energy and activating the parasympathetic nervous system which shifts escalating thoughts to bodily presence avoiding full dissociation.

Moving with half closed or closed eyes as in authentic movement is essential for cultivating an inward focus. Having closed eyes inhibits the strong visual pull which can result in individuals being drawn out into their environment. Attention is towards the interaction between sensation, emotions, images and thoughts, which supports body with mind connectivity. This attention to inner embodied experience helps the mover to become conscious of, and receptive to, the interoceptive response leading to feelings of control, agency and emotional resilience. By promoting kind attention to the moving body, and in stillness, with an exploratory interest (rather than emotional reactivity and negative appraisal) in sensations, even if distressing, the monitoring of signals from interoceptive awareness is aided and accurate perception trained.

Hyperarousal is due to feeling unsafe and is often found in chronic anxiety. It requires a modification of practices to safely train a more accurate perception of internal bodily sensations. For example, for those too anxious to close eyes or even half close them to arrive at an inward focus, as an alternative it is suggested they gaze down at their abdomen, seeing it rise and fall with their breath. Thereafter, if they wish, scaffolding them into half closing eyes to feel the rise and fall of that movement from within whilst ensuring they are aware that their eyes can be opened at any time.

A witness, the one with eyes open, benignly supports the one who moves. She also has an inward focus of attention in that, although "seeing" the action, there is an awareness of its impact on her, that is, the impact on their body, imagination, feelings, sensory experience and thoughts. The mirror neurones are fired up in the presence of the action seen and echo the movement microscopically which, in turn, stimulates a felt response in the witness.

Accessing feelings or memories through language solely, as in the talking therapies, has severe limitations whereas embodied practices can bring forth an understanding of sensory information, for example, physical sensations and impulses, imagery, feelings or sounds that evoke stories of the past and of the present moment.

We know interoception regulates anxiety which is when the nervous system is hyper-aroused. When the ability to sense and interpret bodily signals accurately improves, the self-regulation of anxiety improves. Authentic movement fosters this by allowing individuals to explore their emotions stored in the body memory and be curious about their sensations in a safe, non-judgemental space. Developing a balanced interoceptive awareness through movement can help prevent overwhelming bodily sensations from triggering anxiety.

Adapted Authentic Movement for Supporting Student Anxiety

The practice of aAM can reduce anxiety for students by encouraging a mindful, embodied experience which shifts them away from anxious thoughts and into their body in the present-moment. This can activate the parasympathetic nervous system (the "rest and digest" state), reducing stress and anxiety.

The body plays a crucial role in emotional regulation. Physical sensations, such as muscle tension, beathing or heart rate, can influence our emotional states. In aAM as a mover the participant employs their inner witness and interoception and through this embodied method, which invites attention to the physical sensation of moving, has an experience. The witness also uses their observing self or inner witness to "see" their mover and notice any impact of the action on them. The mover returns after a short movement piece followed by a transitional period (Bracegirdle, 2023) in which movers and witnesses have individual self-reflection time for writing and/or mark-making. Then they both come together where there is the subsequent self-referential languaging of the experience of moving (specifying any actions recalled) reported to the witness. If the mover desires, they can invite the witness to make an offering based on their experience in the presence of the movement/action seen (and/or sounds heard, interactions seen) and which have already been spoken about by the mover previously. All languaging is self-referential and in the present tense.

In aAM the mover through interoception notices an impulse to move or a sensation which in turn sets up an impulse to move and then purposefully expresses it through the body, often just through hand gestures. This is then witnessed by the facilitator, or later another participant, without judgement or interpretation. Meaning evolves from the symbol formation arising from these gestures both as experienced and witnessed and subsequently in the verbal exchange and/or via any writing and/or mark-making. This process may result in a greater accuracy in the perception of the sensory experience and the role it plays in emotional states as well as the relationship the participant has with their body (body image).

It is important to note that the facilitator has previously trained as a dance movement psychotherapy and in TBMA. Therefore, they have the capacity, skills, knowledge and understanding to safely hold the group to enable participation. The safe and trusted other helps participants to feel a sense of belonging and connection. These feelings of safety are represented in the insula. Without safety, playing and being curious with, for example, sensations and/or bodily symptoms cannot take place. Feeling safe is probably the first step in developing accurate interoceptive awareness and interoception appears to develop initially in the context of the early attachment relationship (Oldroyd et al., 2019).

The research and practice-based evidence of TBMA was both quantitative and qualitative. It was conducted when TBMA was delivered in the NHS for primary care patients with chronic bodily symptoms for which tests/scans return normal then termed medically unexplained symptoms (MUS) (Payne & Brooks, 2016, 2017, 2018, 2019, 2020; Payne et al., 2020). Outcomes were reduced symptom distress, anxiety and depression and increased wellbeing, activity and global functioning all of which were sustained at follow-ups at three and six months.

The argument has been made for TBMA and students experiencing stress and MUS (co-morbid anxiety and/or depression) (Payne, 2022). In this context TBMA aims to promote self-management so patients feel more in control to live well, an internal locus of control. It addresses the body/mind (mind-body) split in Western health care, patients and society, stressing a holistic, biopsychosocial model (Borrell-Carrió et al., 2004). The practices honour both conscious and unconscious processes whereby sensation, perception, emotion and cognition are integrated.

A preliminary pre/post study of four 90-minute sessions of TBMA with an external group facilitator was undertaken as a collaboration between the University of Hertfordshire and Newcastle University, which showed encouraging outcomes. The aim was to explore the possibility of interoception practices employed in TBMA reducing stress/anxiety in a small sample of the students who self-identified as overly stressed or anxious and to test the acceptability of TBMA and the measurements. Quantitative data were collected for generalized anxiety via GAD7; body awareness via BAQ; depression via PHQ9; body perception via BPQ; and interoception via MAIA; together with a cortisol test (pre and post intervention). Qualitative data were collected by conducting semi-structured interviews (post intervention) asking whether the TBMA intervention changed participants' interoceptive body awareness, and whether they thought it helped with their stress, anxiety and wellbeing. The data were thematically analysed (Braun & Clarke, 2021). Findings suggest a relationship between TBMA and greater interoceptive awareness. Participants from a range of marginalized groups thought it reduced their stress and anxiety levels and improved social connectedness and wellbeing. However, no direct, causal connection can be assumed between greater interoceptive awareness and improved mental health since the sample was too small to look for effects. Findings were supported by questionnaire scores suggesting decreased depression, anxiety and stress, and improved wellbeing and interoceptive body awareness. The cortisol measures were inconclusive.

Therefore, there is a strong argument of formulating that by engaging the insula and its interceptive function through the bodymindfulness practices available in TBMA, and specifically aAM anxiety may be regulated as the accuracy awareness improves. Furthermore, the relational element in aAM dyadic, triadic and small groupwork may foster change in early unhelpful attachment patterns by engaging in an equitable relationship with a trusted other (the facilitator firstly, then a peer as witnesses).

Here are a few examples of individual and dyadic practices which may scaffold participants into the practice of aAM to support interoception.

Practice Examples

Practice 1

The group facilitator may offer the following practice in the first session undertaken by each participant individually, without a witness to begin with. Later in the programme it may be offered with a silent then speaking witness. The spontaneous, gentle movement is entirely in the control of the mover. It helps to reduce tension, overactivation and thus anxiety and encourages attunement to the embodied sensations.

Aim: To connect the breath with movement to increase interoceptive awareness and calm the nervous system.

1. Each participant is invited to find a quiet space and stand, sit or lie down.
2. If possible, half close or fully close eyes (or alternatively have an inner focus) and focus on the breath without changing it.
3. Begin noticing the body subtly moves with each breath (ribcage expanding, belly rising).
4. Allow the breath to initiate some small movements, maybe rising and sinking the torso with the breath, swaying, opening and closing arms, a shift in posture, or a slight rocking motion.
5. Gradually begin to exaggerate these movements, making them larger, use all the personal space, let them flow intuitively.
6. Continue for five minutes, staying present with the bodily felt sense and any sensations experienced as you move.
7. Reflections in pairs or in the group. Use the personal journal to reflect on the practice.

Practice 2

This is another practice for the first few sessions of the programme. Grounding through weight and gravity to reduce dissociation and overwhelm. Participants are invited to find a space and lie down on their back (mats can be used if available). This practice helps regulate anxiety by increasing bodily presence and reducing dissociation.

Aim: To reconnect with bodily presence and feel safe in the body.

1. Close or half close eyes. Feel the support of the floor.
2. Breath slowly and deeply × three.
3. Sense the weight of the body on the floor.
4. Press heels, gluts, back, upper back, back of head and then arms in turn into the floor and release.

5. Begin some gentle movements like rocking, floating hands in the air or stretching legs. The breath supports the movement.
6. Is there any part of the body where there is tension? Exaggerate the tension, move into it and then release.
7. Breathe deeply and slowly, sensing the weight of your body.

Practice 3

Anxiety can build up and the body may hold onto these unprocessed emotions. Movement allows these emotions to surface and integrate.

Aim: To prevent emotional suppression, release stored stress and provide a safe way to process feelings.

1. Standing or sitting or lying, close or half close eyes. Breathe.
2. With the mind's eye scan from top to toe of the body. Ask participants to identify where they feel tension or unease (the facilitator could offer a full body scan here).
3. Let that sensation initiate movement. For example, if feeling heavy in the chest, maybe press into it, stretch it or shake it out.
4. If an emotion arises, allow it to express itself through movement (for example, stomping if frustration, curling inward if sadness).
5. If needed, vocalize with the movement such as a sigh, hum or natural sounds.
6. Journal any personal reflections for five minutes.
7. The facilitator brings the practice to a close and invites comments and reflections.

Practice 4

This practice is all about containment and expansion with a view to help to regulate overwhelm.

Aim: To balance the nervous system by exploring containment (feeling grounded) and expansion (feeling free).

1. Begin standing or sitting and wrapping arms around the torso in a self-hug (containment).
2. Notice how this feels, for example, safe, soothing or restricted.
3. The inward breath accompanies a slow opening and stretching of the arms going outward, growing and spreading the body (expansion).
4. Now on the outward breath sink and retreat towards the centre of the body.
5. Repeat this, alternating between these states in a personalized rhythm a) contracting inward, then b) expanding outward with the out breath and inward with the in breath to support the movement.
5. Journal any reflections for five minutes.
6. Reflect in pairs and/or the large group.

Practice 5

This dyadic or individual practice can help to deepen the connection between bodily sensations and expressive movement, fostering trust in bodily wisdom. The facilitator may offer this practice with or without a silent (non-speaking external witness) witness. It can help discharge stuck tension and emotions, reducing anxiety-driven bodily tension.

Aim: Using hands only to develop inner impulse exploration to build body/movement confidence, trust and emotional release.

1. The mover half closes their eyes so only a little light shows through the eyelids and stands or sits in a comfortable position.
2. The mover scans their body for subtle sensations, for example, tightness, warmth, tingling or an urge to move.
3. They let these sensations guide their gestures – might be as small as moving fingers or as large as stretching or shaking.
4. They move without judgement, just moving spontaneously in response to any inner impulses.
5. If emotions arise, allow them to be expressed through movements.
6. This phase of action continues for two minutes, then pauses for a transition phase of five minutes to reflect on the experience by making marks on paper or writing in the personal journal.

If there has been a witness present, they can also write or make marks in the transition period of five minutes. The mover then can share with their witness all the actions recalled, languaging them in the present tense, specifically any which stood out and adding any images, thoughts, feelings etc. accompanying them. The witness listens attentively, however as a silent witness does not make an offering at this stage. Change roles.

NB. The preceding practice can be repeated using the whole body (or just hands) with a speaking witness. The mover may invite an offering from their witness following the transition phase. The witness can share the impact of the movement on them using the present tense and self-referential languaging.

Practice 6

This practice is an exercise in learning how to speak about the past in the present tense using self-referential languaging. It might need to be introduced several times early in the practice before new learners are easily able to drop into speaking in the present tense.

1. In pairs, each take a turn to share with the other their journey to the group that day.
2. Speak in the present tense throughout as if it were happening in the immediacy.
3. Speak of the actions, any associated memories, feelings, thoughts etc.

4. Use "I", "me", "my" terms only.
5. The listener does not interrupt or offer any comment. They can nod and show interest but be present to the communication without judgement.
6. Discuss any barriers, how it felt etc.

Practice 7

This practice enables participants to explore the notion of eyes closed when in the role of the mover and eyes open when in the role of a witness. It is a preparatory exercise for embodying the two roles later.

1. In pairs take turns to be the one with eyes open in the presence of the other one with eyes closed.
2. Notice what happens within you as you receive the one with eyes open or the one with eyes closed.
3. Take two minutes to experience this practice.
4. Discuss in pairs or fours, in a group specifically for those with eyes open and another group specifically for those who had eyes closed before returning to the pair and changing roles.
5. After the next round split into the above groups again to discuss the experience.
6. All return to the main group to explore what came up for participants in each role.

Practice 8

Previous practices have scaffolded learners into feeling safe in the group and in the protocols for learning the ground form in dyads whereby the mover is witnessed in their movement which supports emotional regulation by integrating emotions in a safe, facilitated space. This would take place toward the end of the programme when participants are body confident and have learned most elements of the basic ground form, the rituals and languaging. It could be that the movers in the group are restricted to movement of hands only, for example, depending on how body confident they are. They may be seated in chairs or cushions or standing, with their witness in front of them. The time duration can be shorter or longer as felt appropriate for the learners' needs at the time. It is advisable though to being with a short time frame such as three minutes, gradually expanding it to longer and longer as learners feel safer and become more body confident in the roles.

Aim: To feel safe enough to explore spontaneous movement in the presence of a non-judgemental witness.

1. In a trusted dyad one takes the role of "mover", the other "witness".
2. For two, three or five minutes (depending on the confidence of movers by this stage) the mover moves (or remains in stillness) beginning by making eye contact with their witness then closing/half closing their eyes. Taking a few deep

breaths, they wait until they notice an impulse to move (or not), and/or make sound. They follow where their body leads them with their mind's eye.
3. The witness with eyes open, benignly regards their mover, being with them in their movement or stillness, without interpreting or judging but being present and attentive, holding the space.
4. In the five-minute transition phase both write or make marks on paper before the mover returns to share (in the present tense) any actions which felt significant.
5. They return to their dyad where the mover speaks about their movement and any associated images etc. They may ask for an offering from the witness if they wish. If they do not ask the witness does not provide any offering. If invited, the witness shares the impact of the movement on them in the present tense using self-referential language.
6. Change roles.
7. Reflections in the large group including any journal/art making where there is resonance.

Summary

The Equality Challenge Unit (2014) found half of students experiencing mental health difficulties had not received support, as almost half with difficulties were unwilling to disclose/seek treatment due to stigma, fearing other students thinking less of them or of receiving unfair treatment from their institution. The biggest challenges for students with mental health difficulties seeking help were fearing judgements and being shown as weak (Byrom, 2014). Using aAM in a TBMA programme circumnavigates these barriers since it engages students based on a self-management programme for anxiety, framed as training, workshops or classes rather than as a mental health intervention so avoids stigma/judgement making access and acceptability easier. This extra-curricular intervention may be more able to attract and recruit hard-to-reach students (often due to their barriers to help-seeking), and it is anticipated TBMA would be scalable for all young people experiencing anxiety. The practices at the end are examples of how to scaffold non-movers experiencing anxiety into the roles of mover and witness so eventually they are confident to practise the ground form fully.

Note: For further information please see the chapter on Training in Authentic Movement in this volume and the book by Helen Payne and Susan Brooks titled *Management of Distressing Bodily Symptoms in Health: The BodyMind Approach using a Biopsychosocial Model* published by Routledge, 2025.

References

Adler, J. (2002). *Offering from the conscious body: The discipline of authentic movement.* Inner Traditions Press.
Advance HE. (2025). *A competence framework for responding to students in distress.* https://www.advance-he.ac.uk/knowledge-hub/competency-framework-responding-students-distress

Agnafors, S., Barmark, B., & Sydsjö, G. (2020). Mental health and academic performance: A study on selection and causation effects from childhood to early adulthood. *Social Psychiatry and Psychiatric Epidemiology*, *56*(5), 857–866. https://doi.org/10.1007/s00127-020-01934-5

Allman, J. M., Tetreault, N. A., Hakeem, A. Y., Manaye, K. F., Semendeferi, K., Erwin, J. M., Park, S., Goubert, V., & Hof, P. R. (2011). The von Economo neurons in the frontoinsular and anterior cingulate cortex. *Annals of the New York Academy of Sciences*, *1225*(1), 59–71. https://doi.org/10.1111/j.1749-6632.2011.06011.x

Atack, P. (2018). *Mental health concerns for 35% int'l students*. https://bit.ly/3apQ2mB

Auerbach, R. P., Mortier, P., Bruffaerts, R., Alonso, J., Benjet, C., Cuijpers, P., Demyttenaere, K., Ebert, D. D., Green, J. G., Hasking, P., & Kessler, R. C. (2018). The WHO world mental health surveys international college student project: Prevalence and distribution of mental disorders. *Journal of Abnormal Psychology*, *127*(7), 623–638. https://doi.org/10.1037/abn0000362

Bandelow, B., & Michaelis, S. (2022). Epidemiology of anxiety disorders in the 21st century. *Anxiety*, *17*(3), 327–335.

Bantjes, J., Hunt, X., & Stein, D. J. (2022). Public health approaches to promoting university students' mental health: A global perspective. *Current Psychiatry Reports*, *24*(12), 809–818. https://doi.org/10.1007/s11920-022-01387-4

Barsalou, L. W., Simmons, W. K., Barbey, A. K., & Wilson, C. D. (2003). Grounding conceptual knowledge in modality-specific systems. *Trends in Cognitive Sciences*, *7*(I2), 84–91.

Beck, M. (2025). *Beyond anxiety: Curiosity, creativity and finding your life's purpose*. Open Field.

Boath, E., Good, R., Tsaroucha, A., Stewart, T., Pitch, S., & Boughey, A. J. (2017). Tapping your way to success: Using emotional freedom techniques (EFT) to reduce anxiety and improve communication skills in social work students. *Social Work Education*, *36*(6), 715–730. https://doi.org/10.1080/02615479.2017.1297394

Borrell-Carrió, F., Suchman, A. L., & Epstein, R. M. (2004). The biopsychosocial model 25 years later: Principles, practice, and scientific inquiry. *The Annals of Family Medicine*, *2*(6), 576–582.

Bornemann, B., Herbert, B. M., Mehling, W. E., & Singer, T. (2015). Differential changes in self-reported aspects of interoceptive awareness through 3 months of contemplative training. *Frontiers in Psychology*, *5*, 1504.

Bommer, C., Sullivan, S., Campbell, K., Ahola, Z., Agarwal, S., O'Rourke, A., Jung, H. S., Gibson, A., Leverson, G., & Liepert, A. E. (2017). Pre-simulation orientation for medical trainees: An approach to decrease anxiety and improve confidence and performance. *The American Journal of Surgery*, *215*(2), 266–271. https://doi.org/10.1016/j.amjsurg.2017.09.038

Bracegirdle, C. (2023). A mover's practice of transition in authentic movement: An embodied non-dual lived experience. *Body Movement and Dance in Psychotherapy*, Free to download. https://doi.org/10.1080/17432979.2023.2254834

Braun, V., & Clarke, V. (2021). *Thematic analysis: A practical guide*. Sage.

Broglia, E., Millings, A., & Barkham, M. (2017). The counseling centre assessment of psychological symptoms in a UK student population. *Clinical Psychology & Psychotherapy*, *24*(5), 1178–1188.

Bughi, S. A., Sumcad, J., & Bughi, S. (2006). Effect of brief behavioral intervention program in managing stress in medical students from two southern California universities. *Medical Education Online*, *11*(1), 4593. https://doi.org/10.3402/meo.v11i.4593

Busby, E. (2019). *Why do black students with mental health problems do less well than their peers at university?* https://bit.ly/2QH1yTt 30

Byrom, N. (2014). *Grand challenges*. Student Minds.

Campbell, F., Blank, L., Cantrell, A., Baxter, S., Blackmore, C., Dixon, J., & Goyder, E. (2022, December). Factors that influence mental health of university students in the UK: A systematic review. *BMC Public Health*, *22*(1), 1–22.

Chen, W. G., Schloesser, D., Arensdorf, A. M., Simmons, J. M., Cui, C., Valentino, R., Gnadt, J. W., Nielsen, L., Hillaire-Clarke, C. S., Spruance, V., & Langevin, H. M. (2021). The emerging science of interoception: Sensing, integrating, interpreting, and regulating signals within the self. *Trends in Neurosciences, 44*(1), 3–16. https://doi.org/10.1016/j.tins.2020.10.007

Clarke, J., & Draper, S. (2020). Intermittent mindfulness practice can be beneficial, and daily practice can be harmful. An in depth, mixed methods study of the "Calm" app's (mostly positive) effects. *Internet Interventions, 19*, Article 100293. https://doi.org/10.1016/j.invent.2019.100293

Craig, A. (2002). How do you feel? Interoception: Sense of the physiological condition of the body. *Nature Reviews Neuroscience, 3*, 655–666. https://doi.org/10.1038/nrn894

(Bud) Craig, A. (2009). How do you feel – now? The anterior insula and human awareness. *Nature Reviews Neuroscience, 10*, 59–70. https://doi.org/10.1038/nrn2555

Creswell, J. D. (2017). Mindfulness interventions. *Annual Review of Psychology, 68*, 491–516. https://doi.org/10.1146/annurev-psych-042716-051139

Csordas, T. J. (1999). Embodiment and cultural phenomenology. In G. Weiss & H. F. Haber (Eds.), *Perspectives on embodiment: The interaction of nature and culture* (pp. 143–162). Routledge.

Dael, N., Mortillaro, M., & Scherer, K. R. (2012). Emotion expression in body action and posture. *Emotion, 12*(5), 1085–1101. https://doi.org/10.1037/a0025737

De Pury, J., & Dicks, A. (2021). *Stepchange: Mentally healthy universities*. Retrieved July 10, 2023, from https://www.universitiesuk.ac.uk/sites/default/files/uploads/Reports/uuk-stepchange-mhu.pdf

Demirel, G., Evcili, F., Kaya, N., & Doganer, A. (2020). The effect of episiotomy repair simulation on the anxiety and self-efficacy levels of midwifery students. *Journal of Midwifery & Reproductive Health, 8*(1), 2050–2057. https://doi.org/10.22038/jmrh.2019.42024.1479

Eisenberg, D. E., Golberstein, E., & Hunt, B. H. (2009). Mental health and academic success in college. *The B.E. Journal of Economic Analysis & Policy, 9*(1), 40.

Equality Challenge Unit. (2014). *Understanding adjustments: Supporting staff and students who are experiencing mental health difficulties*. Retrieved January 1, 2022, from https://www.ecu.ac.uk/publications/understanding-adjustments-mental-health/

Farb, N., Daubenmier, J., Price, C. J., Gard, T., Kerr, C., Dunn, B. D., Klein, A. C., Paulus, M. P., & Mehling, W. E. (2015). Interoception, contemplative practice, and health. *Frontiers in Psychology, 6*, 763.

Farb, N. A., Segal, Z. V., & Anderson, A. K. (2013). Mindfulness meditation training alters cortical representations of interoceptive attention. *Social Cognitive and Affective Neuroscience, 8*, 15–26. https://doi.org/10.1093/scan/nss066

Fernandez, A., Howse, E., Rubio-Valera, M., Thorncraft, K., Noone, J., Luu, X., Veness, B., Leech, M., Llewellyn, G., & Salvador-Carulla, L. (2016). Setting-based interventions to promote mental health at the university: A systematic review. *International Journal of Public Health, 61*(7), 797–807. https://doi.org/10.1007/s00038-016-0846-4

Fissler, M., Winnebeck, E., Schroeter, T., Gummersbach, M., Huntenburg, J. M., Gaertner, M., & Barnhofer, T. (2016). An investigation of the effects of brief mindfulness training on self-reported interoceptive awareness, the ability to decenter, and their role in the reduction of depressive symptoms. *Mindfulness, 7*, 1170–1181.

Fogel, A. (2009). *Body sense: The science and practice of embodied self-awareness.* W. W. Norton & Company.

Freeston, M., & Komes, J. (2023, June). Revisiting uncertainty as a felt sense of unsafety: The somatic error theory of intolerance of uncertainty. *Journal of Behavior Therapy and Experimental Psychiatry, 79*, 101827. https://doi.org/10.1016/j.jbtep.2022.101827. Epub 2022 December 5. PMID: 36512913.

Friston, K., Daunizeau, J., & Kiebel, S. J. (2009). Reinforcement learning or active inference? *PLoS ONE, 4*, e6421, https://doi.org/10.1371/journal.pone.0006421

Gibson, J. (2019). Mindfulness, interoception, and the body: A contemporary perspective. *Frontiers in Psychology, 10,* 2012.

Gray, A. (2018). Roots, rhythm, reciprocity: Polyvagal-informed dance movement therapy for survivors of trauma. In S. W. Porges & D. Dana (Eds.), *Clinical applications of the polyvagal theory* (pp. 321–354). W. W. Norton & Company.

Hahm, N., Augustin, S., Bade, C., Ammer-Wies, A., & Bahramsoltani, M. (2016). Test anxiety: Evaluation of a low-threshold seminar-based intervention for veterinary students. *Journal of Veterinary Medical Education, 43*(1), 47–57. https://doi.org/10.3138/jvme.0215-029R1

Halloran, D. A. (2017). *Examining the effect of virtual simulation on anxiety experienced by pediatric nursing students* [Doctoral dissertation, Cappella University]. Retrieved August 10, 2021, from http://search.ebscohost.com/login.aspx?direct=true&db=cin20&AN=129468774&site=ehost-live

Harrison, O. K., Köchli, L., Marino, S., Luechinger, R., Hennel, F., Brand, K., Hess, A. J., Frässle, S., Iglesias, S., Vinckier, F., & Stephan, K. E. (2021). Interoception of breathing and its relationship with anxiety. *Neuron, 109*(24), 4080–4093.e8. https://doi.org/10.1016/j.neuron.2021.09.045

Hassed, C., De Lisle, S., Sullivan, G., & Pier, C. (2009). Enhancing the health of medical students: Outcomes of an integrated mindfulness and lifestyle program. *Advances in Health Sciences Education, 14*(3), 387–398. https://doi.org/10.1007/s10459-008-9125-3

Herbert, B. M., & Pollatos, O. (2012). The body in the mind: On the relationship between interoception. *Topics in Cognitive Science, 4*(4), 692–704. https://doi.org/10.1111/j.1756-8765.2012.01189.x

Higher Education Statistical Unit. (2020). https://explore-education-statistics.service.gov.uk/find-statistics/education-and-training-statistics-for-the-uk

Hughes, G. J., & Byrom, N. C. (2019). Managing student mental health: Challenges faced by academics on professional healthcare courses. *Journal of Advanced Nursing, 75,* 1539–1548.

Kessler, R. C., Berglund, P., Demler, O., Jin, R., Merikangas, K. R., & Walters, E. (2005). Prevalence and age-of-onset distributions of DSM-IV disorders in the National Comorbidity Survey. *Archives of General Psychiatry, 62*(6), 593–602.

Kessler, R. C., McGonagle, K. A., Zhao, S., Nelson, C. B., Hughes, M., Eshleman, S., Wittchen, H. U., & Kendler, K. S. (1994, January). Lifetime and 12-month prevalence of DSM-III-R psychiatric disorders in the United States. Results from the National Comorbidity Survey. *Archives of General Psychiatry, 51*(1), 8–19. https://doi.org/10.1001/archpsyc.1994.03950010008002

Khalsa, S. S., & Feinstein, S. J. (2018). The somatic error hypothesis of anxiety. In M. Tsakiris & H. De-Preester (Eds.), *The interoceptive mind* (pp. 144–164). Oxford University Press. https://doi.org/10.1093/oso/9780198811930.003.0008

Khalsa, S. S., Feinstein, J. S., Simmons, W. K., & Paulus, M. P. (2018, June). Taking aim at interoception's role in mental health. *Biological Psychiatry: Cognitive Neuroscience and Neuroimaging, 3*(6), 496–498.

Koch, S. C., & Fuchs, T. (2011). Embodied arts therapies. *The Arts in Psychotherapy, 38*(4), 276–280. https://doi.org/10.1016/j.aip.2011.08.007

Laurie, J., & Blandford, A. (2016). Making time for mindfulness. *International Journal of Medical Informatics, 96,* 38–50. https://doi.org/10.1016/j.ijmedinf.2016.02.010

Lewis, J., & Bolton, P. (2023). *Student mental health in England: Statistics, policy, and guidance.* https://commonslibrary.parliament.uk/research-briengs/cbp-8593/

Lomas, T., Cartwright, T., Edginton, T., & Ridge, D. (2014). A qualitative summary of experiential challenges associated with meditation practice. *Mindfulness, 6,* 1–13. https://doi.org/10.1007/s12671-014-0329-8

Malchiodi, C. A. (2023). *Handbook of expressive arts therapy*. The Guildford Press.
Mark in Style. (2021). *Worrying college student mental health statistics*. Retrieved January 28, 2025, from https://markinstyle.co.uk/college-student-mental-health-statistics/
Mehling, W. E., Wrubel, J., Daubenmier, J. J., Price, C. J., Kerr, C. E., Silow, T., Gopisetty, V., & Stewart, A. L. (2011). Body awareness: A phenomenological inquiry into the common ground of mind-body therapies. *Philosophy, Ethics, and Humanities in Medicine, 6*, 1–12. https://doi.org/10.1186/1747-5341-6-6
Merleau-Ponty, M. (1962). *The phenomenology of perception*. Gallimard.
Mind. (2014). *Understanding mental health problems*. Retrieved July 23, 2023, from http://www.mind.org.uk
Morrissey, B., & Sager, P. (Eds.). (2022). *Intimacy in emptiness: Collected writings of Janet Adler*. Inner Traditions Press.
NatWest. (2020). *NatWest student living index*. https://bit.ly/37FrCEu
NHS Digital. (2016). https://digital.nhs.uk/data-and-information/publications/statistical/health-survey-for-england/health-survey-for-england-2016
NHS Digital. (2022). *Psychological therapies, annual report on the use of IAPT services, 2021–2022*. Retrieved July 22, 2023, from http://www.digital.nhs.uk
NHS Digital. (2023, November). *Mental health children and young people in England report: Wave 4 follow up to 2017 survey*. https://bit.ly/4it46Nt
Nord, C. L., & Garfinkel, S. N. (2022). Interoceptive pathways to understand & treat mental health conditions. *Trends in Cognitive Sciences, 26*(6), 499–513. https://doi.org/10.1016/j.tics.2022.03.004
Oldroyd, K., Pasupathi, M., & Wainryb, C. (2019). Social antecedents to the development of interoception: Attachment related processes are associated with interoception. *Frontiers in Psychology, 10*, Article 712. https://doi.org/10.3389/fpsyg.2019.00712
ONS Census 2021–22. (2022). *Coronavirus and first year higher education students*. https://www.ons.gov.uk/peoplepopulationandcommunity/healthandsocialcare/healthandwellbeing/bulletins/coronavirusandfirstyearhighereducationstudentsengland/previousReleases
Paulus, M. P., & Stein, M. B. (2010). Interoception in anxiety & depression. *Brain Structure and Function, 214*, 451–463. https://doi.org/10.1007/s00429-010-0258-9
Payne, H. (Ed.). (1992). *Dance movement therapy: Theory and practice*. Routledge.
Payne, H. (Ed.). (2006). *Dance movement therapy: Theory, research and practice*. Routledge.
Payne, H. (2017a). Reliable change in outcomes from The BodyMind Approach with people who have medically unexplained symptoms/somatic symptom disorder in primary healthcare. In H. Payne (Ed.), *Essentials of dance movement psychotherapy*. Routledge.
Payne, H. (2017b). Transferring research from a university into the National Health Service; implications for impact. *Health Research Systems and Policy, 15*, 56. https://doi.org/10.1186/s12961-017-0219-3
Payne, H. (2022). The BodyMind Approach® to support students in higher education: Relationships between student stress, medically unexplained physical symptoms and mental health. *Innovations in Education and Teaching International, 59*(4), 483–494. https://doi.org/10.1080/14703297.2021.1878052
Payne, H., & Brooks, S. (2016). Clinical outcomes and cost benefits from The BodyMind Approach for patients with medically unexplained symptoms in primary health care in England: Practice-based evidence. *Arts in Psychotherapy, 47*, 55–65.
Payne, H., & Brooks, S. (2017). Moving on: The BodyMind Approach™ for medically unexplained symptoms. *Public Mental Health Journal, 10*(2).
Payne, H., & Brooks, S. (2018). Different strokes for different folks: The BodyMind Approach as a learning tool for patients with medically unexplained symptoms to self-manage. *Frontiers in Psychology, 9*. https://doi.org/10.3389/fpsyg.2018.02222. http://journal.frontiersin.org/article/10.3389/fpsyg.2018.02222/full?

Payne, H., & Brooks, S. (2019). Medically unexplained symptoms and attachment theory: The BodyMind Approach®. *Frontiers in Psychology, 10*, 1818. https://doi.org/10.3389/fpsyg.2019.01818

Payne, H., & Brooks, S. (2020, December). A qualitative study of the views of patients with medically unexplained symptoms on The BodyMind Approach®: Employing embodied methods and arts practices for self-management. *Frontiers in Psychology, Health Psychology, 11*, 554566.

Payne, H., & Brooks, S. (2025). *Managing distressing bodily symptoms in health: The BodyMind Approach using a biopsychosocial model*. Routledge.

Payne, H., Roberts, A., & Jarvis, J. (2020). The BodyMind Approach as transformative learning to promote self-management for patients with medically unexplained symptoms. *Transformative Education, 18*(2), 114–137. https://doi.org/10.1177/1541344619883892

Payne, H., & Stott, D. (2010). Change in the moving bodymind: Quantitative results from a pilot study on the use of the BodyMind approach (BMA) to psychotherapeutic group work with patients with medically unexplained symptoms (MUSs). *Counselling & Psychotherapy Research, 10*(4), 295–306. https://doi.org/10.1080/14733140903551645

Periera, S., Reay, K., Bottell, J., Walker, L., & Dzikiti, C. (2019). *University student mental health survey*. Insight Network Dig.In. https://assets.website-files.com/602d05d13b303dec233e5ce3/60305923a557c3641f1a7808_Mental%20Health%20Report%202019%20(2020).pdf

Petzschner, F. H., Garfinkel, S. N., Paulus, M. P., Koch, C., & Khalsa, S. S. (2021). Computational models of interoception and body regulation. *Trends in Neurosciences, 44*, 63–76.

Philippi, C. L., & Koenigs, M. (2014, July). The neuropsychology of self-reflection in psychiatric illness. *Journal of Psychiatric Research, 54*, 55–63. https://doi.org/10.1016/j.jpsychires.2014.03.004

Pollatos, O., Traut-Mattausch, E., Schroeder, H., & Schandry, R. (2007). Interoceptive awareness mediates the relationship between anxiety and the intensity of unpleasant feelings. *Journal of Anxiety Disorders, 21*(7), 931–943. https://doi.org/10.1016/j.janxdis.2006.12.004

Public Health England. (2018). *Health matters: Reducing health inequalities in mental illness*. https://www.gov.uk/government/publications/health-matters-reducing-health-inequalities-in-mental-illness/health-matters-reducing-health-inequalities-in-mental-illness

Public Health England. (2022). *COVID-19 mental health and wellbeing surveillance*. Retrieved December 4, 2024, from https://bit.ly/49nFFgx

Quadt, L., Garfinkel, S. N., Mulcahy, J. S., Larsson, D. E., Silva, M., Jones, A. M., Strauss, C., & Critchley, H. D. (2021). Interoceptive training to target anxiety in autistic adults: A single-center, superiority randomized controlled trial. *EClinicalMedicine, 39*, 101042. https://doi.org/10.1016/j.eclinm.2021.101042

Ramasubramanian, S. (2017). Mindfulness, stress coping and everyday resilience among emerging youth in a university setting: A mixed methods approach. *International Journal of Adolescence and Youth, 22*(3), 308–321. https://doi.org/10.1080/02673843.2016.1175361

Ramluggun, P., Jackson, D., & Usher, P. (2020). Supporting students with disabilities in preregistration nursing programmes. *International Journal of Mental Health Nursing, 30*, 353–356.

Ramón-Arbués E, Gea-Caballero, V., Granada-López, J. M., Juárez-Vela, R., Pellicer-García, B., & Antón-Solanas, I. (2020). Prevalence of depression, anxiety and stress and their associated factors in college students. *International Journal of Environmental Research and Public Health, 17*(19), 7001.

Ross, J. G., & Carney, H. (2017). The effect of formative capstone simulation scenarios on novice nursing students' anxiety and self-confidence related to initial clinical practicum. *Clinical Simulation in Nursing, 13*(3), 116–120. https://doi.org/10.1016/j.ecns.2016.11.001

Sanders, M. (2023). *Student mental health in 2023: Who is struggling and how the situation is changing*. King's College. https://www.kcl.ac.uk/policy-institute/assets/student-mental-health-in-2023.pdf

Seth, A. K., & Friston, K. J. (2016). Active interoceptive inference and the emotional brain. *Philosophical Transactions of the Royal Society B: Biological Sciences, 371*(1708), 20160007. https://doi.org/10.1098/rstb.2016.0007

Shatkin, J. P., Diamond, U., Zhao, Y., DiMeglio, J., Chodaczek, M., & Bruzzese, J.-M. (2016). Effects of a risk and resilience course on stress, coping skills, and cognitive strategies in college students. *Teaching of Psychology, 43*(3), 204–210. https://doi.org/10.1177/0098628316649457

Solano Durán, P., Morales, J.-P., & Huepe, D. (2024). Interoceptive awareness in a clinical setting: The need to bring interoceptive perspectives into clinical evaluation. *Frontiers in Psychology, 15*, 1244701. https://doi.org/10.3389/fpsyg.2024.1244701

Stephan, K. E., Manjaly, Z. M., Mathys, C. D., Weber, L. A., Paliwal, S., Gard, T., Tittgemeyer, M., Fleming, S. M., Haker, H., Seth, A. K., & Petzschner, F. (2016). Allostatic self-efficacy: A metacognitive theory of dyshomeostasis-induced fatigue and depression. *Frontiers in Human Neuroscience, 10*, 550.

Student Minds. (2022). *Research briefing*. Retrieved July 3, 2023, from https://www.studentminds.org.uk/uploads/3/7/8/4/3784584/2208_public_facing_research_findings.pdf

Sugawara, A., Terasawa, Y., Katsunuma, R., & Sekiguchi, A. (2020). Effects of interoceptive training on decision making, anxiety & somatic symptoms. *BioPsychoSocial Medicine, 14*, 7. https://doi.org/10.1186/s13030-020-00179-7

Thompson, E. (2007). *Mind in life: Biology, phenomenology, and the sciences of mind*. Harvard University Press.

Thompson, E., & Stapleton, M. (2009). Making sense of sense-making: Reflections on enactive and extended mind theories. *Topoi, 28*, 23–30.

Thorley, C. (2017). *Not by degrees: Improving student mental health in the UK's Universities*. Institute for Public Policy Research. Retrieved June 11, 2023, from https://www.ippr.org/research/publications/not-by-degrees

Tihanyi, B. T., Böőr, P., Emanuelsen, L., & Köteles, F. (2016). Mediators between yoga practice and psychological well-being mindfulness, body awareness and satisfaction with body image. *European Journal of Mental Health, 11*, 112–127. https://doi.org/10.5708/EJMH.11.2016.1-2.7

Todd, J., & Aspell, J. E. (2022). Mindfulness, interoception and the body (editorial). *Brain Sciences, 12*(6), 696.

University and College Admissions Service. (2021). *Report on student mental health*. Retrieved June 30, 2023, from https://www.ucas.com/files/ucas-student-mental-health-report-2021

Varela, F. J., Thompson, E., & Rosch, E. (1991). *The embodied mind: Cognitive science and human experience*. The MIT Press.

World Health Organization. (2022). *World mental health report: Transforming mental health for all*. Retrieved January 18, 2025, from https://www.who.int/publications/i/item/9789240049338

YouGov. (2016). *Female and LGBT students most likely to develop mental health issues at university*. https://yougov.co.uk/society/articles/16156-quarter-britains-students-are-afflicted-mental-hea

Zang, J., Peng, C., & Chen, C. (2024). Mental health and academic performance of college students: Knowledge in the field of mental health, self-control, and learning in college. *Acta Psychologica, 248*, 104351.

Chapter 11

Training in Authentic Movement

Abstract

This chapter provides for an understanding of the development of authentic movement training. Furthermore, it details my personal background, how it prepared me for training in authentic movement as a context for my practice and to illustrate my positionality with reference to the book's content. An overview of the authentic movement training course I provide is described together with those available in various other countries.

Introduction

Since the 1980s in the USA there have been courses in higher education for training dance movement therapists some of which have included an introduction to authentic movement. There have also been specialist centres where DMTs and others can embark on intensive training in authentic movement. For example, the Mary Starks Whitehouse Institute in Northampton, Massachusetts, USA (1981–1983) was founded in 1981 by Janet Adler in honour of her teacher and was the first to offer the study and practice of authentic movement. Then in 1993 DMT Neala Haze and Jungian analyst and DMT Tina Stromsted co-founded the Authentic Movement Institute in Berkeley, California, inviting senior colleagues Jungian analyst and DMT Dr. Joan Chodorow and DMT and scholar of mysticism Dr. Janet Adler to join them. It offered a three-year intensive training in the study and practice of authentic movement for therapists, artists, body-oriented practitioners and educators. It delivered an interweaving of the creative, psychological and sacred. These programmes were supplemented by ongoing supervision for AMI graduates who wished to teach AM and/or incorporate it into their clinical work.

Within the curriculum Joan Chodorow and Jungian analyst Dr. Louis Stewart also offered seminars in active imagination in movement and the creative arts, the roots of authentic movement. The faculty continued to teach both independently and collaboratively following its closure in 2004. Students from this Institute are among those teaching and practising authentic movement today in a wide range of countries. It was at this Institute that Janet developed her model The Discipline of Authentic Movement (Adler, 1987, 2002) which grew from her PhD in mysticism in 1992 (Adler, 1995). The model has as one of its goals the development of the

DOI: 10.4324/9781003479413-12

conscious body (Adler, 2015) and is characterized by a focus on mystical practice, development of the inner witness, languaging and rituals. In 2013 Janet then
founded Circles of Four, another intensive training programme still going today for
those who wish to teach the Discipline of Authentic Movement.

Applications of authentic movement have been in various contexts such as
psychotherapy, a somatic art form, in education, as mysticism, the transpersonal,
in eco-psychology, sacred dance, as a spiritual discipline, contemplative/medi-
tative practice, and arts-based practices including in dance performance. This
volume has not focussed on the transpersonal and the numinous so much as its
relevance to psychotherapy practice and mental health. However, it must be said
mystical elements are found in many of these applications arising unintentionally
and spontaneously.

We know creativity can support personal transformation (Beck, 2025). The
access to the imagination creativity brings sheds light on unconscious processes. It
is not solely the self-directed movement spontaneously arising from the unconscious
body but the use of art materials and creative writing in the transition which bring
creativity to the foreground in the practice of authentic movement. The movement
can evoke feelings, thoughts/stories, sensations and images in both the witness and
mover which can be a source for writing, clay modelling, collage or mark-making
on paper, for example, in transition. Training courses would be wise to include arts
materials and writing in their training programmes whatever the application. For
some participants, the writing undertaken during transition becomes poetry (Bracegirdle, 2023). Authentic movement is a creative process manifesting that which is
unknown to come about and, hopefully, be seen.

My Background

My first experience of non-directive expressive movement came through the study
of Laban's Modern Educational Dance in the 1970s, first as the basis of a specialist physical education degree teacher training programme and later at the Laban
Centre in Addlestone, Surrey, as well as when it moved to New Cross, London,
England. This was so different from the ballet I had experienced growing up with
its tight technical requirements (encouraged by my mother, a former ballerina).
In the Laban dance method, I learned to follow where my body took me, whether
individually, in a group relationship or as a dyad. Music was often our accompa-
niment as well as stimuli such as an image for inspiring our impulses to move in
relationship to each other with specific efforts etc. Sometimes there followed a
sharing of our creative dance to our peers to encourage self-reflection and learning from each other (Payne, 2020; Payne & Costas, 2021). The one-year intensive programme at the Laban Centre provided me with the opportunity to study
movement observation with one of Laban's students, Marion North (North, 1972),
dance therapy with Kedzie Penfield, movement for special education with Walli
Meier as well as classes in post-modern dance. As an adult, living near London
I also went to classes in "New Dance" including Contact Improvisation with Steve

Paxton and Lisa Nelson. Classes at The Place, London in contemporary dance such as Limon, Graham, Cunningham were a staple part of my daily life in the late 1970s and early 1980s.

I was first introduced to inwardly focussed attention in meditation with closed eyes in the 1980s when I spent two years living and working at the Salisbury Centre (founded by Winniford Rushford, a Jungian analyst), still operating today. It is a non-denominational spiritual community in Edinburgh, Scotland. The centre offered exploration of different forms of spiritual, sustainable and creative possibilities in a setting where there are opportunities to become part of a community of others aspiring to live a balanced, compassionate and heart-centred lifestyle. There was a wonderful studio at the centre where I was encouraged to set up a private practice in dance movement therapy/DMT as it was termed then, in the UK now called dance movement psychotherapy/DMP. As a member of the core team, I had the opportunity to participate in, for example, dream groups, various spiritual practices and somatic workshops. Meditation formed part of each day. At that time also I learned the extended form of Tai Chi Chuan. It was at this time I engaged in a training in group analysis at the Scottish Institute for Human Relations, Edinburgh. This provided me with the foundations required for working with group process in group psychotherapy and training circles. Additionally, alongside studies in humanistic and psychodynamic psychotherapy I frequented Christian and Buddhist silent retreats, learning in particular the walking meditation, moving-in-the-present-moment. I learned about the observing self without judgement or discernment from these experiences.

In tandem to my practice in DMT I took various academic qualifications after the specialist physical education teacher training. Whilst full time in the later 1970s to early 1980s as the movement specialist in special schools I began exploring movement as a form of communication with autistic, mild learning disabled and emotionally distressed children. At that time, I studied development movement for children with Sherborne (2001) in a few short courses. She was also a PE specialist who studied with Rudolf Laban. In 1976, I was offered a fully funded sabbatical for a year at the Laban Centre augmenting my Laban Movement Analysis skills with Marian North (1972), another student of Laban, and special education movement skills with Walli Meir. During this time, I also undertook a year of Alexander Technique (alignment in everyday movement, where I spent about a year moving up and down from sitting to standing and back to sitting). Then, when back in special education, I spent two years part time on a postgraduate diploma in special education 1978–1980 whilst developing my own form of dance movement therapy.

Whilst in Durham (and later in Scotland) 1980–1986 working full time lecturing on BEds for physical education teaching (dance modules) I decided to embark on an MPhil at Manchester University. The aim was to take a closer look at my part time DMT practice with young offenders 1982–1986 (Payne, 1999a, 2003). This was how I began learning about qualitative research, later to be built upon in a PhD.

In Scotland I practised as a DMT with young people with eating disorders as well as with young offenders. By the time I had begun working in Scotland I had already visualized the design if a curriculum for a postgraduate training in DMT (Payne, 1985). In 1986, I had become a senior lecturer at Hertfordshire College of Art and Design (HCAD) on the MA in art therapy, and the dramatherapy MA. It was here that I initiated and led the first UK PGDip/MA in dance movement therapy at HCAD validated by the Council for National Academic Awards in 1987. This came on the back of an enormous effort by many volunteers to plough the pathway for the formation of the professional Association of Dance Movement (Psycho)therapy, UK (see Payne, 2024 for further details on how DMT became a profession in the UK).

The experience of qualitative research with young offenders lay the foundations for my PhD at the Institute of Education, University of London. The setting for the study was the postgraduate training in DMT at HCAD which I was leading. The topic was the two-year DMT personal development experiential group and its relationship to post qualification practice as a DMT (Payne, 1999b, 2001a, 2001b, 2002, 2004, 2006). I finished this research in 1996 when employed as a senior lecturer on the MA in counselling at the University of Hertfordshire which had taken over HCAD by then. Thereafter, from 2003, as a Reader, I embarked on research for supporting people with undiagnosed distressing somatic symptoms and The BodyMind Approach (see Chapter 9 on adapted authentic movement), later being conferred as a Chair in Psychotherapy (known in the UK as holding the title of Professor) from 2007. The paucity of research into authentic movement hinders its development significantly. There are a few studies, for example Stromsted (2001), Goldhahn (2007); Tantia (2012); García-Díaz (2018); Lucchi (2018); and Selu (2020) but these are only the beginnings of the contribution to knowledge and practice that can be made by authentic movement. A recent pilot study (Peng et al., 2025) points towards an exciting trajectory exploring how authentic movement can foster healing from developmental trauma.

Intensive personal therapy included person-centred psychotherapy, Rogerian psychotherapy, Jungian analysis and a Winnicottian analysis. I attended many workshops at the Open Centre, Community and Quesiter in London. Some of the innovative approaches for personal growth I engaged in included Reichian Therapy; others were somatic practices such as Feldenkrais Movement, Rolfing, Re-birthing, Trager and Focussing, which had come to the UK from the Esalen Institute in California. I also attended a course in the Bartenieff Technique with Kedzie Penfield, a US dance therapist based in Scotland. Later I engaged with Shamanic traditions with Caitlin Matthews, a Celtic shaman, another avenue of inward attention and altered states together with courses with Marian Woodman (1988). With reference to Woodman's work, I mentioned the importance of psychospiritual transformation via DMP in the postscript in Payne (2006). Authentic movement also provides opportunities for souls to be revealed and contact with the divine made whereby change is supported to become fully integrated through surrender.

This extensive background provided specific tools, knowledge, skills and understanding to prepare me to undertake the authentic movement training with Janet Adler, augmenting my practice as a dance movement therapist.

However, authentic movement was not completely new to me. I was first intro-duced to authentic movement by Mary Starks Whitehouse in 1978 when I attended her workshop at an American Dance Therapy Conference in Seatle, Washington, USA. I also attended another with Zoe Avstreih (2017) which further consolidated my interest in this powerful form. Subsequently, in 1990 Kedzie and I invited Janet to the UK to share her practice of authentic movement, and she arrived in England in 1992. We arranged the venue and administered the event (we could not arrange for good weather unfortunately!) inviting around 20 senior DMT colleagues from the UK and the continent to this, the first of what would be many intensive summer school trainings during the 1990s in warmer climes. During these years I began to tentatively integrate authentic movement into my private psychotherapy practice, I had become registered with the United Kingdom Council for Psychotherapy as a psychotherapist in 1992 (Humanistic and Integrative College). When individuals came for dance movement psychotherapy I offered to teach them the ground form. I was their witness. Then later, I delivered weekend workshops as an informal training for some for about five years in a local holistic health centre. Participants came from both around the UK and abroad, mostly trained in DMT but also some gestalt therapists, counsellors, others with an interest for professional/personal development and for a year or so a Buddhist monk attended. The therapists wanted to learn how to integrate AM into their practice, while others came for personal growth and spiritual practice. It became clear by the 2003 that a more systematic training was required.

Training at The Empty Studio[1]

In 1992, I accepted a part-time post to teach on the MA in counselling (person centred and psychodynamic) at the University of Hertfordshire. Since I had experi-ence designing training programmes in higher education, I set about bringing to fruition a university certificate and diploma in counselling as feeders for the MA in counselling programme. I was a member of the core teaching staff and went on to share my passion for research by initiating and leading a new MA in counselling inquiry programme.

Therefore, it was relatively straightforward for me to design a post qualification training in authentic movement. In contrast to prescriptive curriculum found in most training courses I felt this one needed to be practice-led and individualized, tailor-made to each student's rhythm of learning which would also be dependent on their interests and background to a greater degree. It had to mirror the quali-ties found in authentic movement, democratically fashioned within an ethos of relationality, respect and engaging with truth. Rather than solely academic learn-ing, experiential learning became the focus. The programme which takes three to four years on average has been delivered for over two decades now, and about 25 students have become certified. Additionally, many participants come for short intensives from time to time, which is enough for them. They do not wish to train to deliver AM as such but engage with the open circles for their own personal growth.

The Empty Studio training programme is detailed in the following:
The training is 240 contact/practice hours comprised of the following options:

- Attendance at online and f2f open circles, weekends and/or intensive residential retreats.
- Tutorials.
- Supervision.
- 1.5 hours presentation to peers.
- Individual f2f or online authentic movement sessions with me as their witness.
- Intensive sessions over two or three hours f2f or online with me as their witness.
- One or two day, f2f residential intensive with me as their witness.
- Dyadic practice minimum two hours per month throughout the duration of the training with someone who is interested to learn authentic movement.
- Act as sole witness for a group movement session and receive feedback from tutor and peers.
- Lead the co-production design of the closing ritual in the final group after they have completed the requirements above.

Additionally, specified reading is required throughout and a seminar to peers delivered on a relevant topic in which the student has an interest. The student is requested to log all the hours of practice, and there is peer and tutor assessment of their facilitation of a circle over half a day on one of the f2f workshops to be judged against set criteria. Post the half-day facilitation session within a month they submit a self-assessment document, together with feedback from tutor and peers on their facilitation including capacity, competence, attitude and attributes.

Students are only ready to make an entirely independent offering as authentic movement teachers, psychotherapists/counsellors or artists once we both agree they are ready. Preparedness is not solely about the hours of practice. If readiness is agreed, then the student is certified as trained and ready to practise independently.

It is acknowledged by those having trained as a DMP in the UK that the short introduction to AM on a DMP training does not qualify the practitioner to use as a form of embodied consciousness in psychotherapy or to teach AM. That is why the training is a CPD top up for DMPs in the UK and beyond. Participants also attend for personal and professional development. They will not train but come for the in-depth experience; they must have a suitable background, though. Screening prior to admittance to a circle is vital; therefore, an application form delineates for example, the applicant's previous training, memberships, practice, their background and any health considerations.

Open circles, i.e., open to those which include experienced practitioners, trainees and those new to the discipline, are the format for the delivery of the training. In each f2f circle there may be certified alumni authentic movement teachers attending to keep their practice in flow. Some participants new or newer to authentic movement can benefit from having more experienced practitioners present. Experienced practitioners learn from the naive questions from those beginning their authentic movement practice as in the beginner's mind. I find the learning opportunities are so much richer with this strategy.

The training is not based on a developmental model, rather more as a holistic, gestalt where moving and witnessing come together strengthening each role at the same time. Both inner witness and inner mover are honed during the training. Trainees learn to follow their bodily intuition, and embodied presence is cultivated. During their time as witnesses, somatic counter-transferences are identified and any interpretation of the mover's inner experience (such as feelings, thoughts, sensations etc.) removed. Projections, interpretations and judgements onto the mover are owned or avoided entirely so they begin to see movers more clearly and with honesty from their direct experience. During the training in their role as a mover the student begins to become more aware of their inner witness as they move in the large group or other group formats with the outer speaking witness making offerings to them over many, many classes. Similarly, when in the role of the outer speaking witness they learn to identify their inner mover, as their mirror neurones are activated during the mover's action. At the point of activation, the witness may experience images, memories, thoughts/stories, feelings or sensations etc. This attending to the inner experience and then languaging it in the speaking witness offering also takes many hours of practice. With people who have a contemplative practice or a background in the arts therapies or psychotherapists/counsellors, often the inner mover and inner witness become more quickly established. The silent witness role is essential to occupy over a long period of time to appreciate the need for containment.

Each open circle accommodates those new to the discipline by beginning with the ground form, the languaging and cultivating their presence, building up to the breathing or long circle towards the end of an intensive. Much of the practice is movers moving together in a group with me as their witness to demonstrate the languaging and ritualistic practices. Dyadic, triadic and circles of four formats are introduced to build towards the larger collective circles. The format of four members with three witnesses to one mover can support the confidence required for group formatted circles with a greater number of free-floating witnesses as found in the breathing or long circle. This format also offers opportunities for the role of silent witness to be occupied. Furthermore, groups of four can provide for three movers and one witness preparing additionally for group formats where there will be more movers to witness.

Additionally, during the pandemic I experimented with a colleague practising authentic movement online. Due to my learning from those sessions, I now offer one day online circles focussing on the delivery of authentic movement, teaching methods to ensure successful digital delivery. Trainees may attend these online days to add to their practice and use the contact hours towards the training requirement hours. Please see website for details: https://authenticmovementcirclesblog.wordpress.com/

Finally, as an international teacher of the discipline of authentic movement my intention is to endeavour to teach in a way that is respectful of the culture and language of that country, including Taiwan, China, South Korea, Hong Kong, Switzerland, India, Australia, Norway, Italy, Turkey, Spain, Slovakia, Slovenia, Estonia and Lithuania.

Authentic Movement as a Platform for Creativity

If you recall, earlier I mentioned sometimes poetry surfaces following the mover's speaking and the witness's offering. The poems in the examples that follow arise after the mover has spoken about their movement experience to their witness and received the offering from their witness. The poems also arise from notes written during transition, whether as a mover or a witness, when writing out whichever movements are remembered begins the formation of a poem which may be completed later after the dialoguing with the witness. The actual movements, accompanying kinaesthetic sensations and emotional responses may all contribute to the creation of a poem.

The examples that follow illustrate both the mover's poems and the witness's offerings. The poems have been composed in the light of the mover's writing during transition, their conscious recollection of their movements and any accompanying content, the witness's offering and any subsequent dialoguing with the witness.

Feeling Along the Floor

Moving backwards
focusing on feet
sliding, pushing
pulling, smoothing
feeling along the floor;
finding strength
touching power
gathering the texture
of every movement
feeling along the floor;
standing still
to feel connections
rooting down
throughout the body
while bending forwards
as gliding hands
feel along the floor;
brush away

wipe hands together
ridding each other
and this body
of all that's unwanted
but keeping the presence
of absence within
feeling along the floor.

Witness Offering:

My mover begins by sliding her feet over the slippery floor, pulling them in and pushing them out, one by one, and turning backwards as she travels around the space. She is focusing on her feet and feeling the texture of the smooth surface. I am drawn into the focus, it feels intense, there is strength in the pulling in and pushing out. She stands with feet apart and tips forward. I see her go down and sweep her hands across the floor, then wiping them on each other as though to get rid of something unwanted she had picked up from the surface (my interpretation). I see her sit and contact her body with her hands, stroking her legs, her feet, her arms, head, and face – wiping tears from her cheeks. Then, seeing something in her hands, she looks hard at it and yet offers it to others, sharing it with outstretched hands.

Beating the Bounds

Rolling roughly
across the floor
feeling
breathing me
hands cup down
over the body
touching
sensing me
here
but not here
shout out
this
screaming me
filling up
escaping out

all the struggles
surrounding me
with an ache
of sorrow
powerfully
pervading me
sit waiting
till fingertips
circle round the floor
right round left
to meet the other
left round right
to meet again
marking
reaching
beating the bounds
of me
now so present
within this space
settling in solitude
yet not
for being seen
in this latest grief
confirms
all that is
and all that
cannot be.

Witness Offering:

I see a mover spin around, raise arms, with hands cupped, up in an offering to the sky. She goes down to the floor and shouts which surprises me. I see her hands making a circle around my mover as though setting a boundary (my interpretation). I see her sitting on a rock with water around her, a stream perhaps, and the current is bumping up against the stone on which she sits in contemplation. Hands move, one over the other to build a wall in front of her (my interpretation). I see hands spiralling around each other and feel calm in their presence. My mover stretches her body out long across the floor, prone, resting until the time is ended. She is now rolling long and thin quickly. I can feel my body boundary against the floor.

Surrounding Sorrow

Walking pacing circling
quickly around feeling a rhythm with the ground to spin
this body down to initiate
the seeing
of what can't be found; sitting here hands discover growing vines
curving round hands girding arms wrapping around me as imagined shoots
    and encircling limbs enclose this body
in surrounding sorrow to caress the pain with the love
that flows in the tears that softly
softly release the fear
of all
that must remain unknown.

The Unseen Pivot

Feet stamp anger forcefully out imprinting
frustration's muttering sighs as fury is raised
up to the sky where hands reach the endless sadness hiding beside
so fall back down
to stab the ground where flailing cries shout
yes, yes, yes, revealing the howls from years gone by for acceptance
needs be fully owned in the unseen pivot that holds the key faithfully
sustaining me.

Witness Offering:

I see my mover walking in circles around the space. She spins then goes down.
I see something precious in her hands, she cups it carefully and longingly. It
becomes a baby in her arms which she soothes with a rocking motion. She's
looking down to the baby lovingly. Her arms open and hands begin folding
over each other. I imagine a vine climbing up a tree (my interpretation) as
each hand replaces the other back-to-back in a soft and careful manner. My
mover rises into the vertical stamping her feet in a Spanish dance. Hands up
high she turns and stamps letting out sounds a couple of times. A dance of
anger or frustration (my interpretation). She goes down again to the floor, fist
banging the surface. A cry rings out. "Yes" is shouted in a rhythm, tears fall.
Sitting, a hand off something to the world then it retreats as a fist, holding
onto the offering, it withdraws it. Her hand is on her heart during this time.
I feel moved.

Let Loose

Standing still hands over eyes
arms push palms out while
rocking this body from side to side;
one hand reaches high
to catch something unseen and takes it
down to the floor
where outstretched fingers of that holding hand
are suddenly pinned fixed to the ground so pull back
to find no release
to undo the bond
that holds me here
for tightening muscles find no freedom
from this holding earth
so my other hand swipes underneath and liberates
my whole body;
rolling over in relief I lie back
straightening my spine to feel the response
of this body; arms swing up to lift into sitting where
hands explore around in circles tracing over and over across the floor feeling
    the repetition of being stuck
in the beat
of my rapping ring; frustration
guides hands to drum my head in the same fixed throbbing beat as my mouth
    shouts out
all that's been locked in
until . . . calm at last
I shift into gentler moves with fingertips
meeting fingertips
as these opposing members make billowing
breathing flying shapes
with ballooning hands; the swell and flutter
of a brand, new butterfly emerges
in the lifting
in the breathing in the moving of rippling turns
for what was caught
is now let loose as freed fingers
investigate each other quietly sensing
this tranquil rhythm
replaying the release
from grief's powerful
lingering shadows.

Witness Offering:

Turning around herself and rocking side to side I see alternate arms reaching up and over, going down to the floor. This is repeated several times as though bringing something from above into the earth (my interpretation). I see my mover go down to the floor and spin around herself. First one way then the other. She leans over herself, and one hand, in tension, shakes and stops. She sits up and brings her hands to her ears. Is it a scream I hear? I see a need to protect herself from a sound (my interpretation). Hair over face I see a dog or a horse's head. Hands come towards her, and she explores them, backs and fronts. Then she makes a "butterfly" (my interpretation) with them opening and closing its wings until she releases it into the sky. She repeats this. Exploring the floor gathering something very nourishing, honey perhaps, putting it on her hands and arms in a healing bathing process (my interpretation). She is being kind to herself (my projection), the excess is wiped off. Hands stir something faster and faster. Then one hand slaps it in the middle – kill it dead.

This Passionate Body

Breathing
feeling breath
fill up within
and empty out
while
waiting for this body
to move;
hands cover ears
holding my head
to spin around
to feel the air
within and without;
bending forward
down to the ground
I sit
pull up my knees
and whirl around
to feel my breath
to feel my pulse

to feel the rhythm
tapped out with my ring
upon the floor;
suddenly
fists bang the ground
beating all the losses out
as crying takes over
turning this body
flat on my stomach
I shake with the sobbing
of aching loss;
sitting again
with legs to one side
this passionate frame
is dragged
back and forth
by determined arms
pushing and pulling
to feel the moving
to feel the strength
to feel the heart
of surviving and living
feeling this body
shouting out grieving.
Sitting on the floor
quietness follows
my head lifts up
feeling the light without
yet seeing it within;
my right hand
reaches up
to catch the light
and gently guide
it slowly down
as if to take more in;
rolling over
turning around
hands cover my eyes
but do not stop
this seeing
where
touching my body

stroking my skin
enables a sensing
of these breathing muscles
feeding this body
with feeling
within the aliveness
of being seen
and seeing.

Witness Offering:

My mover goes down to the floor stretches out on her back, then rolls onto her front. She's lying there. Suddenly she sits up. Has someone called her? She sits cross legged now. Is she in school? She's waiting for permission to get up. She goes back to the floor again rolling sideways and then gets to her knees. Tapping hands on knees a rhythm begins. Tapping hands on her sides. Standing now, hand on heart, she is tapping rhythms of heartbeats (my interpretation). Feet have a rhythm too, a dance begins. Now she goes down to the floor again and gathers magic dust with her fingers and lets it go through them. I feel my body boundaries as my mover rolls side to side on the floor and slides on her front and back. Forward and back. Standing she walks forward and back – looking at where she has gone before – balancing carefully she makes sure the floor is secure before stepping onto it.

Other Training Programmes

Members of the International Teachers Inquiry Network for Authentic Movement have kindly sent their programmes as resources for readers from other countries interested in AM training, short courses or groups.

India

The following programmes in authentic movement are currently offered by Brinda Jacob-Janvrin, Founder & Managing Trustee, + 91 9845236242 | www.smartmove.co.in

Sakshi (Witness): This is an ongoing group that began in 2020. Each module is for six months, and during this module, we meet once a month for a three-hour session. We are now in the 5th edition of Sakshi and next time around we plan to meet for one full day (six-hour session + one-hour lunch break). We are a 15-member group, and most of the members have been a part of the group since 2020. At the beginning of each module, we do open for new members who either have prior experience of AM or their own inner work practice. This group has really deepened over the years and is now a powerful container within which so much unfolds.

The Desire retreat is an immersive four-day residential retreat set in nature. It is an utterly intimate, sensual and restorative practice that is designed to awaken the fullness and expansiveness of the Eros and re-ignite the flow of energy and sensitivity in our inner world. Authentic movement practices are an integral part of this exploration, and along with our moving body, we will also get an opportunity to explore our dreaming body.

This work is a powerful antidote to the chaos surrounding us. We live in a world that privileges Logos over Eros, Power over Love, and Mind over Body, creating a polarized and divided condition within our psyche, which is reflected in the world around us. Learning to engage with and honour our desire allows us to break this vicious patriarchal condition of "either/or" and move towards the more inclusive and feminine approach of "yes, and".

Spiralling into Desire – Live performance X Video art: Spiralling into Desire documents a woman's descent into her deep body to access and retrieve her true autonomy. Movement, video art, text and sound populate the liminal landscape into which the audience is gently invited. The sharing also draws parallels from the first epic poem "The descent of Innana". The work is set at the intersection of the arts, psychology and spirituality. Inspired by Brinda's practice of authentic movement and natural dreamwork, the performance builds on both – the creative process and the witnessing process, as it explores the question "how do we hold desire in our bodies?"

The performance premiered in March 2024 and has been sharing in Bangalore and as a short film "Spiralling into Desire" which brings together mover Brinda Jacob-Janvrin and filmmakers Roohi Dixit and Ziba Bhagwagar to explore and document the Desire process. In this exploration of the authentic movement process, the camera is the witness and the relationship between filmmaker and mover is one of deep compassion. The movement x film collaboration in its current iteration of 15 minutes is produced by the Studio for Movement Arts and Therapies Trust, in collaboration with Zero Rules, and is supported by Goethe-Institut/Max Mueller Bhavan Bangalore. It was selected to screen at the following country's film festivals: UK, Australia, Mexico, Russia, Puerto Rico, India, Columbia, Nepal, Greece and Brazil. The film was also screened online in India and in person at, for example, the Goethe-Institut/Max Mueller Bhavan, often followed by a Q&A, or a short two-hour AM workshop, exploring desire. https://thedesireproject.in/

The Expressive Body was created by Dr. Kate Donohue and Brinda Jacob-Janvrin, and titled Expressive Body: Through Wounding, Trauma, Healing, and Well-being. The one-year advanced training programme invites participants to engage deeply with their personal process while grounding the same in EXA theories. Held in a Jungian expressive arts framework, trainees will begin by exploring their relationship to the archetype of the feminine. Starting with their own Motherline, trainees will learn about their personal, cultural and archetypal cords to the sacred feminine. With this archetypal thread lacing the year, participants will become fluent in these two imagistic approaches as well as receive relevant supervision on their work. Authentic movement is an integral module in this training programme. https://smartmove.co.in/expressive-body/

Individual AM sessions of one-hour, authentic movement sessions for clients are offered.

Upcoming projects: We at SMART (Studio for Movement Arts and Therapies) are currently conceptualizing a programme that delves into societal structures of caste and gender and their impact on mental health, through a depth psychology perspective. Authentic movement will be a part of this programme.

China

Inspirees Institute started to offer training in authentic movement since 2023. The programme includes both mystical practice originally from Janet Alder's approach as well as clinical applications. Our mission is to establish a Chinese-speaking community of authentic movement practitioners and contribute to the global development of this discipline. In 2023 Inspirees organized Authentic Movement Summit (curated by Prof. Helen Payne) under the World Arts & Embodiment Forum (WAEF, 2023), attracting 273 participants and 23 presenters. Read more about Inspirees' training and retreat programme https://www.inspirees.com/authentic-movement/. Contact education@inspirees.com

Brasil and Portugal

Soraya George, www.movimentoautentico.com @movimentoautentico – Instagram

For more than ten years I have offered authentic movement in a dance college as part of a special programme called: Therapy through Movement – Body and Subjectivation.

I am regularly invited to teach and speak about AM in various departments at universities, including Dance, Arts and Psychology, as well as in training programmes like Body Mind Movement and the Jungian analyst programme.

Together with a partner, Guto Macedo, I co-founded the International Center of Authentic Movement (CIMA – Centro Internacional do Movimento Autêntico), where I have offered different groups for practice and study continuously for nearly 24 years. And for the past five years, I have also been teaching the Discipline of Authentic Movement. What is present in the relationship between practitioner and facilitator? What can we see together, and at what point in the pathway are we in the learning process?

My website features videos and workshops I offer in Brasil and Portugal. There are also articles written by my students, who are connecting AM with dance, performance, somatic practices, psychology, psycho(therapies), and African and indigenous themes.

Grounded in Janet's teachings, we as a collective (students, practitioners, teachers/facilitators) are investigating and incorporating Brasilian words to make connections, come closer, relate to what we have been experiencing. This exploration touches on themes of colonialism, gender, ritual (African and Indigenous spirituality), and the performance of direct spoken words, with spirituality and art-activism.

New Zealand

E. Connor Kelly, eckellydance@gmail.com

In the first few years after I moved to New Zealand in 2003 I began offering local three-hour workshops in town perhaps monthly and at Creative Arts Therapies conferences in Auckland and then regularly in Auckland sometimes for a full day. Eventually I was able to lead a few retreats locally in 2011 and then at a retreat centre from 2015 through 2019. I moved to Guam in 2016 and developed an online training with a colleague in Auckland. We began offering this in 2017. We did this for a few years offering six small group sessions over five months with several individual or supervision sessions. I continued to return to New Zealand annually and included stops in Australia during those years pre-Covid with two-day workshops in Queensland, Sydney and Melbourne.

When Covid came, I continued offering a series online and added online retreats (a three-hour session Saturday and a three-hour session Sunday). I offered a few of those over a two-year period. Then returning to New Zealand I began offering a series of five sessions online that I call practice sessions. Within those sessions I have some ongoing students who have been with me awhile who understand that this process is long term. A few years ago, some of the DMT students in training thought that they could use authentic movement in their practicum sessions with very little training. I am on the Dance Therapy Association of Australia (DTAA) professional membership committee, and we have made a statement that this is not appropriate for students, and we consider AM an advanced practice. I am planning to go to Australia next year and offer further training through DTAA and include at least a day as an introduction to using authentic movement in therapy. There are some peer groups practising who would like more input from me which is good.

When people inquire with me about training, I tell them this is a long-term practice, and I do not offer a certificate to say they are qualified. Some of these people seem to just want a certificate and I am just not going to do that, as you know this is a long-term practice, a wisdom practice.

Russia

Irina Biryukova, BC-DMT; iradmt@gmail.com

In 2018 a new two-year continuous advanced training in authentic movement was established at the DMP department of the Institute of Practical Psychology & Psychoanalysis in Moscow by Irina. Among her teachers are Joan Chodorow, Tina Stromsted, Patrizia Pollaro and others. The programme "Authentic Movement as a psychotherapeutic modality" is for experienced DMTs with over five years of clinical DMT practice, over 35 years old with no less than three years and 150 hours of own authentic movement practice.

The training is 220 academic hours and combines intensive seminars with own authentic movement practice, theoretical and supervision seminars. Discussions of literature on authentic movement are also a vital part of the training.

In the end there is a written essay to obtain certification. As a result, graduates integrate authentic movement in their clinical practice or lead one-to-one sessions, groups or can use authentic movement in supervision.

Besides general notions of the evolution of the form of authentic movement the training is focused on following issues:

1) The development of skills of tracking bodily experience in the presence of the other and its connection to emotions and personal stories/memories/dreams. Active imagination in movement.
2) The constant deepening of one's own mover's experience and the development of containment skills of difficult experiences as the basis of therapeutic contact.
3) Exploration of witnessing phenomena in authentic movement and in therapeutic practice (embodied presence, openness, body consciousness, widening awareness, use of language, containment and expression, ways to keep body/mind/soul connection etc.).
4) Mover-witness relationship issues.
5) The development of collective (group) skills witnessing.
6) Working with projection and projective identification in authentic movement and in therapeutic process.
7) Working with group dynamics in the context of authentic movement practice.
8) Ways to integrate skills that the practice of authentic movement gives into their own DMT and psychotherapeutic practice.

USA

Tina Stromsted, Ph.D., Tina@AuthenticMovement-BodySoul.com

I am a Jungian psychoanalyst, board-certified dance/movement therapist, somatics educator, consultant and author who works with the interwoven relationships with ourselves, others and the natural world. I have a private practice in San Francisco, where I offer Jungian analysis, creative depth work, authentic movement and other forms of dance/movement and somatic psychotherapy. With international virtual consultation, I mentor authentic movement teachers, mental health clinicians, health professionals and creative artists.

For the past four decades, I have taught authentic movement and related depth-oriented somatic and creative arts approaches in many parts of the world. Having co-taught with Joan Chodorow for decades and assisted Janet Adler for several years, I offered international Authentic Movement Intensives in Tuscany,

Italy over a 34-year period. As a long-time clinical and somatic psychology faculty member in master's and doctoral programmes, I introduced authentic movement in graduate school programmes beginning in the 1980s. In 1993, I co-founded the Authentic Movement Institute (AMI) with Dance/Movement Therapist Neala Haze. We invited senior colleagues Dr. Joan Chodorow and Dr. Janet Adler to join us, followed by additional faculty and guest presenters who worked with special populations in offering three-year intensive trainings programmes in authentic movement until we closed the doors in 2004.

I currently teach at international conferences and lead workshops in person and online that blend authentic movement, depth psychology, somatic psychology, DreamDancing ®, Embodied Alchemy ® and creative arts therapy for healing and transformation. Having trained and worked with Jungian analyst Marion Woodman since the 1980s I was invited to co-lead her BodySoul Rhythms® Leadership Training Program in the US and Canada. Beginning in 1995, I conducted research that culminated in my doctoral dissertation titled "Re-inhabiting the Female Body: Authentic Movement as a Gateway to Transformation". Currently I chair the teaching team for the International Association of Analytical Psychology (IAAP) initiated by Joan Chodorow, Marion Woodman and others teaching active imagination in movement (the roots of authentic movement) since 2000. I am the Director of Soul's Body® Center and faculty at the C.G. Jung Institute of San Francisco, the Marion Woodman Foundation and Jung Platform.

To view my upcoming virtual and in-person offerings, please visit my website: https://authenticmovement-bodysoul.com/

My virtual courses, seminars and workshops are always available on my website (https://authenticmovement-bodysoul.com/trainings/) and on the Jung Platform (https://jungplatform.com/teacher/tina-stromsted).

You can also access the AMI website as an archival resource: https://www.authenticmovementinstitute.com/

My book *Soul's Body: Active Imagination, Authentic Movement, & Embodiment in Psychotherapy* was published by Routledge in August 2025.

Japan

Yukari 崎山ゆかり, sakiyama@mukogawa-u.ac.jp

I have had the opportunity to facilitate authentic movement on a regular basis over the past few years. Although we only meet four times a year, we call it the "Mind and Body Becoming Oneself" group. I am in charge of a study group for psychiatrists and clinical psychologists to learn about movement-based approaches. All of us are professionals in the field of interpersonal assistance. Each meeting lasts two hours, with the first half of the meeting spent experiencing specific movement approaches, and the second half of each meeting being AM time. Since the last meeting, graduate students who want to become psychologists have joined us. This group was founded by a certified Jungian analyst, a graduate professor, with me and his colleague.

South Korea

Hinbaram ParkSunYoug, whitedancesun@gmail.com

The Dance Movement Therapy Center in Sejong City, Korea, conducts an intensive course for eight weeks on Saturdays and Sundays. This programme, conducted by R-DMT KyungSuk Yoo and SunYoung Park, and study the theory of AM online every Friday night for eight weeks. They study the process of active imagination, the role of the mover/witness and what you can learn through authentic movement. This course is currently being conducted with 12 counselling psychologists.

In addition, at the Healing & Counseling Graduate School located in Seoul, graduate students in the Department of Counseling Psychology take one course on authentic movement per year. It is conducted once a week for 2.5 hours for a total of 15 weeks, and the main textbook is *Dance Movement Therapy and Depth Psychology* by Joan Chodorow and *Authentic Movement 1, 2* by Patricia Pallero, and they study the theory and practise. This class has nine students in this semester.

Argentina

Karin Fleischer, karinflei@hotmail.com

Training programme: Authentic Movement as Embodied Active Imagination.

I started the programme in the year 2000, under the supervision of Janet Adler and Joan Chodorow. It involved regular practice, intensive retreats and theoretical seminars, informed by the developments of Mary Starks Whitehouse, Janet Adler and Joan Chodorow, as well as basic concepts of analytical psychology. Within this framework, authentic movement was explored as a creative practice and as a therapeutic approach.

The intensive format has allowed participants to come from different countries, such as: Uruguay, Chile, Perú, Colombia, México, Venezuela, Puerto Rico, Spain, Finland, Greece, among others. A similar programme was developed throughout five years in Perú, and next year will begin in México.

At the present, I continue to work with advanced authentic movement students who are also sharing the practice. I am offering in-depth continuing study and exploration of Authentic Movement as Embodied Active Imagination with a clinical orientation as well as supervision within a Jungian framework.

Summary

This chapter highlighted my background and the training in authentic movement which I offer in the UK. Further details of other training programmes around the world as well as those authentic movement practitioners offering individual and group classes are provided as a resource for the reader.

Acknowledgments: Thanks to members of the International Teachers Inquiry Network for Authentic Movement for the input on their professional authentic movement opportunities and to Dr. Christina Bracegirdle for sharing her poetry in this chapter.

Note

1 This is the name of my studio at my home into which we moved in 2009.

References

Adler, J. (1987). Who is the witness, a description of authentic movement. *Contact Quarterly*, *12*(1), 20–29.

Adler, J. (1995). *Arching backwards: The mystical initiation of a contemporary woman.* Inner Traditions.

Adler, J. (2002). *Offering from the conscious body, the discipline of authentic movement.* Inner Traditions.

Adler, J. (2015). The mandorla and the discipline of authentic movement. *Journal of Dance & Somatic Practices*, *7*(2), 217–227.

Avstreih, Z. (2017). Authentic movement and the relationship of embodied spirituality to health and wellbeing. In V. Karkou, S. Oliver, & S. Lycouris (Eds.), *The Oxford handbook of dance and wellbeing* (pp. 165–179). Oxford University Press. https://doi.org/10.1093/oxfordhb/9780199949298.013.9

Beck, M. (2025). *Beyond anxiety: Curiosity, creativity, and finding your life's purpose.* Penguin.

Bracegirdle, C. (2023). A mover's practice of transition in authentic movement: An embodied non-dual lived experience. *Body, Movement and Dance in Psychotherapy*, *19*(4), 381–396. https://doi.org/10.1080/17432979.2023.2254834

García-Díaz, S. (2018). The effect of the practice of authentic movement on the emotional state. *The Arts in Psychotherapy*, *58*, 17–26. https://doi.org/10.1016/j.aip.2018.03.004

Goldhahn, E. (2007). *Shared habitats, the MoverWitness paradigm* (Submitted in partial fulfilment of a doctorate). Dartington College of Arts and University of Plymouth.

Lucchi, B. (2018). Authentic movement as a training modality for private practice clinicians. *American Journal of Dance Therapy*, *40*(2), 300–317. https://doi.org/10.1007/s10465-018-9287-3

North, M. (1972). *Personality assessment through movement.* MacDonald & Evans.

Payne, H. (1985). An innovation in education: A proposed course in dance movement therapy (postgraduate). *The Scottish Journal of Physical Education*, *1*, 3–4.

Payne, H. (1999a). The use of dance movement therapy with troubled youth. In C. Schaefer (Ed.), *Innovative psychotherapy techniques in child and adolescent therapy* (Revised 2nd ed., pp. 30–60). John Wiley Interscience.

Payne, H. (1999b). Personal development groups in the training of counsellors and therapists: A review of the research. *The European Journal of Psychotherapy, Counselling and Health*, *2*(1), 55–68.

Payne, H. (2001a). A comparison between personal development groups in arts and psychotherapy training: An international survey. *Online International Journal for Arts Therapies,* University of Derby.

Payne, H. (2001b). Students' experiences of a dance movement therapy group: The question of safety. *The European Journal of Psychotherapy, Counselling and Health*, *4*(2), 167–292.

Payne, H. (2002). Ferocious polar bears: Student perceptions of a dance movement therapy group. *German Dance Therapy Journal*, *1*(22), 60–77. (in German).

Payne, H. (2003). Shut in, shut out: Movement therapy with young people labelled delinquent (a psychodynamic perspective) In H. Payne (Ed.), *Dance movement therapy: Theory & practice*. Routledge. (7th reprint).

Payne, H. (2004). Becoming a client, becoming a practitioner: Student narratives from a dance movement therapy group. *British Journal of Guidance & Counselling*, *32*(4), 512–532.

Payne, H. (2006). The lived experience of students in a dance movement therapy group: Loss, physical contact and the DMT approach. In H. Payne (ed.), *Dance movement therapy: Theory, research and practice*. Routledge.

Payne, H. (2020). *Creative dance and movement in groupwork*. Routledge.

Payne, H. (2024). The association of dance movement psychotherapy UK: Becoming a profession. *Body, Movement and Dance in Psychotherapy*, 1–37. https://doi.org/10.1080/17432979.2024.2429565

Payne, H., & Costas, B. (2021). Creative dance as experiential learning in state primary education: The potential benefits for children. *Journal of Experiential Education, 44*(3).

Peng, L., Payne, H., & Grey, B. (2025). Healing developmental trauma: A pilot study on the discipline of authentic movement and attachment in adult females. (In review).

Selu, E. (2020). Authentic movement as a movement meditation: Support for immune mediated inflammatory disease. *International Body Psychotherapy Journal, 19*(1), 55–63.

Sherborne, V. (2001). *Developmental movement for children*. Worth Publishing.

Stromsted, T. (2001). Re-inhabiting the female body: Authentic Movement as a gateway to transformation. *The Arts in Psychotherapy, 28*(1), 39–55.

Tantia, J. (2012). Authentic movement and the autonomic nervous system: A preliminary investigation. *American Journal of Dance Therapy, 34*(1), 53–73. https://doi.org/10.1007/s10465-012-9131-0

Woodman, M. (1988). *The pregnant virgin: A process of psychological transformation*. Inner City Books.

Photograph 12.1 Two witnesses contemplate the empty space
Credit: Photography by Lucie Payne

Chapter 12

Epilogue

This book has been a culmination of my studies, research and practice in the discipline of Authentic Movement (Adler, 2002, Morrissey & Sager, 2022). Several chapters have been previously published, although updated versions appear in this book, and others are new works illustrating my current thinking, research and practice.

The chapters bring together almost all my professional life's experience in this methodology, tracking my life's work in research, theory, practice and teaching authentic movement over three decades. Since 1978 when I participated in workshops on authentic movement with Mary Starks Whitehouse and Zoe Avstreih at an American Dance Therapy conference, I have grown my study and practice of authentic movement in several ways. The seed was sown at that conference. Mary's legacy lived on when I studied intensively with one of her students, Janet Adler through the 1990s. From then I began integrating authentic movement into my private psychotherapy. In the early 2000s I also delivered workshops in AM engaging dance movement, gestalt and body psychotherapists as well as others with a coaching, spiritual or artistic quest, or for personal and/or professional development. Later my offering has been more structured, aimed at training clinicians to apply the discipline in clinical settings (mostly private practice) and/or as facilitators/teachers, accepting only those already trained in psychotherapy (mostly dance movement psychotherapists) and with at least five years of experience working with adult groups. Acceptance into the programme requires the completion of a more detailed application form, and sometimes an interview. Upon successful completion trainees go on to integrate the discipline in clinical practice, supervision and/or teaching/facilitating in groups.

For my postdoctoral research in 2004 I undertook a research project with people experiencing medically unexplained symptoms (now under the umbrella of body distress disorder). The facilitators (all of whom were dance movement psychotherapists) for the research groups had been trained by me in authentic movement. It was made clear this was to be the main practice (albeit tailored to the population) to support the participants' self-management of symptoms. This and subsequent studies led to the development of The BodyMind Approach (Payne & Brooks, 2025). The training in The BodyMind Approach teaches practitioners how I have adapted authentic movement to the layperson to minimize self-consciousness and lack of body confidence often experienced by people when moving expressively in a group setting.

DOI: 10.4324/9781003479413-13

More recently I have made a case for TBMA drawing heavily on authentic movement, and its unique way of cultivating interoception, for supporting students in higher education with chronic anxiety.

This volume charts my professional work in authentic movement and provides the reader with a chronological journey through all the trajectories into which I have taken authentic movement. Following the Introduction where I outline and describe the formats, rituals and strategies for safely practising authentic movement, in Chapter 1 illustrative examples of the ground form and group formats where movers and witnesses speak are presented. Next is an integration of Casement's ideas on the internal supervisor with those of the inner witness and inner mover in authentic movement in Chapter 2; groups and the transpersonal (Chapter 3); the body as container and expressor (Chapter 4); bodies becoming conscious (Chapter 5); psycho-neurology (Chapter 6); nature connectedness (Chapter 7); relational integrative psychotherapy (Chapter 8); undiagnosed somatic, or medically unexplained, symptoms (Chapter 9); anxiety and interoception (Chapter 10); and training (Chapter 11) followed by this, the Epilogue.

Throughout this trajectory my background in DMP clinical practice with emotionally distressed children, autistic verbal and nonverbal children and adolescents, young offenders and functioning adults, have informed my approach to the discipline of authentic movement. My personal process, alongside my professional practice and training, have been contained within person-centred psychotherapy, psychodynamic psychotherapy and in particular many years of Jungian analysis and a Winnicottian analysis. Additionally, silent meditation retreats/practice and previous training in research, group analysis, psychotherapy, creative dance and somatic practices, for example, have become integrated into my specific methodology. Fortunately, authentic movement can evolve organically within each practitioner's field of work and become one with their backgrounds, so it becomes moulded and refined in ways relevant to their context.

I hope you, dear reader, have found this book of interest and stimulating for your own development in the application of theory and/or practice of authentic movement.

Looking to the Future

There is much to be considered in authentic movement going forward. The term "authentic" can be viewed as problematic and limited as an explanatory title of the discipline. Whitehouse states, "you can only do your own work if you are going to be authentic" (cited in Sherman, 1999, p. 29). Adler states the term "authentic" refers to movements that emerge spontaneously and genuinely from within, unfiltered by pretence or external influence. They are unplanned. However, the movement is only one part of the discipline. It is unfortunate there is no acknowledgement of the importance of the authenticity of the witness.

The term MoverWitness was first employed by Goldhahn (2007) from a visual arts-and performance-based, phenomenological perspective renaming it the "MoverWitness exchange" which covers the sharing and languaging between mover and witness in subsequent publications (Goldhahn, 2009, 2022). Adler, following Goldhahn, has explained the evolution of witnessing/witness consciousness, with the concept of "MoverWitness" as the more advanced element (Morrissey & Sager, 2022, p. 211). This is where the empty mover and empty witness become as one. Or, as Adler states, "representing grace, unitive consciousness within mover and witness and their relationship" (Morrissey & Sager, 2022, p. 211).

The theoretical elements need exploration, for example through research which is crucial to the development and application of authentic movement. Reflections on practice could be illustrative of its evolving nature and delivery in a range of settings. The democratic nature of authentic movement could be explored with reference to the current political scene as the new world order evolves. Decolonization is another concern which could inform this practice as it evolves. Since authentic movement is a relational methodology, adult attachment patterns offer an intriguing area of research. Peng et al. (2025) describe a qualitative pilot study with women in China undertaking an authentic movement training programme which had encouraging outcomes. A further main study is currently underway. Additionally, Goldhahn (2022) raises the issue of white privilege's impact within this form, for example it is mostly white, middle-class women who practise authentic movement. Finally, we rarely find men participating in AM, which is such a loss to the discipline. These are all important issues meriting engagement in meaningful conversations and research. I look forward to the next generation's participation in, and contributions to, this beautiful and powerful discipline which cultivates embodied consciousness. It does not need to be framed as a mystical practice, it can be whatever you intend it to be, an art form, a somatic practice, psychotherapy, experiential learning or contemplation for example. I urge you to step into the unknown space of authentic movement to see what you can become to the benefit of our world!

References

Adler, J. (2002). *The Discipline of Authentic Movement*. Inner Traditions Press.

Goldhahn, E. (2007). *Shared habitats, the MoverWitness paradigm* (Submitted in partial fulfilment for a doctorate). Dartington College of Arts and University of Plymouth.

Goldhahn, E. (2009). Is authentic a meaningful name for the practice of authentic movement? *American Journal of Dance Therapy, 31*(1), 53–63.

Goldhahn, E. (2022). *Reflections on authentic movement: Theory, practice and arts-led research*. Routledge.

Morrissey, B., & Sager, P. (Eds.). (2022). *Intimacy in Emptiness: An evolution of embodied consciousness. Collected writings of Janet Adler*. Inner Traditions.

Payne, H., & Brooks, S. (2025). *Manging distressing bodily symptoms: The BodyMind Approach using a biopsychosocial model*. Routledge.

Peng, L., Payne, H., & Grey, B. (2025). Healing developmental trauma: A pilot study on the discipline of authentic movement and attachment in adult females. (In review).

Sherman, F. (1999). In conversation with Mary Whitehouse. In P. Pallaro (Ed.), *Authentic movement: Essays by Mary Starks Whitehouse, Janet Adler and Joan Chodorow*. Jessica Kingsley.

If we dare to travel down the bridge from our head to our body, we may find our soul in the darkness and we may find the questions which will quicken her, opening every call as we bring her to consciousness. Body becomes embodiment, sight becomes insight.

Woodman, M. (1990). *The Ravaged Bridegroom: Masculinity in Women* (p. 177). Inner City Books

Abbreviations

AM	The Discipline of Authentic Movement
aAM	Adapted Authentic Movement
DMP	Dance Movement Psychotherapy
DMT	Dance Movement Therapy
DSM	Diagnostic Statistical Manual of Mental Disorders
ES	Embodied Simulation
F2F	Face to Face
GP	General Practitioner/Physician
HE	Higher Education
LGBTQ+	Lesbian, Gay, Bisexual, Transgender, and Queer (or questioning)
LMA	Laban Movement Analysis
MUS	Undiagnosed/Medically Unexplained Symptoms
NHS	National Health Service
TBMA	The BodyMind Approach
UCAS	Universities and Colleges Admissions Service
UK	United Kingdom

Appendix
Resources

Professional Associations for Dance Movement Therapy

American Dance Therapy Association, Inc. Contact for inquiries re dance therapy alternate route registry, the ADTA Journal, Videos/Films on Authentic Movement & Dance/Movement Therapy. 10632 Little Patuxent Parkway, Suite 108, Columbia, MD 21044, Tel. (410) 997–4040. Fax: (410) 997–4048, Email: info@ADTA.org. http://www.ADTA.org

Association for Dance Movement Psychotherapy UK (ADMP UK) http://admp.org.uk/

European Association of Body Psychotherapy. http://www.eabp.org

European Association of Dance Movement Therapy. http://www.eadmt.com/

Professional Journals

The Arts in Psychotherapy Journal. https://www.journals.elsevier.com/the-arts-in-psychotherapy/

Body, Movement and Dance in Psychotherapy: An International Journal for Theory, Research and Practice. Published by Taylor & Francis Email: subscriptions@tandf.co.uk. http://www.tandf.co.uk/journals/titles/17432979.asp

The Jung Journal: Culture & Psyche. https://www.jstor.org/journal/jungjcultpsyc

Somatics: Magazine-Journal of the Mind/Body Arts and Sciences. 1516 Grant Ave., Suite # 212, Novato, CA. 94945. Tel. (415) 892–0617. Fax: (415) 892–4388. http://www.somaticsed.com

Spring Journal. https://www.springpublications.com/springjournal_index.html

Other Relevant Organizations

Authentic Movement Open Circles. https://authenticmovementcirclesblog.wordpress.com/

Authentic Movement Community Blog: http://authenticmovementcommunity.blogspot.com/. Facebook Group: https://www.facebook.com/groups/48153313102/

Center for Movement Education and Research. Alternate Route Training Courses in Dance. https://cmer.info/

Discipline of Authentic Movement – Circles of Four. www.disciplineofauthentic-movement.com/

International Association for Creative Arts in Therapy and Education (IACAET). www.iacaet.org

International Association for Analytical Psychology. A resource for Jungian Depth Psychology, the Journal, newsletter, conference information, and international analyst members. http://www.iaap.org/

International Expressive Arts Therapy Association. P.O. Box 320399, San Francisco, CA 94132. Tel. (415) 522–8959. http://www.ieata.org

International Somatic Movement Education & Therapy Association. http://www.ismeta.org/

Marion Woodman Foundation. https://www.mwfbodysoulrhythms.org/

Movement Therapy. http://www.movement-education.org

Soul's Body Center. www.AuthenticMovement-BodySoul.com

Index

Note: Pages in *italics* refer to figures, pages in **bold** refer to tables.

For Product Safety Concerns and Information please contact our EU
representative GPSR@taylorandfrancis.com
Taylor & Francis Verlag GmbH, Kaufingerstraße 24, 80331 München, Germany

www.ingramcontent.com/pod-product-compliance
Lightning Source LLC
Chambersburg PA
CBHW052002270326
41929CB00015B/2750

9 781032 766430